A SHORT TEXTBOOK OF
ORTHOPAEDICS AND TRAUMATOLOGY

UNIVERSITY MEDICAL TEXTS

General Editor

SELWYN TAYLOR, D.M., M.Ch., F.R.C.S.
Dean, Royal Postgraduate Medical School
Surgeon, Hammersmith Hospital

A Short Textbook of Medicine
Fourth Edition
J. C. HOUSTON, M.D., F.R.C.P.
Physician and Dean of the Medical School, Guy's Hospital

C. L. JOINER, M.D., F.R.C.P.
Physician, Guy's Hospital

J. R. TROUNCE, M.D., F.R.C.P.
Professor of Therapeutics, Guy's Hospital Medical School

A Short Textbook of Surgery
Second Edition
SELWYN TAYLOR, D.M., M.Ch., F.R.C.S.
Dean, Royal Postgraduate Medical School
Surgeon, Hammersmith Hospital

L. T. COTTON, M.Ch., F.R.C.S.
Surgeon, King's College Hospital

A Short Textbook of Medical Microbiology
Second Edition
D. C. TURK, D.M., M.R.C.P., M.C.Path.
Consultant Clinical Bacteriologist to the Radcliffe Infirmary
Honorary Consultant to the Oxford Public Health Laboratory

I. A. PORTER, M.D., M.C.Path.
Consultant Bacteriologist to the Ayrshire Area Laboratory Service
Formerly Senior Lecturer in Bacteriology, University of Newcastle-upon-Tyne

A Short Textbook of Chemical Pathology
Second Edition
D. N. BARON, M.D., D.Sc., M.R.C.P., F.C.Path.
Professor of Chemical Pathology, Royal Free Hospital School of Medicine

A Short Textbook of Gynaecology and Obstetrics
G. D. PINKER, M.B., F.R.C.S., F.R.C.O.G.
Consultant Gynaecological Surgeon and Obstetrician, St. Mary's Hospital

D. W. T. ROBERTS, M.Chir., F.R.C.S., F.R.C.O.G.
Consultant Obstetrician and Gynaecologist, St. George's Hospital

A Short Textbook of Psychiatry
W. L. LINFORD REES, B.Sc., M.D., F.R.C.P., D.P.M.
Professor of Psychiatry, St. Bartholomew's Hospital Medical College, London

A SHORT TEXTBOOK
OF
ORTHOPAEDICS
AND
TRAUMATOLOGY

J. N. ASTON, M.B., F.R.C.S.

Orthopaedic Surgeon, St Bartholomew's Hospital, London

THE ENGLISH UNIVERSITIES PRESS LTD

CONTRIBUTORS:

JAMES O. ROBINSON
M.D., M.Ch., F.R.C.S.
Surgeon, St. Bartholomew's Hospital, London

R. CAMPBELL CONNOLLY
F.R.C.S.
Neurosurgeon, St. Bartholomew's Hospital, London

ISBN 0 340 05106 X Paper
ISBN 0 340 05107 8 Boards

First published 1967
Reprinted (with revisions) 1969, 1971, 1972, 1973, 1974

The English Universities Press Ltd
St Paul's House, Warwick Lane, London EC4P 4AH

Printed and bound in Singapore by
Hoong Fatt Press, 9 Harper Road, Singapore 13.

EDITOR'S FOREWORD

A Short Textbook of Orthopaedics and Traumatology is a most welcome addition to the University Medical Texts. Those who know this series well will already have noted that the Short Textbook of Surgery includes an introduction to the subject of fractures and orthopaedics, but this new book covers the subject much more thoroughly and is an extremely acceptable and convenient volume.

Each of the textbooks in this series has been prepared with the object of providing an authoritative up-to-date account of its particular subject in as inexpensive a form as possible. Advances in surgery occur so swiftly today that a new edition will be required within a few years and it is clearly unwise to produce a large and durable textbook which of necessity will be out of date in the foreseeable future.

The student of surgery will find here an excellent introduction to orthopaedics and traumatology and the practitioner anxious to keep abreast of the times will also find it a refreshing textbook to consult. The author is particularly to be congratulated on the extreme clarity of his presentation.

SELWYN TAYLOR.

AUTHOR'S PREFACE

The speciality known as 'orthopaedics' is essentially that concerned with abnormalities of the locomotor system, and therefore many of the problems with which it is associated have a mechanical basis. While, with the general improvement in medicine as a whole, some orthopaedic conditions, such as those resulting from tuberculosis of bones and joints, or muscle paralysis due to anterior poliomyelitis, are getting less frequent, many others are becoming more important because larger numbers of people are surviving with generalised diseases which affect the locomotor system.

Injuries, similarly, will remain a major problem in the future not only because trauma will inevitably persist in the community, but also because, firstly, the general advance in age of the population means that falls and the like in the elderly are more common, and, secondly, increasing mechanisation at home, at work, and in transportation means that serious multiple injuries are becoming more frequent. As trauma, while by no means restricted to the locomotor system, affects this part of the body most frequently, it is convenient to have a short textbook which deals with both orthopaedics and injuries. The medical student can thus have a small and inexpensive textbook which covers both subjects—such is the intention of this volume.

The author is most grateful for the help he has received from his colleagues in the preparation of this work. Particularly, to Mr. J. O. Robinson, surgeon at St. Bartholomew's Hospital for contributing the chapter on Abdominal Injuries, and to Mr. R. Campbell Connolly, neurosurgeon at St. Bartholomew's for his chapter on Head Injuries. Mr. I. M. Hill, thoracic surgeon to St. Bartholomew's Hospital went through and gave most helpful advice on the chapter dealing with Chest Injuries, and Mr. R. L. G. Dawson, surgeon to the Plastic Surgery Centre at Mount Vernon Hospital very kindly assisted in the portion dealing with Skin Loss in the first chapter of the Trauma Section.

In addition, the author would like to thank all those who have assisted in the preparation of this work, including the publishers, the general editor Mr. Selwyn Taylor, and the secretaries. Finally, he would like to express his gratitude to all those who assisted him in his own training in orthopaedic surgery.

J. N. ASTON.

St. Bartholomew's Hospital,
  London.

TRAUMA

CHAPTER ONE

TRAUMA—INTRODUCTION

Summary

PRINCIPLES OF FIRST AID

1. Initial Assessment
(a) Local
(b) General

2. Initial Treatment
Local—
(a) Splintage of Fractures
   (i) In The Leg
   (ii) In The Arm
(b) Dressing of Wounds
(c) Control of Bleeding

3. Resuscitation
(a) Control of Pain
(b) Maintenance of Blood Pressure

ANTI-TETANIC MEASURES
LATER MANAGEMENT

1. General

2. Local—Wound Surgery
(a) Incisional Wounds
(b) Crushing Injuries

MANAGEMENT OF SKIN LOSS

1. Free Grafts
(a) Split Skin
(b) Full Thickness (Wolfe)

2. Flap Grafts

3

INTRODUCTION

Two factors are tending to make the management of trauma in modern times increasingly important. Firstly mechanisation, particularly in transport, where the severity and frequency of road accidents increase with the speed of vehicles. Secondly the ageing population, as, due to improved medical treatment and social conditions, many more people reach old age. In the elderly, owing to a combination of loss of locomotor control and senile osteoporosis, falls become more common and more serious.

PRINCIPLES OF FIRST AID

The main aim in First Aid is the saving of the patient's life and the prevention of further damage to the patient. *Locally*, it consists of the splintage of injured parts and the control of bleeding. Open wounds should be covered by a clean dressing to prevent further contamination. Splintage reduces pain, and where a fracture is present, reduces the risk of further injury to soft tissues by the broken bone ends. Bleeding can usually be adequately controlled by firm pressure. Only where a major artery has been cleanly divided is a tourniquet indicated.

General measures are directed towards minimising shock by keeping the patient warm, and reducing movement to a minimum. The preservation of a good airway is important in unconscious cases.

On admission to the casualty department of a hospital, management of the severely injured patient may be considered under three headings:

1. Initial assessment both of the local injuries and the general condition.
2. Initial treatment.
3. Resuscitation.

1. INITIAL ASSESSMENT

Immediately on arrival in the hospital casualty department, the patient should be subject to a rapid, but thorough examination, which must be conducted with the utmost gentleness. This has two aims—firstly to diagnose the nature of the injuries sustained, and secondly to decide their relative priority in treatment. Examination, therefore, falls into two parts —local and general.

(*a*) Local Examination

The fact that a major fracture has occurred is usually obvious, and actual bony details will be obtained upon radiological examination. Similarly, a soft tissue injury can be seen at once, and at this stage, its true extent can wait. The most important aspect is to check the arterial blood flow beyond the site of injury, as, if impaired, this must be restored within three to four hours from the time of the accident if permanent ischaemic changes are to be avoided. The state of the peripheral nerves in the injured part should also be checked where possible on arrival at hospital, thus providing a 'base line' against which future progress can be assessed, though this may be impracticable in severely shocked or unconscious patients.

(b) General Examination

A rapid, but complete general examination directly the patient is brought into the casualty department is essential, as otherwise the presence of some obvious injury—for example a compound fracture in a limb—may cause a more serious lesion, such as a ruptured intra-abdominal viscus, to be overlooked. This is particularly necessary in an unconscious patient.

Also, included in the general examination, must be a recording of the blood pressure and pulse rate. This is not only required in the assessment of the general condition on admission, but also so that any deterioration or improvement may be appreciated.

X-rays. Only rarely is it necessary to subject the seriously injured patient to a radiological examination immediately upon arrival in hospital. Usually it can be deferred until he is fit enough to be transferred to the ward, where it may conveniently be carried out on the way—provided he is not moved from the stretcher upon which he lies. In severely shocked patients it may be wiser to wait, and take films with a portable machine under general anaesthesia in the operating theatre, after resuscitatory measures have been taken. Portable films in the operating theatre are also indicated to check the position of fractures after manipulation.

2. INITIAL TREATMENT

In most instances this is a continuation of the first aid measures, and can be considered under two headings—local treatment of the injured part, and general treatment of the patient as a whole.

Local Treatment. This has three aspects—the splintage of fractures, dressing of wounds, and control of bleeding.

(a) Splintage of Fractures

Splintage, at this stage, is required to control pain, and prevent further injury to the part. It is important to appreciate that at this early stage it is not associated with attempts to reduce the fracture. Various methods may be employed:

(i) *In The Leg.* The simplest measure is to bandage the injured limb to its un-injured neighbour. To provide added support, in thigh injuries, a wooden splint, which extends from the axilla to the ankle, may be applied along the affected side, being bandaged to the trunk and both lower limbs. This is known as a 'Long Liston' splint.

A more effective method for use in fractures of the femoral shaft is by the use of a Thomas splint. This consists of a padded ring to go round the top of the thigh, with a metal rod extending down the outer side of the limb, bent across beyond the foot, with a notch to which cords may be tied, and then up the inner side. The leg is attached to the splint by 'extension' adhesive plaster with cords as shown in Figure 1, purchase being obtained above by pressure of the ring against the ischial tuberosity.

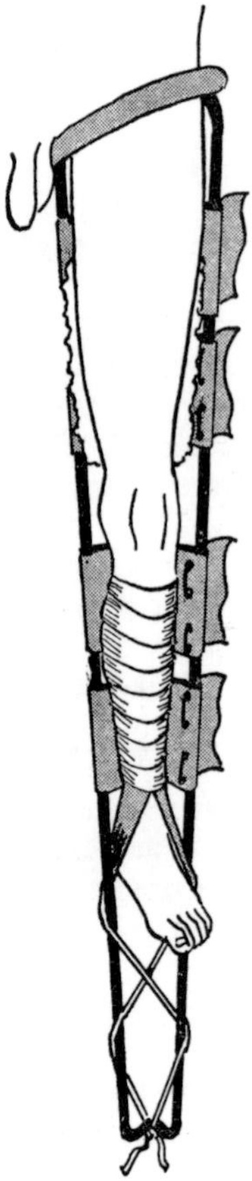

For injuries below the knee, plaster-of-Paris slabs, in six-inch widths, provide a useful method of temporary splintage. These take the form of a 'U' by being applied to one side of the limb from mid thigh level, round the sole of the foot, and up the opposite side. Care must be taken not to bandage such slabs too tightly as increasing swelling may lead to interference with circulation.

(ii) *In The Arm.* The simplest method is to bandage the injured limb to the chest, with the elbow flexed, leaving the hand free where possible, and with a pad of wool in the axilla. For forearm injuries, a plaster-of-Paris slab, extending from the upper arm to the metacarpal heads on the dorsum of the wrist with the elbow flexed at a right angle provides good immobilisation. For wrist injuries, a plaster slab, extending from just below the elbow to the metacarpal heads, may also be used. A Carr's wooden splint (Fig. 2) is also often satisfactory as a temporary measure.

FIG. 1. Thomas splint, using 'fixed' skin traction

(b) Dressing of Wounds

At the stage when the patient is first brought in to the casualty department disturbance of the wound must be minimal and, after the initial inspection, it should be merely covered by a sterile gauze pad and left until definitive treatment is undertaken, usually in the operating theatre.

(c) Control of Bleeding

In the majority of instances, bleeding does not provide as great a problem as might be anticipated. The reasons are two-fold; firstly, unless a wound has been caused by a sharp instrument the injured tissues will be crushed and the smooth muscle in major blood-vessel walls go into spasm; secondly, in a severely shocked patient blood pressure is low, thereby reducing blood flow. In most cases, therefore, bleeding can be adequately controlled by firm direct pressure applied to the wound, which can be achieved by the use of a large pad of wool and a crêpe bandage.

If bleeding is profuse from a lacerated wound, owing to injury to major blood vessels, whenever possible after the patient has reached hospital, direct digital pressure should be applied to the region of the vessels above the wound until preparations for more definitive wound haemostasis are complete. Only rarely is a *tourniquet* necessary. On those occasions when it is required, care must be taken that it is applied well above

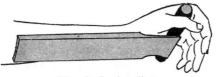

FIG. 2. Carr's splint

the wound, over muscle, so that main nerve trunks are not damaged by direct pressure. It must be tight enough to arrest both arterial and venous blood flow, otherwise, by merely obstructing venous return, it will cause congestion, and can actually increase the blood loss. When a tourniquet is used, it is essential to note the time of application, and if it has to be maintained for longer than one hour before further action can be taken, it must be released briefly, every hour, to avoid the risk of ischaemic damage to the limb.

3. RESUSCITATION

Resuscitatory measures fall into two categories—the control of pain, and the maintenance of an adequate blood pressure by means of blood transfusions if necessary and bed rest.

(a) Control of Pain

Disturbance of the patient must be minimal. Clothing is loosened or cut away sufficiently to allow a proper initial examination, but the patient should not be fully undressed or moved from the stretcher upon which he entered hospital until he is either anaesthetised ready to be placed on the operating table if surgery is required, or, if not, until he is put to bed in the ward.

Adequate analgesia must be obtained, which usually means the administration of morphine. To ensure rapid absorption, especially when the blood pressure is low, this should be given by intra-muscular or even intravenous injection. The dose should be 10–15 mg ($\frac{1}{6}$–$\frac{1}{4}$ grain). When morphine is used care must be taken to ensure that a second dose is not accidentally given.

(b) Maintenance of Blood Pressure

In the less severely injured, control of pain and avoidance of unnecessary disturbance suffices to prevent a significant fall in blood pressure, but if there is any doubt, intravenous fluids should be administered, of which there is a choice of four—isotonic (normal), saline, polysaccharide solutions of high molecular weight, plasma, and whole blood.

Normal Saline. This is convenient because of its easy availability, but has only limited use in the treatment of severe shock, as saline is of low molecular weight, so that the fluid given is therefore rapidly lost.

Polysaccharide Solutions. The high molecular weight of the substances contained in these solutions prevents their rapid loss, and they can, therefore, provide an artificial substitute for plasma. They are useful in practice, because as long as the fluid is kept sterile, they can be stored indefinitely without risk of deterioration, and so can be kept always available for immediate use. Examples are 'Dextran' and 'Rheomakredex'.

Plasma. This is blood serum, from which the cells have been extracted. Its protein content, therefore, renders it the best means of restoring blood volume, though it lacks the oxygen carrying power of the red blood corpuscles.

Whole Blood. This is the ideal material for use to restore blood volume in cases of severe blood loss, because not only does it restore the fluid content, but also the oxygen carrying capacity of the blood. It must, however, be compatible with the blood of the patient to whom it is administered. For this reason, in a casualty department, only universally compatible Group 'O', Rhesus Negative blood, is given to patients who need blood immediately upon arrival in hospital, and a small stock of blood in this group should be kept available for emergency use in all hospitals liable to receive major accidents. Where massive haemorrhage has taken place, whole blood provides by far the most effective means of treatment, and transfusion should be started forthwith.

The quantity of fluid required, and the rate of its administration, will vary from case to case, but in a shocked patient brought into a casualty department up to three pints may be given without hesitation, the first as rapidly as possible. The actual quantity needed can be decided after the patient has been transferred to a ward.

ANTI-TETANIC MEASURES

Measures to combat tetanus must be taken in all patients brought to hospital with open wounds. The universal use of tetanus antiserum (A.T.S.) is not now advised, and the following steps should be taken:

(i) In purely superficial wounds, if contaminated with soil, tetanus toxoid (to produce an active immunity) should be given.

(ii) In clean but larger wounds without a large quantity of devitalised tissue, and where early surgical cleansing is possible, both toxoid and a wide-spectrum antibiotic should be administered.

(iii) Where there are large wounds present, heavily contaminated, and with much devitalised tissue present, both anti-toxin (A.T.S.), anti-biotics, and toxoid should be employed. Whenever A.T.S. is given, a preliminary small dose should be injected subcutaneously to see if a reaction occurs.

Where active immunity is desired, the patient should be encouraged to attend hospital or his own doctor for two booster doses at intervals of six weeks and six months respectively.

LATER MANAGEMENT

1. GENERAL

As soon as the initial measures are completed, the patient should be moved to a w~rd. Ideally, this should be a resuscitation ward, linked with the casualty department, and where all the facilities necessary to deal with such patients are available.

In severely injured cases, the patient should remain upon the stretcher on which he arrived at the hospital, and this should not be moved from a suitable trolley. The transfusion set up in the casualty department should still be running. Resuscitatory treatment is continued, and the blood pressure and pulse rate are charted. When the patient is fit he is moved to the operating theatre.

In the theatre the patient is anaesthetised. In view of the probability that the stomach will not be empty, a sucker, connected up, must be available beside the anaesthetist, and endotracheal anaesthesia is always employed. Only when the patient is unconscious should he be undressed and transferred from the stretcher to the operating table.

Apart from specific procedures required for individual lesions, considered elsewhere in the appropriate sections, initial surgery consists of the treatment of soft-tissue wounds, and the reduction and splintage of fractures.

2. LOCAL

Soft-tissue wounds are of two types—incisional wounds, where tissues have been simply divided, and crushing injuries. In many cases there will be a mixture of both. In addition, as a result of shearing forces, frank skin loss may occur, leaving the deeper tissues intact.

(a) Incisional Wounds

Unless there has been a delay of over eight hours from the time of injury, incisional wounds are treated by *primary suture*. The wound is cleansed, and obviously devitalised tissue excised both from the skin edges and deeper layers and haemostasis secured, following which it is carefully closed in layers. When it is both large and deep, a small drain may be inserted. At the conclusion a pressure dressing is applied, and in large wounds of the limbs a temporary plaster-of-Paris slab splint may profitably be employed. Local and general wide-spectrum anti-biotics should be administered in all but trivial cases.

If primary suture is not possible, either because the patient's general condition does not permit surgery within eight hours of injury, or because he did not reach hospital in time, then after cleansing, excision of dead tissue, and haemostasis, the wound is packed open. Four to seven days later, if the wound is now clean, the skin edges are freshened and the wound is closed. This is known as *delayed primary suture*. Tension of the sutures must be avoided, if necessary either by making relaxing incisions parallel to the line of the wound, or by the use of split skin grafts (Thiersch grafts) to cover areas where the skin edges could only be approximated under tension.

Where sepsis is present, wound closure must be deferred until this is under control. Then the granulation tissue which will have formed must be curetted away, dead tissue removed, and wound edges excised, being undercut if necessary, after which the wound is sutured where possible without tension. This is *secondary suture*. If a skin defect is left, this must be covered either by split skin grafts, or a full thickness flap or pedicle.

(b) Crushing Injuries

Minor crushing injuries, such as may follow direct blows, produce only bruising, which is due to damage to the capillary blood vessels in the subcutaneous fat, and causes local swelling and blue coloration of the skin. A collection of fluid blood in the tissues is known as a *haematoma*. Occasionally when large and tense, drainage of a haematoma through a small incision may be employed.

When an injury is due to a more severe crushing force, particularly if there is also a shearing element present, both skin and deeper tissue will be destroyed. In such cases, suture is impossible and primary treatment consists of excision of all non-viable material. Where possible, the raw area is then covered with split skin grafts. If this is not practicable, then the wound is packed open and skin cover provided as soon as possible.

MANAGEMENT OF SKIN LOSS

There are two basic methods of replacing skin loss, either by the use of free grafts or by flaps. With free grafts, the skin is taken directly from the donor site and applied to the recipient area. The graft then being dependent for survival upon direct oxygenation from its new bed. Where a flap is employed, the skin for grafting remains attached to the area from which it has been raised by its base, thereby retaining its blood supply. Only when new vessels have grown into the flap from the recipient site is it detached from the donor area.

1. FREE GRAFTS

These may be either split skin or full thickness skin.

(*a*) Split Skin Grafts

In this, strips of partial thickness skin, consisting of epidermis and part of the dermal layer, but nowhere extending down to the subcutaneous fatty tissue, are cut using a special flat knife. These are then applied directly to the recipient area, which has been cleaned and rawed up in preparation. The grafts are held in place by firm even pressure so that blood cannot collect beneath and raise them from the recipient site. Because part of the dermis remains, full regeneration of skin follows in the donor area.

Indications. Split skin provides a very satisfactory immediate treatment for areas of skin loss, but as there sometimes is no subcutaneous fat, the grafted part is adherent to deeper structures, and liable to injury, so that it has no place as a permanent measure in the management of skin loss in areas subject to pressure. As it is cosmetically ugly, it also has no place in the definitive treatment of facial injuries. It has, however, a very useful function in the replacement of skin in donor areas from which flaps have been taken to provide full thickness skin elsewhere.

(*b*) Full Thickness (Wolfe) Grafts

These are grafts in which the whole thickness of dermis down to the subcutaneous fat is included, thereby providing a slightly firmer cover.

Its main use, therefore, is in replacing small areas of skin loss in the hand and face.

2. FLAP GRAFTS

Skin flaps may be used to provide full thickness skin cover to denuded areas in three ways. Firstly, where the area to be covered is not very large, use may be made of the natural elasticity in the skin by turning one side of the raw area into a flap, and swinging it across to meet the opposite edge (*Rotation Flap*).

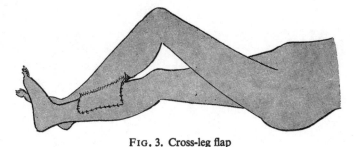

FIG. 3. Cross-leg flap

Secondly, in the extremities, a flap may be raised at one site and the affected limb brought to it. Thus, in the case of a hand, a pedicle may be raised from the abdominal wall, and sutured to the denuded area by approximating the limb to it. In the leg, a denuded area in one foot may be covered by raising a flap from the opposite calf (*Cross-Leg Flap*, Fig. 3).

Thirdly, a flap may be raised from the chest or abdominal wall, remaining attached at either end, the two edges of the central portion being sutured together to form a tube. This can then later be detached at one end and swung across to reach the recipient area, where it can be opened out once more (*tubed pedicle graft*). This method is of particular value in replacement of skin on the legs or arms. Occasionally the tube is moved by stages from the abdomen to the forearm, and then from the forearm to the face.

I. FRACTURES

A. A TYPICAL FRACTURE (Fig. 4).

When normal living bone is subjected to sufficient violence to cause it to break, considerable damage inevitably occurs to the soft tissue structures which surround it. The periosteum will be stripped from the bone, and torn through on the side opposite to that to which the injuring force

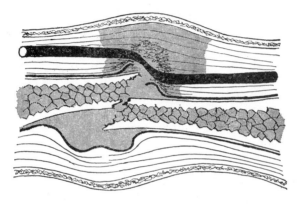

FIG. 4. A typical fracture showing tear in periosteum concomitant soft tissue damage which occurs

was applied. Blood vessels contained in the bone and periosteum are ruptured, and a haematoma forms round the fracture site. Blood also escapes through the rent in the periosteum into the surrounding muscles, producing a variable degree of swelling.

Union of Fractures

Bone-forming cells, known as *osteoblasts*, are poured out into the fracture haematoma both from the bone ends, and from the deeper layers of the periosteum, into the fracture haematoma. This, as it clots, takes on the appearance of thick and rather coarse granulation tissue, due to the deposition in it of calcium phosphate. This is known as *callus*. Gradually the callus hardens, and it becomes remoulded to form mature bone.

Clinical Features of Fractures

The presence of a fracture should be suspected if, following an injury, the patient complains of severe localised pain and tenderness in the region of a bone. Examination will confirm the tenderness and localised pain on

15

movement, and in addition swelling can usually be seen. Abnormal mobility at the site of injury and crepitus between the broken bone ends are patho-gnomonic of a fracture, though neither should deliberately be sought, as local damage and shock may be increased thereby.

Clinically, union of the fracture can be tested by absence of local tender-ness at the fracture site, the bone feeling rigid and causing no discomfort on attempting to bend it. Radiologically a fracture can be said to be united when bony trabeculae can be seen crossing the fracture site. In addition, the shadow of well-defined fusiform callus beneath the periosteum can usually be seen.

B. TYPES OF FRACTURE

Various terms are employed to describe different types of fracture:

(i) A *simple* fracture is one in which there is no skin wound directly communicating with the bone at the fracture site. It must be stressed that this term does not imply that the fracture will be easy to manage, or will unite rapidly. Skin damage may be present, but it does not link with the actual fracture site.

(ii) A *compound* fracture is one where there is a skin wound directly communicating with the bone ends. For practical purposes there are two types—either the broken bone may burst through the skin from within, or the injuring force may directly damage the skin, so that the wound leads down to the fracture. Compound fractures are always due to con-siderable violence, but of the two methods of causation, the second is the more serious because the direct damage to soft parts is greater, and there will be more contamination of the wound from outside.

(iii) A *comminuted* fracture is present when the bone has been broken into more than two fragments. Where there is a third fragment, of tri-angular shape, present on the convex side of the fracture, this is known as a 'butterfly' fragment.

(iv) A *'greenstick'* fracture is an incomplete fracture occurring when a long bone is broken on the convex side, but buckled on the concave. They can only occur in the growing bones of children, where there is some springiness present.

Also occurring in children are *fracture-separations of the epiphysis*. These result from injuries to long bones near their ends, where the epi-physis is avulsed through the epiphyseal line, on the concave side taking a triangular fragment of the diaphasis with it. Only rarely is the epiphysis alone avulsed.

(v) A *pathological* fracture is one occurring in a bone rendered abnorm-ally fragile because of a pathological process already taking place within it. In practice, these are of two types—those occurring through a local area of bone destruction, such as a neoplastic deposit, and those which may occur in any bone of an individual who has a general weakness throughout the skeleton, such as crush fractures of vertebrae occurring in elderly individuals who have generalised senile osteoporosis (p. 293) or in children with fragilitas ossium. (p. 197).

(vi) A *stress* fracture, similar to that occurring in metal subjected to repeated strains in the same direction, may occur in bones subject to abnormal stress, as in the shaft of the second metatarsal, where there is reversal of the metatarsal arch—a 'March Fracture' (p. 153).

C. MECHANISM OF PRODUCTION OF FRACTURES

Fractures result from either direct or indirect violence.

Those due to *direct* violence occur where the injuring force is applied directly to the bone at the site of fracture, either from a severe blow or a crushing force. Compound fractures therefore more commonly follow direct violence, and such fracture lines are either transverse or comminuted.

Fractures due to *indirect* violence usually follow rotational injuries, and the fracture line will be oblique or spiral. An appreciation, from the shape of the fracture line, of the direction of the causative rotatory force, will facilitate the reduction of the fracture, which is achieved by rotating the limb in the opposite direction.

D. COMPLICATIONS OF FRACTURES

These fall broadly into two categories—those resulting from the problem of obtaining sound bony union in good position, and those due to associated soft tissue lesions.

(i) Complications Associated with Union

These are of two types: those in which sound union is obtained, but the resulting position is unsatisfactory—Mal-union—and those where bony union is retarded—Delayed or Non-union.

(a) *Mal-union*

A fracture may be united in bad position either because the bone ends overlap, leading to shortening, or because the bone ends unite with an angular deformity, or because they unite in a position of rotation in the longitudinal plane. The significance varies according to the bone involved. On the whole, mal-union is of less importance in the upper limb, because in the leg, shortening, unless compensated for by a raised shoe, will cause a limp, and also as a result of altered stresses on the spinal column, may lead to various back troubles. Angular deformities in the leg, particularly in the sagital plane, are also important, because the altered alignment in weight bearing joints will cause later degenerative changes.

In the arm, minor deformities are important in fractures of the radial and ulnar shafts, as considerable restriction of rotation at the wrist may result. A valgus deformity of the elbow may be important, by causing irritation of the ulnar nerve as it goes round the medial epicondyle of the humerus.

An occasional cause of late deformities following injuries in childhood is due to premature epiphyseal fusion, due to a crushing injury of the epiphyseal cartilage. This is most commonly seen in the ankle, where forced adduction may cause crushing of the lower tibial epiphysis on its medial side, so that the normal growth in the lower fibular epiphyses gradually produces a varus deformity of the ankle.

(b) Delayed and Non-union

The rate of union in fractures is closely related to the local blood supply. At sites where it is abundant union rarely presents a problem. At other sites, where the anatomical arrangements of the vessels is such that a fracture interrupts the blood supply to one fragment, union normally is slow, and perfect immobilisation must be maintained until there is clinical and radiological evidence of union. Examples are fractures through the femoral neck, the waist of the scaphoid, and the neck of the talus. In each case, if the blood supply to one fragment—the femoral head, the proximal pole of scaphoid, or the body of the talus—is completely cut off, *avascular necrosis* will follow. This is first shown radiologically by apparent increase in bone density, in fact due to relative osteoporosis in the surrounding bone which has a normal blood supply, resulting from hyperaemia due to the injury, which cannot affect the fragment which is devoid of circulation. Later, the avascular portion of bone becomes softened, and unless protected for a long period, collapses.

At other sites, the blood supply may be impaired by the severity of the local soft tissue damage. Thus compound fractures, especially those following severe violence, tend to take longer than a simple fracture at the same level. Fractures of the mid-shaft of the tibia often are slow in uniting. This is partly because, if the fracture is below the point of entry of the nutrient vessels the blood supply to the lower fragment is not very full, and partly because, being subcutaneous, damage to the periosteum is often fairly extensive.

When union is taking longer than normal, but before there is definite sclerosis between the bone ends radiologically, a state of *delayed union* is said to exist. Some such cases eventually do unite by bone, in others union never can occur.

Non-union is said to be present when, radiologically, there is an obvious gap between the bone ends, with sclerosis of the fragments. The gap between the ends may be bridged by fibrous tissue, when '*fibrous union*' may be said to have taken place, or a false joint ('*pseudarthrosis*') may form, the bone ends becoming lined by fibro-cartilage. Clinically some movement at the fracture site persists. In the case of fibrous union, this may be a mere jog with some discomfort. When a pseudarthrosis has formed there may be a considerable range of movement which may be relatively painless.

(ii) Complications in Surrounding Soft Tissues

The early complications of a fracture all occur in the surrounding soft tissues, either due to damage from within the bone ends damaging important structures, or from without, as a result of the direct violence of the injury.

(a) *Skin*

In any compound fracture the skin has been damaged. In severe injuries skin loss may be extensive. The management of skin loss in injury is considered on p. 100. As a late result of skin damage at the time of injury, scarring may present a problem, either because the scarred area is tender and the skin liable to break down, or because resulting contractures may lead to residual stiffness and deformity.

Skin necrosis may also occur, due to pressure upon it, either from within by a displaced fragment of bone, or from without by pressure from ill-fitting plaster casts or splints. Blisters commonly occur at fracture sites over areas of severe bruising and swelling. They are usually of no importance, except as an indication of the extent of deeper soft tissue damage, but they may become infected, and if the full thickness of the skin breaks down also, this may spread to deeper tissues.

(b) *Muscle and Tendon*

In most major fractures some damage to the muscles or tendons in close proximity to the bone ends occurs. This, together with the scarring and organisation of the haematoma associated with the fracture site, accounts for much of the stiffness which follows removal of the splintage after the fracture has united. Occasionally, in fractures of the shafts of major long bones, a length of muscle may become trapped between the bone ends, thereby preventing reduction.

Myositis Ossificans. This is ossification in muscle. It is liable to occur as a complication of severe bony injuries in the neighbourhood of the larger joints, and is commonest in the region of the elbow. As a result of the bony injury, the periosteum is torn, and osteoblasts are released into the surrounding muscle. If, as a result of too early mobilisation of the affected joint, particularly if passive movements are practised, healing is delayed, and further osteoblasts are poured out, ossification will occur in muscle attachments. This is first visible radiologically as a vague shadow, but later it becomes more well defined as a clear-cut calcified mass.

(c) *Nerves*

Major nerves may be injured by the broken bone ends, particularly at sites where nerves are closely related to bone, as with the radial nerve where it lies in the musculo-spiral groove in the humerus, or in the region of major joints. Most such lesions result from sudden stretching of the nerve at the moment of injury, no permanent damage is done to the neurones, and full rapid recovery follows (neuropraxia). In more severe cases the nerve fibres lying in their sheaths are pulled apart (neuro-temnesis), the sheaths remaining intact. In these cases the distal portion degenerates, and a new fibre regenerates by growing down the intact sheath. This is a slow process, often taking several months, and unless the muscles paralysed as a result are kept contracting artificially, they will become so wasted and fibrosed by the time the nerve has recovered that severe permanent weakness persists. Occasionally the nerve is completely severed (axontemnesis) when no recovery of nerve function is possible, unless the nerve ends are repaired surgically.

(d) *Blood Vessels*

Major arteries are particularly liable to injury in the region of the elbow and knee joints because, near these levels, the arteries bifurcate and are anchored by muscle attachments. As a result the artery is injured by one of the bone ends. Rarely is the vessel completely divided, usually as a result of irritation it goes into spasm, and the stimulation of the accompanying sympathetic nerves around the vessel causes constriction of the other vessels making up the collateral circulation. Complete gangrene does not ensue, but ischaemic necrosis of muscle fibres occurs, because this is the tissue most dependent upon a good oxygen supply. Quantities of muscle fibres therefore become replaced by fibrous tissue which contracts. In the forearm this produces a typical clinical picture known as *Volkmann's ischaemic contracture*, because the finger flexors are those most severely affected, so that the patient is unable to extend the fingers with the wrist dorsi-flexed, whereas some extension does become possible when the wrist is fully palmar flexed. In the calf this causes rigid clawing of the toes.

(e) *Sudek's Atrophy*

One late soft tissue complication of fractures occurs, known as Sudek's Atrophy. Normally, after a bony injury, as a result of the trauma and of the subsequent immobilisation necessary to allow union in good position, some stiffness and swelling with hyperaemia follows. Occasionally this is exaggerated, the skin is shiny and warm with some swelling and marked stiffness, with pain when any movement is attempted. This is a complication of wrist and foot injuries and is due to over-reaction of the sympathetic nervous system. The frequency appears to be linked with the severity of the bony injury, but it also tends to occur more frequently in nervous patients. Management consists of active movement of the part, in spite of the discomfort so caused; rarely a sympathetic block is required.

E. THE TREATMENT OF FRACTURES

Basically, from the angle of treatment, fractures fall into three groups:

(*a*) Those where treatment is directed primarily towards dealing with the soft tissue lesions, the bony injury being largely ignored. Examples are the flat bones, such as the scapula or ilium, avulsion or fractures of bony outgrowths, such as the transverse processes of vertebrae, or sites where joint surfaces are involved and abundant blood supply makes union almost certain, such as the upper end of the humerus or calcaneum. In all these, treatment consists of early mobilisation of the injured part.

(b) Those where blood supply to the bones is good and union will occur, but unless good alignment is restored and maintained mal-union will follow. The majority of fractures fall into this group.

(c) Those in which not only is splintage necessary to maintain good position, but also, unless complete immobilisation is continued, union of the fracture will not take place. In all these cases the blood supply to one of the fragments is poor.

In practice, therefore, the treatment of the average fracture can be divided into three phases: Reduction—to restore normal bony alignment, Immobilisation—to maintain the reduced position until union has occurred, and finally, Rehabilitation to restore normal function to the injured part, or failing this assist the patient to cope with any residual disability—which is dealt with at the end of this chapter.

(i) Reduction

This aims at restoring bone length and alignment, to overcome both angular and rotatory deformities. This is achieved by either closed manipulation or open operation.

Closed reduction consists firstly of traction to disengage the bony fragments or to overcome their overlap, followed by the manoeuvre required to restore normal alignment. The latter consists of manipulating the limb in the reverse direction to that which caused the fracture. Most injuries of the major long bones result from falls or other forms of indirect violence, with some rotation, and this must be taken into account at the time of reduction.

Open reduction is indicated where either manipulative reduction fails, as when there is some soft tissue interposition between the bone ends, or, where in the overall interests of the patient it is desirable to avoid external splintage of the part. In most cases, therefore, open reduction is associated with some form of internal fixation. Examples of the latter are patients with multiple injuries, where internal fixation or one or more fractures will simplify the overall management, or where early mobilisation of the part is desirable, as in elderly patients with fractures of the upper end of the femur.

(ii) Immobilisation

This may be achieved by either external or internal splintage.

(a) *External Fixation*

In order to achieve complete immobilisation it is necessary to include the joint above and the joint below the fracture, though in many instances, provided the bone ends can be locked in position at the time of reduction, immobilisation of both joints may not be necessary, as in most fractures of the wrist and ankle where the elbow or knee can be left free.

The usual method of external splintage is by a plaster-of-Paris cast, in the application of which three practical points must be borne in mind. Firstly, a skin-tight cast must never be employed where there is a risk of swelling, otherwise the circulation of the limb may be impaired. Secondly, care must be taken to avoid ridges or indentations as the plaster is applied, otherwise when they harden they may cause pressure sores. Thirdly, the plaster should be applied smoothly, evenly, and rapidly so that the whole cast sets in one piece, not in several layers which may crack at a later date.

(b) *Internal Fixation*

In open reduction of a fracture direct manipulation of the broken bone allows perfect restoration of position. This is almost always followed by some form of internal fixation, which ideally should be strong enough to avoid the need for additional external support.

The method employed will depend upon the nature and site of the fracture. Two basic forms of fixation are in use. Firstly, those which obtain their hold by screws which traverse the bony cortex. Sometimes screws are used alone (Fig. 5) or, they are used in conjunction with a

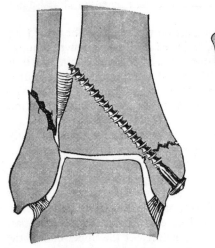

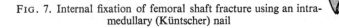

FIG. 5. Internal fixation of fractured medial malleolus using a screw

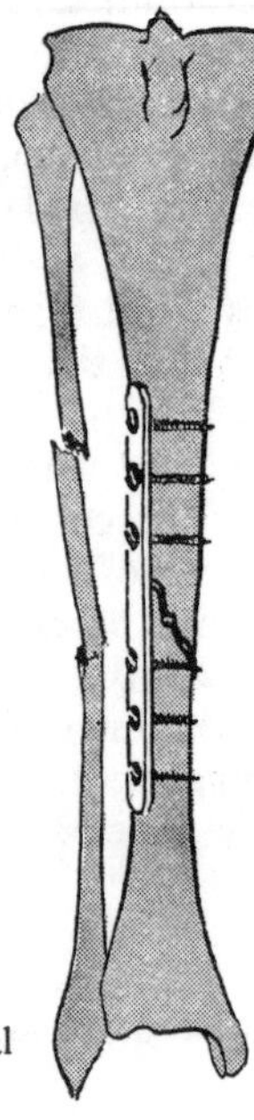

FIG. 6. Internal fixation of fractured tibial shaft using a plate and screws

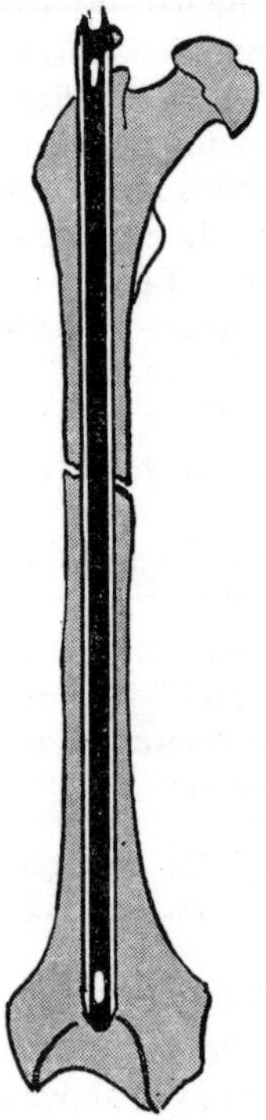

FIG. 7. Internal fixation of femoral shaft fracture using an intra-medullary (Küntscher) nail

strong strip of metal, known as a plate (Fig. 6). Secondly, fixation is obtained by the use of internal splintage traversing the medullary cavity of the bone. These take several forms, ranging from large nails (Fig. 7) to various special types of screw (Fig. 8).

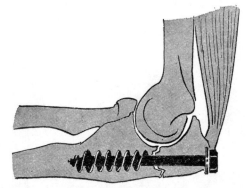

F<small>IG</small>. 8. Internal fixation of fractured olecranon using intramedullary lag screw

The metal used for internal fixation must not only be strong, but also produce no reaction when implanted in the tissues. Those in common use are high-grade stainless steel, a chrome cobalt alloy known as 'Vitallium' and 'Titanium.' If more than one piece of metal is implanted, as when a plate and screws are used, it is important that they are all of the same material. If different metallic implants are employed tissue fluid will set up electrolysis between them so that a reaction in the tissues will follow.

F. TREATMENT OF COMPLICATIONS

In general these will be considered under the two headings—Bony and Soft tissue.

(i) Bony

(a) *Mal-union*

Where there is a degree of mal-union sufficient to cause early or late disability it must be treated by *osteotomy*. That is division of the bone at a suitable site. In the large majority of instances the certificial fracture so caused is held in the corrected position by a suitable form of internal fixation.

(b) *Non-union*

Where non-union is established, or appears to be inevitably developing, *bone grafting* should be employed.

This may take two forms, depending upon the kind of bone employed in the graft. It may be either cortical or cancellous. In both the fracture site is exposed, and the bone ends freshened, the fibrous tissue joining the ends being removed.

Cortical Grafting. In this method a strip of hard cortical bone, usually taken from the subcutaneous surface of the tibia, is used to bridge the gap. In larger bones, such as the femur, tibia, or humerus, a bed in the recipient bone is cut which accurately fits the piece of 'donor' bone. This is known

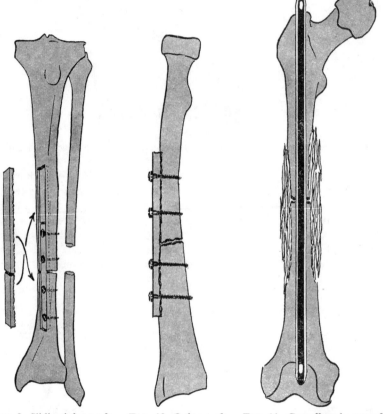

FIG. 9. Sliding inlay graft for fractured tibia

FIG. 10. Onlay graft for fractured radius

FIG. 11. Cancellous bone graft, with intramedullary nail fixation

as '*inlay grafting*'. In the case of the tibia, the donor bone is usually taken from above the fracture site, and then used to bridge the gap by making one continuous groove—a '*sliding inlay graft*' (Fig. 9). Where this is not possible, as in grafting fractures of the radial and ulnar shafts, the recipient area is rawed up and the cortical donor graft is placed upon the bone. This is known as '*onlay grafting*' (Fig. 10).

Whichever method is employed, the graft is anchored in place by screws and cancellous bone chips from the surrounding bone are packed around.

Cancellous Grafting. Here no attempt is made to fix the fracture by the bone graft. Slivers of cancellous bone are taken from the ilium and packed around and across the fracture site. One or two small grooves are cut in the recipient bone so that some of the slivers can be actually made to bridge the gap. In this method it is often desirable to use internal fixation, with either an intramedullary nail (Fig. 11) or plate, to splint the fracture while union is taking place.

As, in fact, a fresh fracture has been created under as ideal circumstances for union as possible, after operation immobilisation must be maintained until union is complete.

(ii) Soft Tissue

The treatment of skin loss and nerve injuries are dealt with elsewhere. Consideration will therefore only be given to the management of myositis ossificans and vascular complications.

Myositis Ossificans. The basic method of treatment for this condition is rest. As the vague shadow of early calcification visible on the first X-rays becomes more clearly demarked as it turns into bone, gentle *active* movements may commence. Rarely, when all the reaction to the injury has entirely settled down, if the mature bone causes a block to some movement excision is justified, but this is not often indicated, because the amount of scarring also present in fact prevents any benefit from this procedure.

Vascular. Where arterial occlusion occurs it is a matter of great urgency to restore normal circulation, if permanent ischaemic changes are to be avoided.

Immediately, all constricting bandages and dressings should be removed, and while the injured part is kept cool, general vasodilatation is encouraged by warmth applied to the patient as a whole. If circulation does not return within a few minutes, the vessel should be explored. Sometimes division of

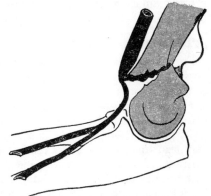

FIG. 12. Supracondylar fracture of humerus showing how the brachical artery may be injured

the deep fascia alone may suffice to relieve pressure on the vessel and allow return of normal circulation. More often, the vessel is in spasm because a fragment of bone is impinged against it (Fig. 12), in which case, if the fracture is reduced, and a solution of some vasolidator such as papaverine instilled around it, circulation may be restored. Failing this, or where obvious vascular damage can be seen, the injured segment of vessel should be excised and the divided ends either sutured or continuity restored by a graft, preferably taken from an autogenous vein. To encourage the rapid development of a collateral circulation, the appropriate cervical or lumbar sympathetic nerves should be temporarily paralysed by infiltration with local anaesthetic.

When ischaemic changes have occurred, the degree of contracture may be minimised by stretching the affected muscles, using spring splintage. Surgery is often required to release contracted muscles. In the forearm, block excision of the ischaemic flexor muscles may release those not involved and thus improve function. In the foot, troublesome clawing of the toes may be overcome by interphalangeal arthrodesis, and division of the tight extensor tendons (Lambrinudi's Operation, p. 190).

II. JOINT INJURIES

A. TYPES

Joint injuries may take four forms—a dislocation, where the articular surfaces are completely displaced from each other; a subluxation, where though displaced, the articular surfaces remain in contact; a sprain, in which there is a tear of the capsular ligament without disturbance of the relationship of the opposing articular surfaces, and a fracture-dislocation where, in order that the articular surfaces may become completely displaced from each other, a fracture of part of one of the bones must have taken place.

(i) Dislocations

For complete separation of the articular surfaces in a normal joint to be possible, the capsule of the joint must be completely torn through. This is, therefore, an injury resulting from considerable violence applied to the joint, and the soft-tissue damage may cause some residual stiffness through scarring. At certain sites where the cavity is shallow, residual capsular laxity may leave an unstable joint or, as in the shoulder, an unhealed rent may lead to recurrent dislocation. Pathological dislocations may occur where there is some inherent ligamentous laxity or abnormal muscle pull, such as in certain neurological disorders leading to paralytic dislocations. Pathological dislocations may also occur where the joint lining has been destroyed by an infective process.

(ii) Subluxations

Partial displacement of the articular surfaces of a joint, with the bones still remaining in contact with each other most commonly occurs in 'plane' joints such as the acromio-clavicular. In these cases residual laxity usually persists.

(iii) Sprains

Tears of the capsular lining of a joint may be of trivial nature, or they may be severe, involving a complete disruption of one of the collateral ligaments in a hinge joint. In the latter case momentary subluxation will have taken place, and unless the ligamentous rent heals recurrent sprains from minor violence may follow.

(iv) Fracture Dislocations

The fracture of the bony margin as it is dislocated may affect any joint, but it is most frequently seen in the more severe rotational injuries of the ankle joint.

B. TREATMENT OF JOINT INJURIES

This is similar in principle to that of fractures. In dislocations, fracture dislocations, and subluxations reduction is required first. This will be followed by a variable period of immobilisation, after which the joint is actively mobilised.

(i) Reduction

In dislocations and fracture dislocations reduction normally requires an anaesthetic, whereas in subluxations, simple pressure applied in the reverse direction to the displacement may suffice—as in the acromio-clavicular joint, where strapping is employed to press the outer end of the clavicle downwards while the humeral shaft and shoulder are pressed upwards (Fig. 13). Open reduction is required less frequently for true dislocations than in fracture dislocations. In fracture dislocations operative reduction may be indicated firstly, to ensure that a smooth articular surface has been restored, thereby avoiding the later development of osteo-arthritis, and, secondly, to maintain accurate reduction of the bony fragment by internal fixation. Sometimes a flap of soft tissue may prevent manipulative reduction of the bony fragment.

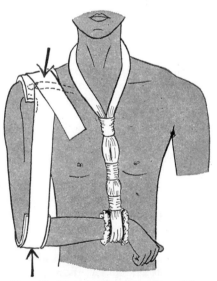

FIG. 13. Strapping for dislocation of the acromio-clavicular joint

In true dislocations operative reduction will only be necessary on the uncommon occasions when the displaced bone becomes 'button-holed' through a rent in the capsule and cannot be reduced by manipulative means.

(ii) Immobilisation

Unlike fractures, where immobilisation must be complete if mal-union or non-union is to be prevented, only in fracture dislocations is perfect immobilisation necessary. After dislocations, subluxations, and sprains, immobilisation is only necessary to prevent movement in the direction which caused the original injury, as in the shoulder, where the usual anterior dislocation is caused by external rotation, which is prevented by bandaging the arm, with the elbow flexed, to the side. Supportive immobilisation is usually only required for two to three weeks.

(iii) Mobilisation

Cautious mobilisation, avoiding strains in the direction which caused the capsular tear, should commence as soon as the initial reaction to the injury has begun to subside. The time will vary according to the natural stability of the affected joint and the rise of residual stiffness. For example, in the fingers, after reduction, the injured digit is strapped to an uninjured neighbour, thereby protecting it from lateral strains, and mobilisation is encouraged at once.

In all cases, movement must be *active*. Passive stretching of any injured part carries the risk of further damage and merely irritates the affected joint.

III. REHABILITATION

Restoration of function is an essential part of the treatment of all injuries. In the majority of cases a full return to normal can be anticipated, and the aim of rehabilitation is to achieve this as rapidly as possible. Less commonly irreparable damage may have occurred at the time of injury so that a full return to normal function cannot be expected.

A. IF NORMAL FUNCTION SHOULD RETURN

In most limb injuries, where full recovery can be expected, all that is required is encouragement to make the patient move all joints in the affected part which do not have to be immobilised. Then, as soon as splintage is removed, the injured limb should be used fairly actively until all the residual discomfort, stiffness, and swelling have disappeared.

In fractures, the immobilisation needed to permit bony union in good position accentuates stiffness caused by the associated soft-tissue damage. The joints below the site of injury are those mainly affected, because the muscles and tendons concerned with their movement will also have been damaged.

Methods of treatment will vary according to the severity of the injury and the mental attitude of the patient. In most cases, where the trauma was not very severe, encouragement to use the injured part normally suffices. Where the injury was more severe, or the patient is unduly nervous, a course of mobilising exercises under physiotherapy supervision, coupled with local heat to overcome muscle spasm, should commence as soon as the period of immobilisation is completed. These exercises are usually better carried out by a group of patients working together in a 'class', as thereby a mild spirit of competition may be introduced, which will help the more nervous individuals. Exercises done against increasing resistance, such as by lifting weights with the affected part are very valuable at a later stage. *Remedial Games* are also often helpful, particularly among younger adult patients, as thereby the exercises are made more enjoyable. *Occupational Therapy*, in which the patient does some interesting, purposeful, and constructive work to overcome residual stiffness and restore self-confidence is also often very useful. *Hydrotherapy* in which the patient carries out exercises against the resistance of water in a warmed pool is also useful in selected cases.

Occasionally, when injuries have been severe, and the patient's normal occupation involves hard physical work, a spell spent in a residential *Rehabilitation Centre* may be valuable, not only because such centres contain the best possible equipment and facilities, but also, unlike most hospital physiotherapy departments, treatment can be given to the patient continuously throughout the whole working day. In addition, firstly, an atmosphere is created which encourages maximal activity, and secondly, skilled assistance can be given to assist the patient to carry out specific activities which his normal occupation requires, and which he finds difficult to carry out.

Minor permanent deformities or joint stiffness may occur, but as a result of the treatment outlined above, do not in practice amount to a real disability.

B. IF A SIGNIFICANT DISABILITY WILL REMAIN

In cases where some permanent disability is anticipated, rehabilitation has two aims: firstly, to minimise the functional affects of that disability and, secondly, to help the patient cope with both the social and physical problems which may arise as a result. The former is dealt with along the lines already described.

The Medical Social Worker (Almoner) can often assist in the social and financial problems which arise as a result of some permanent disability, and suitable employment may be found by registering the patient as disabled with the Ministry of Labour, and referring him to the Disablement Resettlement Officer (D.R.O.).

In selected cases, the patient may be sent to a special residential resettlement centre to be taught a new craft within the limits of his capabilities. Occasionally special appliances may be required to help overcome certain specific disabilities.

CHAPTER THREE

SKELETAL INJURIES OF THE TRUNK

Summary

A. FRACTURES OF THE SPINE

These may occur in three ways, depending upon the mechanism of causation. Firstly, those due to direct blows on the back, leading to fractures of transverse processes, or more rarely, as a result of a direct blow on the mid-line, fractures of spinous processes. Secondly, those due to vertical compression forces, which cause crush fractures of vertebral bodies. Thirdly, those in which there is a combination of a compression force, with an antero-posterior shearing strain leading to a dislocation of one vertebra on another. In practice, therefore, the last type of injury follows when a forced flexion injury to the spine occurs in an individual who is moving forward at speed, as in a motor cyclist, thrown over his handlebars, lands on his head and shoulders. In this injury, the neurological contents of the spinal canal are almost inevitably damaged.

(i) Fractures of Transverse Processes

These follow direct blows, usually in the lumbar region, because in the thoracic spine the ribs are more liable to be fractured, and in the neck the mobility of the head is such that either the spine is undamaged or the force will have been so great as to cause a more severe injury.

The importance of fractures of transverse processes lies, not in the bony injury, or the bruising of muscle which goes with it, but in proximity of abdominal viscera which are often damaged at the same time. The organ most likely to be injured will be the kidney on the side which was struck.

Treatment

The actual fracture is unimportant and requires no specific treatment. To prevent adhesive formation in the muscle which has been damaged, and to help disperse the haematoma which inevitably forms, early mobilisation by gentle exercises is encouraged. As the pain diminishes, the tempo of the exercises should be increased.

Because of the risk of renal, or other intra-abdominal injury, all patients with fractures of lumbar transverse processes should be admitted to hospital for a 24–48 hour period of observation, and their urine examined for fresh blood as a routine measure.

(ii) Crush Fractures of Vertebral Bodies (Fig. 14)

These injuries occur when a vertical compression force is applied to the spinal column, such as when a heavy, bulky object falls upon the patient's shoulders from above, or the patient himself falls from a height landing on his feet. In such cases it is important to exclude injuries elsewhere.

Other injuries caused by falls from a height include fractures of the base of the skull and fractures of the calanea. Less commonly these may be a vertical fracture of the lower end of the tibia caused by the talus being driven upwards, and compression fractures of the condyles of the tibia or

31

femur. Often these other injuries predominate, and unless the spine is checked, crush fractures may be overlooked. This applies particularly to patients who are unconscious with fractures of the base of the skull.

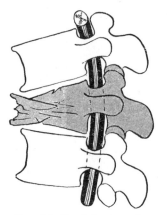

FIG. 14. Crush fracture of a vertebral body

Collapse of a vertebral body is also the commonest type of pathological fracture. This is because, firstly, they are filled with red bone marrow and therefore blood-borne metastatic deposits from a neoplasm elsewhere are particularly liable to settle in a vertebral body, and any generalised skeletal decalcification will also involve vertebral bodies extensively. It is for the latter reason that vertebral collapse affecting several bones is common in elderly persons with senile osteoporosis.

On clinical examination, a crush fracture should be suspected if there is an area of local tenderness over one vertebral spine, which also feels a little more prominent than its neighbours. Irritation of the nerve root at the affected level also often causes referred pain in the region supplied by that nerve.

Complication

Paralytic Ileus. This is a state where, owing to temporary suppression of autonomic nervous function, there is paralysis of the smooth muscle in the bowel. It is a condition which may follow any major injury, but is commoner in injuries of the trunk, particularly where there is a retroperitoneal haematoma which may irritate the sympathetic trunk, such as may occur with any injury to the lumbar spine. There is rapid severe abdominal distension, with copious vomiting and a complete absence of normal bowel sounds. This leads to rapid dehydration and a serious risk of inhalation of stomach contents.

Treatment consists of immediate and continuous gastric suction by a Ryles' tube, and intravenous fluid replacement, with nothing by mouth until there is evidence of return of normal bowel function as shown by the passage of flatus per rectum, and the presence of bowel sounds on abdominal ascultation.

Treatment

This will depend upon the age and general condition of the patient, the level of the lesion, and the amount of bony damage present. In the frail and elderly, management of the general condition will take priority over the local injury, and the possibility of some underlying pathological process requiring specific treatment—such as radiotherapy for a metastatic deposit—must be borne in mind.

Crush fractures of the dorsal spine are rarely serious as the rib-cage provides some support. For the same reason, little active correction of any deformity is possible. Management, therefore, in the young, fit individual consists of an initial period of strict recumbency on a firm bed until the initial pain has subsided, after which extension exercises are commenced. For the first three to four weeks, these are done lying prone, and then, when the patient becomes ambulant, their tempo is increased, and they may be better carried out in the competitive atmosphere of a 'back class'.

In the thoraco-lumbar region, where there is severe crushing of a vertebral body in an otherwise fit patient, reduction should be attempted, because persistent angular deformity at a level where the rigid thoracic spine joins the more mobile lumbar spine will cause considerable residual disability. Reduction is achieved by suspending the prone patient between two tables. In this position a plaster-of-Paris jacket is then applied, extending from the sternal notch to the symphasis pubis. The jacket is retained for twelve weeks, during which time intensive extension exercises are practised, and the patient encouraged to lead as active a life as possible.

In the lower lumbar spine, severe deformity is less likely to occur, so that, after a period of three to four weeks recumbency to allow the initial reaction to subside, with extension exercises in bed, mobility and a period in the 'back class' follows. If later symptoms occur, these can be adequately controlled by the provision of a stout corset.

(iii) Fracture Dislocation of the Spine (Fig. 15)

This is the most severe type of spinal injury in which not only is a vertebral body fractured, but the vertebra above is also displaced on that below, usually in a forward direction. This causes narrowing and distortion of the spinal canal, so that, with the exception of the cervical spine, where the canal is larger than the cord, the neurological contents are also almost always severely injured. The nature and extent of nervous damage varies according to the level of injury, because the spinal cord in adults terminates at the lower border of the first lumbar vertebra, and below this level the nerve roots contained in the canda equina alone will be affected. Lesions above this level will involve both spinal cord and nerve roots. The significance of the level of injury lies in the fact that, as nerve fibres

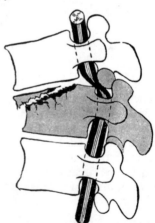

FIG. 15. Fracture dislocation of the spine, showing how the cord is damaged

contained in the roots have myelin sheaths, recovery is potentially possible, the unmyelinated fibres in the cord cannot regenerate (for further details of the neurological aspect see 'Traumatic Paraplegia', p. 34).

Treatment

Management of fracture-dislocations of the spine will be dominated by the neurological situation. In this section only preventative First Aid measures and treatment of the bony injury will be considered.

First Aid. In all spinal injuries the possibility of an unstable spine with the associated risk of incurring damage to the spinal cord as a result of injudicious handling of the patient must be kept constantly to the fore. The greatest care must therefore be taken at no time to flex the patient's spine when he is being moved on to the stretcher, or from the stretcher on to a bed, during the radiological examination, or in any other manoeuvre.

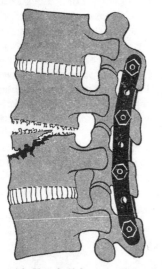

Later Treatment will also be dominated by the neurological situation. Where no serious damage has occurred, because the spine is unstable, immobilisation in a plaster-of-Paris jacket for twelve weeks is advisable to protect the cord from injury. Some months later, when the risk of sudden displacement has passed, spinal fusion of the affected vertebrae is usually indicated.

FIG. 16. Vertebral fracture dislocation held reduced by plate fixation of the spinal processes

Where paraplegia is present, particularly in lesions of the thoracolumbar and lumbar regions, early operative exploration is indicated in order to decompress the nerve roots, in which recovery can take place, and to stabilise the fracture. Permanent damage to the actual spinal cord has almost always occurred. Stabilisation may be obtained by fixation of the two vertebrae above and below the fracture together by the use of two curved plates secured by bolts passing through the spinous processes (Fig. 16). Thereafter, the fracture requires no further treatment and management is directed entirely towards the control of the neurological lesion.

(iv) Traumatic Paraplegia

Immediately after injury there is complete suppression of all neurological activity in the cord below the site of injury. Then, after a variable interval, some reflex activity returns to the isolated distal segment of cord. This initial period of complete inactivity is known as *Spinal Shock*.

At first, therefore, not only is there complete loss of sensation below the level of cord transection—which will, of course, not alter with the passage of time—but also there is flaccid paralysis of all musculature. This includes the smooth muscle of the bladder and lower bowel, so that both distend passively. In the case of the bladder, when the intra-vesical pressure has built up sufficiently to overcome the passive resistance of the sphincters, dribbling overflow incontinence will follow. During this period, with a stagnating pool of urine in the bladder, chronic infection may occur, the organisms entering via the urethra.

After an interval, varying from three weeks to three months, the isolated segment of spinal cord below the lesion begins to recover Reflex activity. Tone begins to return in the paralysed muscles, which change from being flaccid to spastic.

In the bladder, provided the muscle has not been allowed to become overdistended during the initial period of inactivity, and its lining has not become contracted owing to infection, when intra-vesical pressure reaches a certain level, reflex contraction takes place together with reflex relaxation of the sphincters. The result is that urine is passed with a normal stream, and the bladder emptied. This, however, takes place without either the knowledge or control of the patient, and is described as an *Automatic Bladder*.

In the bowel a similar state occurs, so that, provided the patient is neither constipated nor has loose stools, fairly regular evacuation will occur, such as happens after an interval with a colostomy.

In the lower limbs, the return of muscle tone may enable the patient to be taught to stand, and even walk, with suitable apparatus. When this stage has been reached, the application of some stimulus which would normally cause pain provokes an automatic withdrawal reflex, or spasm. If violent this may also cause emptying of the bladder and even evacuation of the rectum. Sometimes, either due to chronic urinary infection, or pressure sores in the skin, these reflex spasms become exaggerated, being provoked by the slightest stimulus, thereby causing the patient a great deal of discomfort and seriously impeding efforts at rehabilitation.

Complications

As already mentioned there are two important complications of traumatic paraplegia. These are chronic urinary infection and pressure sores. The *Pressure Sores* occur because, owing to the absence of sensory stimuli, the patient will not alter the points of pressure as he lies or sits. In addition, during the initial stage of flaccid paralysis, owing to absence of muscle tone, the periferal circulation will not be very brisk, making the skin more delicate than normal. Sores occur over bony points such as the sacrum, great trochanters, malleoli, and heels. If not rapidly and adequately treated, full thickness skin loss down to the underlying bone quickly follows.

Later, when tone has returned, owing to unequal pull in opposing muscle groups, contraction deformities may develop unless care is taken to prevent them. Exaggeration of the normal withdrawal reflex which appears when muscle tone returns may cause severe spasms in the limbs which may gravely interfere with efforts to rehabilitate the patient.

Management

Management of the traumatic paraplegic presents many complicated and specialised aspects, so that where possible such patients are better transferred to a special paraplegic centre as soon as possible. For practical purposes there are two phases: early, during the period of suppression of reflex activity, and later, when this has returned to the isolate segment of the cord.

(a) *Early*. Prevention of pressure sores and control of the urogental system dominates the early phase. Pressure sores can only be avoided by the regular and frequent alteration in position of the patient, with nursing treatment of all anaesthetic bony pressure points. The patient must therefore be turned every two hours by day and night, ideally from the moment of the accident. Established sores should be thoroughly cleaned and all dead tissues excised to encourage healing by granulation tissue. Occasionally skin grafting may be required.

Management of the bladder in the early stage is aimed at control of distension, thereby avoiding the vesical wall becoming stretched, and prevention of infection. Infection occurs because stagnant urine provides a good culture medium for organisms, which can reach the bladder fairly easily by ascending the urethra and passing through the relaxed sphincters. In practice both objects may be achieved either by intermittent catheterisation, conducted under the most perfect aseptic conditions, with regular bladder wash-outs using a mild non-irritant antiseptic lotion, or by the use of tidal drainage, employing an indwelling catheter. A wide spectrum anti-biotic such as oral penicillin—e.g. 'Penbritten', is also administered. Throughout, the external genitalia should be covered by a sterile dressing.

(b) *Later*. The principle aim in management turns to rehabilitation. As tone returns to muscles, it may be possible with suitable calipers and crutches to train the patient to walk after a fashion by swinging both legs through together 'tripod gait'. Nevertheless, most cases will be mainly, if not entirely, dependent upon wheelchairs, and time must be spent in teaching them how to make the most use of these. Some recovery may occur in involved nerve roots (as opposed to the cord) so that electrical stimulation of paralysed muscles should be practised until tone returns.

Where 'automatic' micturition becomes established, it is often possible to stimulate reflex bladder contraction by tickling the end of the penis, or some similar method. At first, to ensure that the bladder is completely empty, a catheter should be passed after voiding, but this can soon be discarded. Bowel movement can, with suitable dietary care, be made fairly regular in much the same way as with a colostomy.

If flexor spasms prove troublesome, they may be due to an irritative focus, such as a pressure sore. If they persist in spite of the removal of any obvious cause, division of the nerves supplying the more powerful muscle groups ('neurectomy') may be required. In extreme cases, intrathecal injection of alcohol may be employed to destroy the isolated segment of cord, thereby reverting to a completely flaccid type of paralysis.

B. INJURIES OF THE CERVICAL SPINE

As the cervical spine is the most mobile part of the vertebral column, it differs in several ways from the spine below it. The main features being that the intervertebral articulations are placed more laterally than elsewhere, and not so far behind the vertebral bodies, so that the nerve roots leave the spinal canal in an antero-lateral direction. The bodies themselves are smaller in relation to the size of the vertebra as a whole, and therefore subluxations and dislocations of one vertebra upon another are more common than elsewhere. There is more room in the canal than in the thoracic region, so that the cord has a greater chance of escaping severe damage than lower down though if it does occur and is not immediately fatal, the patient will have all four limbs involved, and will therefore be quadriplegic.

Injuries to the cervical spine fall into two groups, those due to flexion and those due to extension, though Rotatory forces also often play a part. Injuries of the atlanto-axial region will be considered separately.

(i) Flexion Injuries of the Cervical Spine

These may take three forms: firstly, subluxation of one pair of intervertebral joints with slight forward displacement. This is not a serious injury, though it may cause irritation of a nerve root leading to pain in the arm or side of the neck, depending upon the level. It is also likely to lead to early disc degeneration at this site (p. 180) resulting in cervical spondylosis at a later date.

Secondly, there may be frank dislocation of the intervertebral joints, which may be unilateral or bilateral, with or without a fracture of the vertebral lamina. Dislocation, particularly if unilateral, often results in locking of the facets. Severe irritation of the nerve root emerging at the affected level is almost inevitable, and damage to the spinal cord may also be present in this type of injury.

Thirdly, a crush fracture of a vertebral body may occur. This is rarely serious, and, as explained is less common in the cervical spine than elsewhere.

Treatment

Minor injuries merely require the use of a supporting collar for six to eight weeks, followed by a period of exercises to regain mobility.

More severe injuries require very careful handling from the outset. For this reason all patients attending hospital with neck injuries must not be moved until the extent of the damage is known and the greatest of care taken during the initial radiological examination. The possibility of associated injury to the cervical spine must be borne in mind whenever a patient is brought to hospital unconscious from a head injury. Dislocations of

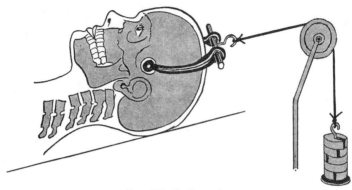

FIG. 17. Skull traction

intervertebral joints should be treated by traction using skull calipers (Fig. 17) inserted under local anaesthesia, so that the patient is not inadvertently moved. By this means the facets may usually be disengaged as considerable weight (up to 30 lb.) may be applied to the skull without causing discomfort. If after a few days radiographs show the dislocation to be reduced, then traction is maintained for a further two or three weeks, after which a 'Minerva' plaster cast, consisting of a jacket extending down the trunk to the iliac crests, and including the head, with a band round the forehead, over the eyebrows (Fig. 18). This will be worn for about twelve weeks.

FIG. 18. 'Minerva' plaster-of-Paris jacket

Occasionally reduction may be difficult, in which case, with skull traction still in place, open reduction is performed with the patient lying prone. At the same time the position is usually stabilised by wiring the vertebrae together, often with the addition of some cancellous bone chips taken from the ilium, so that later, bony fusion occurs.

(ii) Extension Injuries of the Cervical Spine

These occur when the head is violently driven backwards. It is therefore very common in road accidents, where sometimes when the trunk strikes the back of the car seat it is then thrown forwards again—the so-called 'Whip-lash Injury'. Extension injuries often cause no radiological abnormality, the anterior and posterior longitudinal ligaments being torn. Occasionally, possibly owing to momentary pressure from the ligamentin flavum and lamine posteriorly, severe cord damage occurs, even though X-rays appear normal. External injuries should be suspected in patients with evidence of injury to the face suggesting that the head has been knocked backwards.

Treatment

This consists of supporting the head in a firm collar or cervical brace for about ten to twelve weeks, followed by cautious mobilisation.

(iii) Atlanto-Axial Injuries

Three forms commonly occur—firstly, displacement of the atlas on the axis with fracture of the odontoid process (Fig. 19(a)), an injury from which the patient usually survives. Secondly, displacement with dislocation of the odontoid process backwards (Fig. 19(b)), which is almost invariably fatal owing to sudden pressure on the vital centres below the foraman magnum. This is the injury produced by judicial hanging. Thirdly, a vertical blow from driving the head downwards may split the atlas in a lateral direction (Fig. 20).

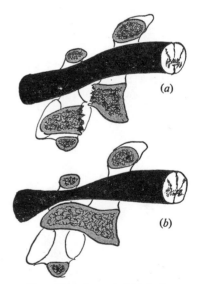

Treatment

Fractures of the odontoid are serious, so the neck is unstable. They are best treated by skull traction for four to six weeks, followed by a 'Minerva' plaster cast. Compression

FIG. 19. Atlanto-Axial injuries
(a) Fracture of the odontoid process
(b) Dislocation of the odontoid

fractures are less serious, and can be adequately controlled in most instances by a firm supporting collar worn continuously for six to eight weeks.

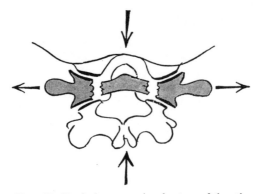

Fig. 20. Vertical compression fracture of the atlas

C. INJURIES OF THE PELVIS

Injuries to the bony pelvis are of two types—firstly, isolated fractures either of the pubic rami or ilium and secondly, double fractures of the pelvic ring. The latter may occur in three forms. The anterior portion of the ring may be broken if all four pubic rami are broken (Fig. 21), the loose portion being driven backwards. Or one side of the pubis may be fractured before and behind, and this then rolls outwards (Fig. 22). Finally, one side of the pelvic ring may be fractured, and not only roll outwards, but also be displaced upwards (Fig. 23).

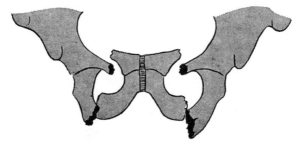

Fig. 21. Fractures of the pubic rami

As with all bony injuries of the trunk, the possibility of visceral damage must be constantly borne in mind. In pelvic injuries this applies with particular force, because the rectum, bladder, and urethra are contained within the pelvic cavity, and, as the membranous urethra passes through the pelvic diaphragm this is especially vulnerable. A distended bladder is also very liable to be ruptured by a blow hard enough to disrupt the pubic bones.

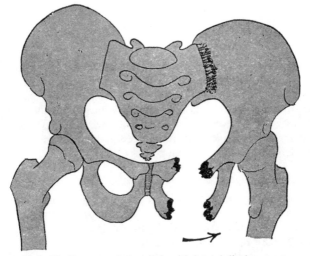

FIG. 22. Fracture of the pelvis with lateral displacement

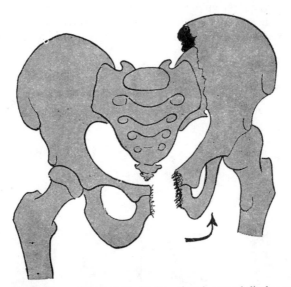

FIG. 23. Fracture of the pelvis with lateral and upward displacement

(i) Isolated Fractures

These follow direct blows and occur, therefore, rather more readily in the more osteoporotic bones of the elderly. Fractures of the ilium alone, while less common than fractures of the pubic rami, usually result from greater trauma and therefore cause more constitutional upset to the

patient. Fractures of the pubic rami on one side only are of little significance unless they extend into the hip joint.

Treatment

After more serious intra-pelvic damage has been excluded, these injuries
should be treated in the same way as severe bruising, by early mobilisation.
Weight bearing can be resumed within a few days, the only exception being
where the fracture line extends into the hip joint. When this has occurred
the joint cavity will have filled with blood (*Haemarthrosis*) and the acetabular articular cartilage may have been damaged, so weight bearing
should be deferred for three to four weeks.

(ii) Fractures of all Four Pubic Rami

Detachment of the whole anterior segment of the pubis follows a severe
blow on the front of the pelvis. Such injuries usually result from road
accidents, or sometimes from falls from a height, when the patient lands
prone, striking this region on some hard object. The significance of injuries
of this nature lies in the grave risk of associated damage to the bladder or
urethra. The membranous urethra as it passes through the pelvic diaphragm is particularly vulnerable. The bony injury is important only if
the fracture line extends into the hip joint, or, in women of child-bearing
age, when residual displacement may obstruct normal delivery of an
infant.

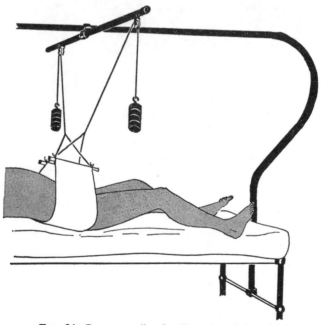

FIG. 24. Cross-over sling for disruption of the pelvis

Treatment

This is mainly symptomatic. An initial period of rest is necessary until the floating fragment begins to become stabilised, because otherwise the opposing pull of the abdominal muscles above, and the hip adductors and intra-pelvic muscles below, cause considerable discomfort. But, as soon as possible, active movements of the lower limbs is begun, the patient remaining in bed for four to six weeks after injury.

Very rarely, if the acetabular articular surfaces have been severely distorted, open operation possibly using a screw to hold reduction is required.

(iii) Lateral Disruption of the Pelvic Ring

In these injuries, as the pelvic ring has been broken both behind and in front of the hip, the natural tendency for the lower limb to roll outwards will open up the pelvis anteriorly. The plane of cleavage in front will be either through both pubic rami on the affected side, or through the pubic symphysis (*Diastasis of the Symphasis pubis*). Behind, the break may be through the ilium, at the sacroiliac joint, or through the ale of the sacrum itself.

Treatment

This is aimed primarily at closing the anterior gap. Three methods may be employed. Firstly, a sling passed beneath the pelvis and suspended, with cords which cross each other, to weights on opposite sides (Fig. 24), thereby providing a continuous circumferential squeeze to the pelvic ring.

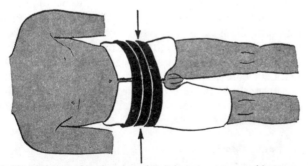

Fig. 25. Short plaster-of-Paris spica with strip cut out to provide compression in pelvic disruption

Secondly, a plaster of-Paris spica cast may be employed, where, in order to achieve the lateral pressure required, a strip is cut out of the front of the spica, and the edges are then brought together by an encircling rubber bandage applied as firmly as possible (Fig. 25). To permit healing, in both methods either the sling or plaster spica should be maintained for four to six weeks. Lastly, when there has been a diastasis of the public symphasis, the gap may be closed surgically by wiring the pubes together. This method allows early mobilisation in bed, but weight bearing on the affected side must be deferred for six to eight weeks to permit the posterior part of the injury to heal.

(iv) Combined Lateral and Upward Displacement

In this, which is the most severe form of pelvic fracture, the displaced fragment, with the lower limb attached, not only has rolled upwards, but is also displaced upwards. To correct this position, therefore, not only must the pelvis be compressed from side to side, but traction must be applied to the affected leg. In such cases the sling method is easiest to employ, with skeletal traction on the leg through a tibial tubercle pin.

COMPLICATIONS OF PELVIC INJURIES

(i) Rupture of the Bladder or Urethra

These are the commonest serious complications of pelvic injuries, and, unless treated immediately, extravasation of urine into the surrounding tissues can be a serious problem, leading to widespread necrosis. In all but minor injuries, therefore, the patient should be told to hold his water, and a catheter passed. If urethral damage has occurred, passage into the bladder will be impossible, no urine will be obtained, but a few drops of blood may appear from the catheter or the urethral orifice on its withdrawal. If the bladder has been ruptured, the catheter will pass freely, but only a few drops of bloodstained urine will be obtained.

Rupture of the urethra is treated by operative exposure through the perineum, when the catheter can be passed across the site of injury into the bladder under direct vision, and the urethra then repaired over it. Postoperatively an indwelling catheter is retained for two to three weeks.

Rupture of the bladder may be either intra-peritoneal, which is likely only to occur when it is full, or extra-peritoneal into the surrounding soft tissues. Treatment consists of supra-pubic opening of the bladder, with repair of the rupture, and the insertion of an indwelling urethral catheter. The abdominal wound is closed with drainage either of the peritoneal cavity or extra-vesical soft tissues.

(ii) Injury of the Rectum and Anus

Occasionally the rectum and anus are involved in severe pelvic fractures. Where this is so, there will be bleeding from the anus, and radiographically there may be fractures through the sacrum or coccyx. Gas shadows outside the rectum may also be visible on X-ray. Most such injuries are extra-peritoneal, when there is intra-peritoneal rupture there will be abdominal rigidity and absent bowel sounds.

Treatment consists of diverting the bowel contents through a colostomy in the descending colon, with repair of the local damage. After the rectal wound has healed, three to four weeks later, the colostomy may usually be closed and normal bowel function restored.

(iii) Injury to the Main Iliac Vessels

The external iliac vessels run round the brim of the pelvic cavity, and are therefore sometimes torn in severe pelvic fractures. This is a serious complication, and fatal internal haemorrhage may occur. In addition there will be obvious circulatory impairment in the leg on the affected side. In such cases an attempt should be made to repair the vessel either by direct suture, or by the use of an arterial graft.

(iv) Injury to the Sciatic Nerve

The sciatic nerve may sometimes receive a traction injury in severe pelvic injuries, with disruption. This is rarely serious, and providing any temporarily paralysed muscles are protected until their motor power returns, full recovery can be expected.

CHAPTER FOUR

CHEST INJURIES

Summary

GENERAL REMARKS

In the management of all chest injuries the maintenance of normal oxygen and carbon dioxide levels in the blood stream must be the dominant feature. This may be disturbed in three ways—the accumulation of pulmonary secretions, impairment of movement in the chest wall, and collapse of the whole or part of a lung. In practice, a combination of all three factors is often present. Chest injuries may result from either a direct blow, a crushing force, a penetrating wound, or blast from an explosion. Diaphragmatic injuries may be associated with both thoracic and intra-abdominal damage.

I. INJURIES TO THE CHEST WALL

These involve fractures either of ribs or sternum.

(i) Single Fracture of a Rib

These result from a direct blow, which in the elderly where some osteoporosis is present may be quite trivial. Rarely a rib may crack during a violent coughing fit.

Until union has commenced sharp local pain is caused not only by movements of the trunk or upper limb on the affected side, but also by deep breathing or coughing with the result that, particularly in the elderly, serious respiratory complications may follow.

Treatment

In fit individuals, supportive non-stretch strapping centred at the level of the injury and extending half way round the chest is usually all that is required. In older patients, or those with multiple injuries elsewhere, when it is important not to impede breathing or coughing in any way, infiltration with local anaesthetics may be employed.

(ii) Multiple Rib Fractures

These are due either to a compression force, or a direct blow with some fairly large object. They are serious injuries, because of the dangers of respiratory impairment. If several ribs are fractured at two sites on the same side, this will drive in part of the chest wall ('*Stove-in Chest*'). This portion will be flail, so that on inspiration, when the rest expands, this portion is sucked inwards, and on expiration it is blown outwards ('*Paradoxical Respiration*').

Treatment

In multiple rib fractures, treatment must be mainly directed to the preservation of respiratory function. This often necessitates the use of an endotracheal tube passed through the larynx for a short period, or by an opening made in the trachea (*Tracheotomy*). By this means, pulmonary secretions may be aspirated and the lungs artificially ventilated. If insufflation is required for more than a short period, a respirator may be employed.

Where paradoxical respiration is present, if a respirator is not used, the flail portion of the chest wall must be stabilised, either by internal fixation of the rib fractures, or by traction using a clip round one of the mobile portions of a rib.

(iii) Fractures of the Sternum

These may follow either a direct blow on the part of the chest or a forceful flexion injury to the thoracic spine. Sternal fractures are liable to be associated with fractures of ribs or disruption of the costal cartilages, (the latter not being evident on radiographs) so that those due to a direct blow often represent a type of 'stove-in chest'.

Management is similar to that described for multiple rib fractures.

II. INJURIES OF THE PLEURA AND LUNG

Under normal circumstances the pleural cavity is a potential space only. The lung is held against the chest wall by negative pressure. If, therefore, either air or fluid enter the pleural cavity, the lung will collapse.

(i) Pneumothorax

Air may enter the pleural cavity either from the lung or major air passages within the chest, or from the outside, through a penetrating wound of the chest wall. A pneumothorax resulting from an injury will be associated with some tissue damage, so that blood is also very liable to be present in the pleural cavity, forming a *haemopneumothorax*.

(a) Closed

This results when air escapes into the pleural cavity from the lung. The lung then collapses, and in most instances the rent heals rapidly, allowing the lung to re-expand. Aspiration of the air will encourage re-expansion, and is indicated in the majority of cases. This is best achieved by intubation of the pleura using a water seal drain.

(b) Open

This results from a penetrating injury to the chest wall, so that air is sucked in from the outside. If the wound is large so that air blows in and out of the pleural cavity freely, movements of the opposite lung will cause the mediastinum to move, greatly impairing respiratory function.

Treatment

The wound must be closed as soon as possible, and covered by an airtight dressing, and the pleural cavity is then drained by a fine catheter into

a water-sealed bottle in which negative pressure is maintained by a pump
if air leak is excessive.

(c) Tension

Occasionally, when there is an open pneumothorax air may be sucked
in on inspiration, but owing to the valve-like nature of the wound in the
lung or chest wall it is not expelled on expiration, so that positive pressure
is built up in the pleural cavity pressing on the mediastinal contents and
moving them across to the unaffected side. This is a very serious condition
which, unless relieved rapidly, will cause death from respiratory insufficiency.

Treatment

Immediate partial relief may be obtained if a wide bore needle is inserted
into the pleura, thereby permitting the air under tension to escape. This
should be followed by catheter underwater drainage of the pleural cavity
using a sucker.

(ii) Haemothorax

This occurs when there is blood in the pleural cavity. Where present,
aspiration is necessary to control pulmonary collapse. If the haemothorax
cannot be completely evacuated in this way, open operation to remove the
clot is indicated, for if it remains there is a risk of infection or permanent
lung and chest wall retraction. All such cases should have chemotherapy
cover. If the clot is not removed at this early stage, later decortication of
the lung is required. After both early and late operation, immediate full
expansion of the lung must be obtained by multiple tube drainage with
suction and vigorous physiotherapy.

(iii) Pulmonary Contusions and Lacerations

Contusions may be due to a compression force either from a solid
object, or from the blast of an explosion. Pulmonary lacerations may be
associated with severe injuries to the chest wall.

In both instances, management essentially consists in the preservation of
adequate oxygenation of the blood until the pulmonary injury has recovered. Local treatment for the lung itself is rarely required, unless a major air
passage is damaged.

If severe, the patient has a tracheotomy, and using a cuffed endotracheal
tube is kept on artificial respiration, with bronchial aspiration at frequent
intervals.

III. INJURIES OF THE HEART AND GREAT VESSELS

With penetrating injuries or antero-posterior compression, cardiac
injury may occur, with bleeding into the pericardium. If this is not relieved,
tamponade will occur, shown by diminishing cardiac output, raised venous
pressure, and paradoxical pulse.

Though tamponade may be relieved by aspiration of the pericardium, if there is any doubt about the situation, immediate thoracotomy with evacuation of the blood and control of the haemorrhage gives the best chance of survival.

Rupture of major blood vessels, often caused by deceleration injuries is not necessarily immediately fatal, and may be suspected if the haemo-thorax is very large and the patient's condition requires unusually large blood transfusion to improve. Early transfer to a unit where major vascular surgery is possible gives the best hope of survival.

CHAPTER FIVE

ABDOMINAL INJURIES
(by J. O. ROBINSON)

Summary

I. ABDOMINAL VISCERA

INJURY to the abdominal viscera may be caused by blunt trauma or penetrating wounds.

Blunt trauma may be due to crushing of the abdominal wall against the rigid spine and sacrum, or sudden and violent compression. It may also be due to a tangential force which causes a viscus to be torn from its pedicle. Indirect trauma, such as an explosion or falling from a height, may produce a sudden violent movement within the abdominal cavity and cause disruption of a hollow viscus, or the tearing of its blood vessels.

Penetrating wounds are less commonly found in civilian life, but may be due to knives, bullets, or foreign materials such as glass, wood, or metal.

DIAGNOSIS

An accurate history of the method whereby the injury was sustained is one of the most important aids to diagnosis. It must be appreciated, however, that this is not always forthcoming as the patient may be unconscious or disorientated by an intracranial lesion or shock. Similarly abdominal physical signs may be minimal or even absent, even when a viscus has ruptured.

The two major effects of either type of abdominal injury are haemorrhage producing *shock* and rupture of a hollow viscus producing *peritonitis* or a combination of both, either of which may be lethal if left untreated.

Established shock is readily recognised in the cold and clammy patient, the rising pulse rate and poor volume, the falling blood pressure, and the shallow rapid respiration. The danger lies in overlooking a minimal degree which may become rapidly severe and irreversible.

Peritonitis is recognised by the immediate onset of an acute and constant abdominal pain which becomes increasingly severe. Haemorrhage alone will cause some degree of peritoneal pain, but it is usually less severe than that due to the spilled content of a ruptured viscus. Vomiting when present, and particularly when it is frequent, is strongly suggestive of intestinal perforation. Tenderness and rigidity, with or without guarding, are usually present and are directly related to the extent of the underlying lesion, but are masked in severe shock and with the loss of consciousness. These signs may be present as the result of reflex spasticity due to a fractured thoracic cage, which in itself does not exclude concomitant intra-abdominal injury. Physical examination of the abdomen may be further confused by contusion and severe bleeding within the layers of the abdominal wall. Distension is a late sign and denotes an ileus accompanying peritonitis, but is also found in extensive trauma to the abdominal parietes, especially if there is retroperitoneal bleeding or injury to the spine or pelvis. Rectal examination should never be omitted to exclude a pelvic peritonitis as shown by the presence of tenderness high up anteriorly. Blood on the examining finger suggests injury to the colon or rectum.

INVESTIGATIONS

These may be invaluable but should not delay exploratory laparotomy if the clinical findings justify this.

(i) Blood

The haemoglobin should be estimated, the patient's blood group determined, and blood cross-matched. The serum anylase level may be helpful in assessing damage to the pancreas. Haematocrit readings are valuable in suspected cases of continuing blood loss. A high white count is indicative of active infection or severe retained haemorrhage.

(ii) Radiological

The chest and abdomen should be X-rayed when possible to see the extent of any thoracic injury, and the presence of air under the diaphragm which indicates rupture of a hollow viscus. It will also show evidence of bone damage and foreign bodies, areas of density occasioned by haematomas and the fluid levels of ileus.

(iii) Abdominal Tap

This is sometimes of value in cases of suspected haemorrhage, particularly from the spleen. Gas, bile, and urine may be withdrawn and carry their obvious significance.

Treatment

An accurate diagnosis should be made as quickly as possible, but treatment must accompany whatever means may be required to determine the full extent of the injury.

Pre-operative

The temperature, pulse rate and volume, blood pressure, and respiration must be recorded every 20 minutes. Severe injuries are more easily cared for under a monitor when possible.

A good airway must be constantly maintained. Other injuries must receive temporary treatment, such as the splinting of fractures. An intravenous infusion of Dextran or Rheomacrodex should be set up as soon as the serum has been taken for grouping and cross-matching. Analgesics must be administered to prevent pain, which will increase the degree of shock. Parenteral anti-biotics should be given to cover the possibilities of a septic peritonitis and the development of bronchopneumonia. A nasogastric tube should be passed to prevent the possible regurgitation of gastric content with subsequent inhalation into the bronchial tree, and a catheter passed into the bladder for drainage and accurate recording of the urinary output.

Operative

Exploratory laparotomy should be carried out as soon as the patient's condition allows, and preferably within four hours of the injury. Unless the exact site of the lesion is known a right or left paramedian incision is the one of choice. The abdominal cavity must be inspected carefully and gently to minimise shock to the patient and further trauma to possibly damaged tissues. Bleeding should be immediately arrested, spilled contents sucked and mopped out, and any ruptured intestine secured with non-crushing clamps to avoid continued leakage. Each organ should then be inspected to exclude concomitant injury.

Post-operative

The blood volume must be restored by blood transfusion during and after surgery. The fluid, electrolytic balance, and plasma protein level must be carefully checked and corrected by intravenous infusions until the patient's gastro-intestinal tract can once again take over from the bio-chemist. The use of intravenous vitamins is of undoubted value in these patients. Gastric aspiration should be continued until there is evidence of intestinal motility as shown by the passage of flatus per rectum and the return of bowel sounds. Solid food is started as soon as a bowel action has occurred, which may be stimulated by the use of suppositories.

A. HOLLOW VISCERA (Gastro-intestinal tract)

The fixed portions of the gastro-intestinal tract are slightly more commonly injured by blunt trauma than by penetrating wounds which tend to involve the small intestine. The stomach is an exception to this rule, for, although it is rarely involved, it is more frequently injured by a foreign body. The duodenum, duodeno-jejunal flexure, the upper 15 cm. of jejunum and the terminal ileum are the sites more frequently damaged by non-penetrating wounds as they are readily compressed against the rigid spine. Rupture of the retroperitoneal portion of the duodenum may give rise to surgical emphysema of the abdominal wall, and the escape of gas around the right kidney will clearly define this organ on radiography. The colon is infrequently damaged, but is more likely to suffer the effects of penetrating than non-penetrating wounds.

Tears in the mesentery produce severe haemorrhage which must be controlled by ligation after which the intestine related to that portion of the mesentery must be observed to ensure that it remains viable. Small perforations of the intestine can usually be closed by a 'purse-string' suture, but larger tears, and always those in the stomach, should be closed in layers in a transverse direction to prevent narrowing of the lumen. Extensive lacerations, pulping of the intestinal wall, or multiple adjacent perforations normally require resection and end-to-end anastomosis. Lesions of the colon are treated in the same way as the small intestine, but the risk of infection is greater: it is, therefore, sometimes advisable to exteriorise the bowel and carry out staged procedures. The formation of a temporary caecostomy after any primary anastomosis following resection for an injured portion of the colon is a wise precaution. The peritoneal cavity should be drained after the closure of any gastro-intestinal perforation or resection and anastomosis particularly if the damage has involved the retroperitoneal tissue where blood collects and forms a good medium for infection.

B. SOLID VISCERA (Spleen, Liver, Pancreas)

(i) Spleen

The spleen is the most commonly injured intra-abdominal viscus following trauma to the trunk or lower thoracic cage. Non-penetrating wounds are much more frequently the cause of rupture of the spleen than penetrating wounds. The characteristic clinical picture is that of intra-abdominal haemorrhage accompanied by shock, followed by paralytic ileus. Tenderness and guarding are usually confined to the left hypochondrium, but may initially be or become generalised. A poorly defined mass may become palpable under the left costal margin, where crepitus may be felt if the ribs have been broken. Pain referred to the top of the shoulder (Kehr's sign) is present in about half the number of cases and is due to irritation of the under-surface of the diaphragm by blood and clot.

Radiography is particularly helpful as it usually demonstrates elevation of the left leaf of the diaphragm, with a large dense shadow beneath it, and depression of the gastric air bubble which may be distorted. An abdominal tap will produce blood, but should only be used in doubtful cases.

Approximately 25% of patients develop acute symptoms and signs of a ruptured spleen but recover rapidly, and may remain apparently well for a period of a few days or even months, when there is a sudden return of the symptoms of severe and acute intra-abdominal bleeding (delayed rupture of the spleen). The interval is most commonly within the first two weeks after the loin injury.

The operative treatment of ruptured spleen is almost invariably splenectomy.

(ii) Liver

The liver is liable to be equally affected by blunt and penetrating injuries because of its size and fixity. Rupture produces profuse haemorrhage with shock and peritonitis. Any leakage of bile will increase the degree of peritonitis.

Treatment is aimed at controlling the haemorrhage, which if severe must be reduced by compressing the hepatic artery and portal vein between the finger and thumb where the vessels course through the free edge of the lesser omentum (Seton Pringle's manoeuvre). Dead and lacerated tissue is removed, obvious vessels are ligated and the liver tissue closed with large blunt needles carrying chromic catgut. Packing with rolls of gauze is to be avoided as it inevitably leads to gross infection, which predisposes to massive secondary haemorrhage when the pack is removed.

(iii) Pancreas

There are no specific clinical manifestations of this rarely injured viscus. Serum amylase estimation is the only useful ancillary investigation, but the level is not always raised immediately after the injury. Injury to the pancreas should always be looked for and may be made evident by the presence of white plaques of fat necrosis on the mesenteries and omentum. If the organ is contused drainage down to the site is adequate, but if there is laceration of the tail this should be removed. Damage to the main duct requires complicated surgery in the form of anastomosis over a T-tube, or even anastomosing a portion of ileum to the distal cut end of the duct.

II. GENITO-URINARY SYSTEM

Injuries to the urinary system are due to either blunt trauma or to a penetrating wound.

A. THE KIDNEY

The kidney may be contused, suffer varying degrees of laceration or be totally avulsed. The main symptoms are those of shock (the extent of which varies with the degree of blood loss or other concomitant injuries), the passage of blood in the urine and pain in the loin. The signs are those of shock, bruising, tenderness, and a palpable mass in the loin, and usually a varying amount of bright red blood in the urine.

Investigations

Apart from estimating the haemoglobin level, grouping and cross-matching blood, an immediate intravenous pyelogram is necessary to establish the presence of renal function on the opposite side, and to assess whether any normal renal pattern can be visualised on the damaged side. If radiography is difficult or impossible to carry out, the presence of one normal kidney can be ascertained by the injection of 5 ml. of 0·4% indigo-carmine intravenously, and observing through a cystoscope the efflux of dye from the ureteric orifice within ten minutes. A faint discolouring of the urine from the suspected side indicates that total avulsion has not occurred.

Treatment

In cases of renal contusion and mild lacerations in which there is minimal shock, no mass in the loin, and only moderate haematuria, symptomatic treatment is all that is necessary. With severe lacerations the shock must be controlled, after which the loin is explored and whenever possible the lacerations sutured. A totally avulsed kidney must of necessity be removed and any co-existent intra-abdominal injury sought.

B. THE URETER

The ureter is only damaged by penetrating wounds, and it is remarkable how often the ureter escapes such trauma. It is recognised by the site of the penetration and the haematuria. In minor cases the ureter is repaired over a T-tube, but in more severe cases the area is drained and at a later stage the defect may be replaced with an isolated segment of ileum.

C. THE BLADDER

The bladder may be ruptured by a penetrating wound, or by a crushing injury, usually when the bladder is full. The leak may be intraperitoneal or extraperitoneal, the latter will be discussed with intrapelvic rupture of the urethra as the treatment is basically the same.

(i) Intraperitoneal Rupture

There is a sudden severe pain accompanied by shock and evidence of lower abdominal peritonitis with tenderness, guarding, and rigidity. There is often an initial leakage of urine per urethram after which no further urine is voided. The pelvis is X-rayed to exclude a fracture.

Treatment

After the shock has been controlled, the lower abdomen is explored, urine sucked out from the peritoneal cavity in which other lesions are sought. Large and accessible rents are closed, but smaller rents are often difficult to find and may be safely left. In either case the bladder is drained by a small suprapubic or urethral catheter, the choice depending on the extent of damage and the degree of haemostasis which has been achieved.

(ii) Extraperitoneal Rupture

It is almost impossible to distinguish clinically this lesion from an intrapelvic rupture of the ureter. The patient although desiring to micturate cannot do so. Increasing pain develops in the suprapubic region where eventually a slow-growing mass develops, which is a haematoma and not a full bladder.

Treatment

The shock is controlled and an X-ray of the pelvis taken to exclude a fracture. A cystourethrogram, using a dilute radio-opaque solution may be gently instilled down the urethra and will demonstrate the site of the tear. A urethral catheter is then gently passed under general anaesthesia. If it passes easily into the bladder, from which a few blood-stained urine drops may drain, it can be assumed that there is a tear in the bladder, but if the catheter fails to pass, the rupture is probably in the membranous urethra, and a small quantity of pure blood will drain.

An extraperitoneal rupture of the bladder necessitates suprapubic exploration, evacuation of the retropubic haematoma, the insertion of a suprapubic catheter, and drainage of the space of Retzius.

Rupture of the intrapelvic portion of the urethra demands the same initial procedure. When the bladder is opened attempts are made to guide the urethral catheter into the bladder, either with a finger inserted through the internal urinary meatus or with two metal bougies, one introduced via the penile urethra, and the other through the internal urinary meatus. A plastic urethral catheter is then inserted and where possible the urethral defect loosely closed, but this is often difficult and is not essential. The bladder is then closed around a suprapubic catheter.

D. THE URETHRA

Injuries to the urethra are uncommon and are either intrapelvic (membranous) as described above, or extrapelvic when they are most commonly due to straddle injuries or kicks in the perineum.

The urine and blood leak through the tear and extravasate into the perineum and scrotum. A few drops of blood-stained urine escape from the external urinary meatus, but the attempted passage of more urine only increases the size of the perineal swelling. Pain is considerable, shock minimal, and the abdominal signs negative unless there is a palpable bladder due to urinary retention.

Investigations

A urethrogram is occasionally useful in demonstrating the site of the tear where the radio-opaque due is seen to pass into the periurethral and perineal tissues.

Treatment

A formal cystostomy is established as soon as possible. The perineum is then exposed with the patient in the lithotomy position, and an incision made over the haematoma or the site of the rupture as visualised radiographically, and the clots evacuated. A metal bougie is then passed along the urethra to the site of the tear which is examined to assess whether the tear is incomplete or complete. An incomplete tear may be sutured loosely with fine chromic catgut, but a complete tear demands mobilisation of the proximal and distal torn ends of the urethra, which are trimmed, an end-to-end anastomosis carried out, and the penile tissue brought loosely together over a soft drain. A urethral catheter should NOT be left *in situ*, but the urine allowed to drain through the suprapubic catheter. At the end of ten days bougies are gently passed over the anastomosis and, if successful, the suprapubic catheter may be removed four days later.

CHAPTER SIX

UPPER LIMB—SHOULDER INJURIES

Summary

A. FRACTURES OF THE CLAVICLE

These occur very commonly throughout life, being seen most frequently in children and young adults. The majority of fractures are situated in the middle third of the bone, and are due to falls on the point of the shoulder. Sometimes fractures of the outer end follow direct blows.

Complications are very uncommon. Rarely the subclavian vessels are trapped as they pass between the clavicle and the first rib.

Treatment

Fractures of the clavicle almost invariably unite rapidly, despite the fact that true splintage is almost impossible. Treatment aims at preventing the bone ends from overlapping by bracing the shoulders back, thereby minimising visible residual deformity. This is achieved by a 'Figure-of-eight' bandage applied firmly while the patient is sitting upright. Large woollen pads are placed anteriorly extending into the axillae to prevent pressure on the skin, muscles, nerves, and vessels (Fig. 26). The bandage is retained for about three weeks and must be re-applied two to three times weekly as otherwise it works loose. Except in the case of young children, a triangular bandage sling to support the point of the elbow is worn for the first ten to fourteen days.

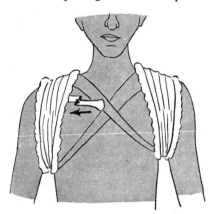

FIG. 26. Figure-of-eight bandage for fractured clavicle

B. DISLOCATION OF THE STERNO-CLAVICULAR JOINT

This injury results from a force which drives the shoulder forwards and inwards. The inner end of the clavicle usually coming to lie anteriorly and below the manubrium. Rarely it is displaced backwards, where it may cause respiratory distress by pressure on the trachea.

Treatment

Reduction is obtained by direct pressure on the bone end, while the shoulder is drawn outwards. It is usually simple to obtain, but maintenance is not so easy, and reliance must be placed upon a firm pad over the joint. Recurrent displacement and subluxation are therefore common, but do not often cause any disability. In the occasional case, surgery is required, and the bone can be anchored either by the use of a fascia lata strip or the tendon of the subclavius muscle.

C. INJURIES TO THE ACROMIO-CLAVICULAR JOINT

These injuries result from blows on the shoulder, forcing it downwards. The joint may be completely dislocated, or merely subluxed. In the latter the strong coraco-clavicular ligament remains intact, whereas in dislocations this must be torn through to allow full displacement. Clinically, apart from obvious marked prominence of the outer end of the clavicle, when the coraco-clavicular ligament has been torn, there will be tenderness and bruising over the coracoid process as well as over the acromio-clavicular joint.

Treatment

This varies according to whether the joint is subluxed or dislocated.

Subluxations require only that the joint is protected, by supporting the arm in a triangular bandage sling for about ten days.

Dislocations are more difficult to treat, as it is necessary to provide downward pressure over the outer end of the clavicle, at the same time raising the shoulder joint. A simple method consists of passing non-stretch zinc oxide strapping over the clavicle, down the upper arm anteriorly, under the flexed elbow, and then up behind to cross the clavicle again (Fig. 13). Felt pads are used to protect the bony points. This strapping should be retained for three weeks. Sometimes reduction is prevented by the outer end of the clavicle becoming trapped above the trapegius muscle. Then operative reduction is necessary, which can be secured by an intramedullary wire passed through the acromion, down the clavicle.

D. FRACTURES OF THE SCAPULA

These injuries, affecting either the neck or body of the bone, follow direct blows on the scapular region. The bony injury is unimportant, and treatment therefore consists of early mobilisation using a sling for protection until the acute pain has subsided.

E. DISLOCATION OF THE SHOULDER

In order to permit a really wide range of movement, the glenoid cavity is shallow, and the shoulder joint depends for stability upon the surrounding soft tissues. Dislocation of the shoulder is, therefore, a very common injury usually resulting from falls on the hand where the arm is abducted. The head of the humerus most commonly is forced out of the glenoid cavity inferiorly and then moves up to lie anteriorly, because, as the body is moving forwards, the shoulder is externally rotated at the same time—

this is *Anterior Dislocation of the Shoulder*. Sometimes the head is driven directly forwards where the cartilaginous labrum glenoidall is torn from its anterior attachment. This leaves a potential cavity into which the head can repeatedly slip if primary healing fails to take place—this is known as *Recurrent Dislocation*. More rarely, the humeral head is displaced behind the glenoid, i.e. there is *Posterior Dislocation*.

(i) Anterior Dislocation

The clinical picture is characteristic. There is flattening of the normal shoulder contour, because the humeral head is absent from the glenoid

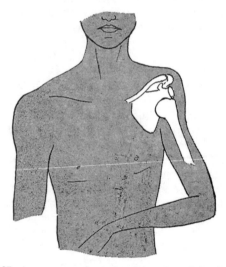

FIG. 27. Appearance of anterior dislocation of the shoulder

and below the deltoid, the arm is held in about 30° of abduction (Fig. 27). Radiologically the head usually lies below the coracoid process (*sub-coracoid* position). Occasionally it remains below the empty glenoid cavity (*sub-glenoid* position).

Complications

The circumflex nerve, as it passes round the neck of the humerus, may be injured with paralysis of the deltoid muscle, shown by inability to abduct the arm actively after reduction. Rarely, when severe violence caused the injury, the brachial plexus, in part or as a whole, may be damaged, as may the axillary vessels. The great tuberosity is sometimes fractured at the same time, which may delay full return of function for a while. Rarely there is an associated fracture through the surgical neck of the humerus, leaving the head lying free in front of the glenoid.

Treatment

Kocher's method of reduction is that normally employed. Under general anaesthetic the arm is fully externally rotated, then, in this position, adducted across the body, and finally, still adducted, it is swung into internal rotation. Alternatively, the Hippocratic method may be used. In this the operator's unbooted foot is placed in the patient's axilla, and with traction on the hand the humeral is gently lowered back into the glenoid.

After reduction, in all but the aged, the arm is supported by a sling and bandaged to the side for three weeks, thus, by preventing external rotation, allowing the capsular tear to heal, and diminish the risk of recurrent dislocation. Following this, a period of exercises to restore movement is usually required.

Circumflex nerve injury, leading to deltoid paralysis is usually only transient, so treatment merely consists in protecting the muscle by holding the arm abducted in a splint (Fig. 28) until it can be actively raised from the splint.

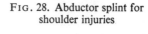

FIG. 28. Abductor splint for shoulder injuries

(ii) Recurrent Dislocation

This is due to the pressure of an unhealed rent in the anterior humeral attachment of the labrum glenoidale, leaving a pocket into which the humeral head can slip when the arm is externally rotated. Associated with this, a notch develops in the head posteriorly where it strikes the margin of the glenoid, as it dislocates (Fig. 29).

Treatment

This is surgical, by repair of the rent in the anterior attachment of the labrum and deliberately restricting the range of external rotation by taking a tuck in the subscapularis tendon and anterior part of the joint capsule. After treatment consists of keeping the arm firmly bound to the side for six weeks.

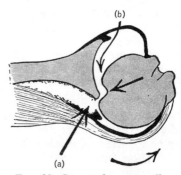
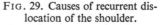

FIG. 29. Causes of recurrent dislocation of the shoulder.
(*a*) Rent in the glenoid labrum
(*b*) Notch in the head of the humerus

(iii) Posterior Dislocation

This injury is comparatively uncommon, and is due to an internal rotation—abduction force. It can be overlooked if only antero-posterior radiographs are taken of the shoulder joint because the head of the humerus, while lying behind the glenoid, may not be displaced medially.

Reduction is obtained by adducting the arm across the trunk, followed by external rotation. If recurrent dislocation occurs, this is best prevented by deepening the posterior glenoid margin by inserting a bone block.

F. FRACTURES OF THE UPPER END OF THE HUMERUS

These are common, and occur at two sites—the greater tuberosity may be fractured alone, or in association with dislocation of the shoulder joint, or the fracture line may pass through the neck of the humerus.

(i) Fractures of the Greater Tuberosity

These common injuries usually result from direct blows on the shoulder itself. Occasionally the tuberosity is avulsed by the contracting supraspinatus muscle, when the abducted arm is forcefully adducted. Middle-aged or elderly people are those mainly affected.

Treatment

The bony injury is largely ignored, the associated soft tissue damage being more important. Invariably, in injuries of this type, there is tearing of the joint capsule and tendons comprising the rotator cuff, with an associated haemarthrosis in the shoulder joint. As soon as the initial reaction to the trauma has subsided, therefore, mobilisation is commenced.

For the first seven to ten days the arm is kept at rest under the clothes in a triangular sling. At the conclusion of this time mobilising exercises are instituted, and practised with increasing intensity until full movement has been regained. Where the fractured tuberosity is associated with dislocation of the shoulder, the bony injury is ignored, and routine treatment for the dislocation, as already outlined earlier (p. 61) is carried out.

(ii) Fractures through the Neck of the Humerus

These may be displaced or undisplaced. Undisplaced fractures of the neck of the humerus are due to direct violence, and are usually seen in the elderly. Displacement takes two forms, the fracture may be either adducted or abducted, depending upon the direction of the causative force (Fig. 30). These fractures tend to occur in rather younger adults. In addition, as already mentioned, fracture-dislocation of the shoulder sometimes occurs, where the humeral head is displaced out of the glenoid cavity, with a fracture through the neck, so that the isolated head is left lying free.

In children, fracture-separation of the upper humeral epiphysis is quite

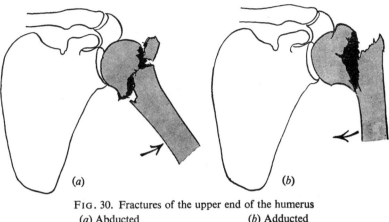

FIG. 30. Fractures of the upper end of the humerus
(a) Abducted   (b) Adducted

common, with varying degrees of angular deformity, because dislocation of the shoulder (as with other joints) rarely occurs in childhood.

Treatment

As with other shoulder injuries, prevention of stiffness is the most important aspect of management. Undisplaced fractures should be protected by bandaging the arm to the side, over a sling for seven to ten days, after which mobilising exercises should be commenced. The tempo of these should be steadily increased as pain and muscle spasm subside, until eventually intensive exercises and games are undertaken in the competitive atmosphere of a physiotherapy 'class'.

Displaced fractures may require reduction, but if redisplacement is to be avoided, this must be followed by immobilisation in the reduced position, thereby increasing the risk of residual stiffness. Moderate degrees of displacement are therefore usually accepted, particularly in the elderly. Adduction fractures are reduced by abducting the arm, while

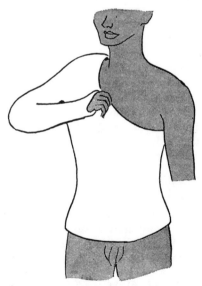

FIG. 31. Plaster-of-Paris shoulder spica

applying gentle traction to disimpact the fragments, after which reduction is maintained by holding the limb abducted either in a splint (Fig. 28) or

in a plaster-of-Paris shoulder spica (Fig. 31) for about four weeks. Abduction fractures are rarely sufficiently displaced to require reduction.
Occasionally, downward traction to disimpact the fragments under general
anaesthesia is necessary, after which the arm is bound to the side over a
pad of wool in the axilla for three or four weeks.

G. SOFT TISSUE INJURIES OF THE SHOULDER

Because the shoulder is largely dependent upon surrounding soft parts
for its stability, these are, naturally, subject to injury. Musculo-tendinous
structures intimately related to the joint are, firstly, the flat muscles arising
from the scapula and inserted into the tuberosities on the humeral head—
the subscapularis, supra-spinatus, infra-spinatus and tires minor, which
together form the 'rotator cuff' and secondly, the tendon of the long head
of the biceps brachii crossing over the head of the humerus within the
joint, to enter the bicipital groove between the greater and lesser tuberosities on its way to join the short head in the arm.

(i) Injuries of the Rotator Cuff (see also p. 254)

Some tearing of the musculo-tendinous fibres of the rotator cuff must
occur when a normal shoulder is dislocated, but this is rarely important.
If, however, in a fall, the abducted arm is forcefully brought to the side,
there may be an extensive tear of the rotator cuff and capsule of the
shoulder. Usually this involves mainly the supra-spinatus tendon, though
other parts of the cuff may also be torn, depending upon the direction of
the fall.

Clinically, there will be marked tenderness over the humeral head and
complete inability to initiate abduction. Soon after injury, however, before
reaction has caused general stiffness in the joint, it may be possible to
demonstrate that if abduction is initiated passively the patient can then
continue to raise his arm actively using the deltoid. In these cases also as
the abducted arm is lowered, sudden pain will be experienced, causing the
arm to drop to the side. This occurs when the torn tendon impinges upon
the under-surface of the acromion.

Treatment

In the elderly, preservation of movement is the most important aspect of
treatment, so that as soon as the initial reaction has subsided, mobilising
exercises are started. In younger patients a spell of three or four weeks on
an abduction splint may allow the tear to heal. Occasionally direct
operative repair of extensive tears is required.

(ii) Rupture of the Long Head of the Biceps

This is an injury of elderly patients, and is associated with attrition of the
tendon of the long head as it passes through the bicipital groove, which
may be somewhat roughened.

Frequently, this occurs almost spontaneously, so that no actual moment of rupture can be recalled, the patient becoming aware of pain in the shoulder, with tenderness over the bicepital groove, and a characteristic bulging of the biceps muscle belly when the elbow is flexed against resistance (Fig. 152, p. 257). Usually, however, there is a specific moment when sudden sharp pain is experienced as the patient is lifting some heavy object.

Treatment

In the large majority of cases no active treatment is indicated. The patient is instructed to continue using his arm as normally as possible, and to ignore the bulge in the arm as the muscle belly contracts. Very rarely in younger persons, the torn lower end of the tendon may be re-attached to the bicepital groove, though no attempts to repair the tendon itself should be made.

CHAPTER SEVEN

UPPER LIMB—INJURIES OF ARM AND ELBOW

Summary

I. FRACTURES OF THE HUMERAL SHAFT

II. INJURIES OF THE ELBOW

General Remarks

A. Fractures of the Lower End of Humerus

    (i) Supr-condylar Fracture

        (*a*) Posterior Displacement
        (*b*) Anterior Displacement

    (ii) Y-shaped Fractures of the Lower End of the Humerus
    (iii) Fractures of the Lateral Humeral Condyle
    (iv) Fractures of the Capitellum
    (v) Avulsion of the Medial Epicondyle

B. Dislocation of the Elbow

C. Fractures of the Olecranon

D. Fractures of the Head of the Radius

E. Fracture of the Neck of the Radius

F. 'Pulled Elbow'

G. Rupture of the Biceps Insertion

I. FRACTURES OF THE HUMERAL SHAFT

THESE occur at all levels, and may result from direct or indirect violence—the former having a transverse or comminuted fracture line, and the latter oblique. Fractures of the humeral shaft occur at all ages, but they are rather less common than fractures of the shafts of the other long bones. Possibly this is because the wide range of movement in the shoulder joint absorbs some of the violence of an injury.

Pathological fractures are common in the humerus. In children, they may occur through a solitary bone cyst, the upper shaft of the humerus being the commonest site for this condition. In adults, the humerus is a common site for carcinomatous metastatic deposits, particularly from neoplasms of the breast or bronchus. Often, a pathological fracture is the first sign of abnormality in the bone, and, in the case of bronchial carcinoma, may also be the presenting symptom of the disease as a whole.

Complications

The radial nerve, being closely related to the bone as it lies in the musculo-spiral groove, is often injured in fractures of the humeral shaft. Usually this is merely bruising—'neuropraxia'—in which full recovery occurs spontaneously after an interval of two to four weeks. Occasionally, however, permanent damage is done to the nerve.

Non-union, while not very common in fractures of the humeral shaft, can present a very great problem in cases in which it does occur, partly owing to the difficulty of providing really adequate immobilisation of the bone.

Treatment

In uncomplicated fractures of the humeral shaft, treatment does not usually provide a problem. Reduction is simple, and minor degrees of overlap or angulation are of less significance in the humerus than in any other long bone. With the patient in sitting, leaning slightly to the injured side, and with the wrist supported so that the elbow is flexed at 90°, the fracture automatically re-aligns itself (Fig. 32). While in this position a plaster-of-Paris slab is applied extending from the

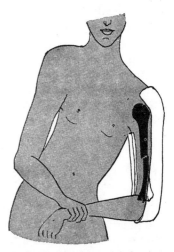

FIG. 32. 'U' plaster slab fixation for fracture of the humeral shaft

axilla, down the inner side of the arm, beneath the elbow, and up the outer side, to end lying over the shoulder in the region of the acromio-clavicular joint. This 'U' plaster slab is secured by a crêpe bandage, applied before it has set. The wrist is then supported in a collar-and-cuff sling. Anaesthesia is not required. Immobilisation is continued for six to eight weeks, after which mobilisation is commenced, with the arm protected by a triangular sling for a further two to three weeks.

Where there is difficulty in obtaining adequate reduction, or where there are multiple injuries elsewhere rendering early mobility desirable, and in most pathological fractures through a neoplastic deposit, internal fixation should be used. The best method is by an intra-medullary nail inserted from above and driven across the fracture site. This is followed by radiotherapy in neoplastic lesions.

Treatment of Complications

(i) *Injury to the Radial Nerve.* The integrity of the radial nerve should be tested in all fractures of the humeral shaft, and if any weakness is discovered the wrist should be supported by a 'cock-up' splint. If paralysis is incomplete, full recovery is almost certain, and all that is required is to protect the affected muscles by splintage, coupled with electrical stimulation to keep them healthy until their nerve supply is restored. Where no recovery takes place after several weeks the nerve should be explored and sutured if divided. As the radial nerve is largely motor, the results of suture are usually good. If suture is impossible, or fails, good function can be restored by transplanting the tendon of Flexor carpi ulnaris into the finger and thumb extensors, and pronator veres into extensor carpi radialis longus.

(ii) *Non-union.* This occurs when the blood supply to the humerus has been impaired, and therefore is commonly associated with severe local trauma. If, after a reasonable interval, union has failed to take place, the fracture should be grafted. An intra-medullary nail is used to provide internal fixation, and cancellous iliae bone clips should be employed as the graft. Post-operatively, to provide added protection, a plaster-of-Paris shoulder spica (Fig. 31) should also be applied.

II. INJURIES OF THE ELBOW

GENERAL REMARKS

It must be appreciated that, while residual stiffness in the elbow is serious, loss of flexion is a much greater disability than loss of extension. Therefore, not only must the elbow never be splinted in extension, but also, when mobilisation is begun, flexion is the more important movement to restore. Further, the weight of the forearm tends to extend the joint passively at the expense of regaining flexion, so the elbow must be supported in a sling until a reasonable range of movement has returned.

Passive movements are to be avoided, as they merely irritate the joint, and so increase the stiffness. Sometimes, where there has been periosteal stripping at the time of injury, myositis ossificans may be provoked by such means.

The close proximity of the main vessels and nerves to the elbow joint must always be borne in mind when dealing with major injuries, and the state of these should be checked regularly.

A. FRACTURES OF THE LOWER END OF THE HUMERUS

The lower end of the humerus may be fractured in several ways, depending upon the direction of force. In a fall on the outstretched hand, the lower end may be driven backwards—a posterior supra-condylar fracture of the humerus. This is a very common injury of childhood, whereas in an adult, a similar force would dislocate the elbow joint. Falls striking the point of the elbow from behind may cause an anterior supra-condylar fracture of the humerus. In a fall directly upon the flexed elbow, the olecranon may split the lower end of the humerus vertically, causing a Y-shaped fracture. If a severe lateral angulatory force is applied to the elbow, the lateral humeral condyle may be displaced upwards. Occasionally the medial humeral epicondyle may be evulsed, an injury of later childhood occurring before this epiphysis joins the main bone.

(i) Supra-condylar Fracture of the Humerus

(a) *Posterior Displacement* (Fig. 12)

As stated, this is a very common injury of childhood, caused by falls upon the outstretched hand. The lower end of the humerus is displaced backwards. All degrees may occur from undisplaced cracks, to complete separation of the lower fragment. Where displacement is severe considerable soft tissue damage may be done.

Complications. (i) The *brachial artery* may be injured by impinging upon the sharp lower end of the main fragment. The vessel is not often torn, through, but the damage to its wall causes it to go into severe spasm, which if not relieved rapidly will lead to permanent ischaemic changes in the forearm and hand, with infraction of muscle, leading to the condition known as Volkmann's Ischaemic Contracture, already described (p. 20). It is important to appreciate that injury to the brachial artery may occur during injudicious attempts at reduction of the fracture.

(ii) *The median nerve* may also be injured by striking the lower end of the main fragment, and occasionally severe damage is done in this way.

(iii) *The ulnar nerve* may be damaged by traction between the point where it passes through the medial inter-muscular septum (above the fracture site) and where it is anchored in its groove below the medial epicondyle of the humerus, or irritation may also occur if the fracture unites with a valgus deformity. This causes late development of weakness in the intrinsic muscles of the hand, and numbness of the fourth and fifth fingers. This complication is known as *Delayed ulnar neuritis*.

(iv) *Myositis ossificans* as already mentioned, may follow injudicious attempts to mobilise the stiff elbow at a later stage.

Treatment

Manipulative reduction is employed, but, because of the risk of injury to the brachial vessels, it should be conducted under full general anaesthesia, with X-ray control, in a properly equipped operating theatre.

Procedure. While an assistant exerts gentle traction on the *flexed* elbow, the surgeon applies steady pressure on the olecranon with his thumbs,

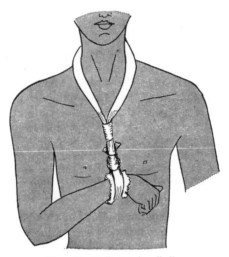

FIG. 33. Collar-and-cuff sling

using his fingers to grasp the arm over the biceps muscle, and then by pressure with his thumbs he cautiously flexes the joint. After reduction, the fracture can be maintained in good position merely by keeping the elbow flexed, thus tightening the posterior humeral periosteum, which while stripped of the bone, was not torn through. However full flexion, if swelling is considerable, may impair the circulation, so that this may have to be deferred for two or three days, and a very careful watch must be kept after reduction on the radial pulse for at least 24 hours. A collar-and-cuff sling (Fig. 33) worn under the clothes, so that it cannot be removed provides sufficient immobilisation, but the added protection of a posterior plaster-of-Paris slab is usually advisable.

Treatment of Complications

(i) *Vascular.* As soon as circulatory impairment is observed, as shown by an absent radial pulse, blue or grey coloration in the fingers, with absent capillary return after pressure on the finger nails, it is urgently necessary to restore blood flow.

Initially, the arm should be rested on a pillow and, to encourage vaso dilatation, the body as a whole should be warmed. A cervical sympathetic block, using 1% novocaine may also encourage vaso dilatation.

If after 30 minutes, there is no return of pulsation, the vessel should be explored. Sometimes mere decompression by division of the deep fascia is sufficient to restore pulsation. Usually, however, the artery must be inspected under direct vision, and any sharp spike of bone removed from it, after which the soft tissues surrounding the vessel should be impregnated with a solution of papaverine. If there is obvious injury to the vessel wall, the damaged segment should be excised. Continuity is restored either by direct suture of the ends, or by an arterial graft.

(ii) *Neurological.* In most cases nerve damage is not severe, and full recovery takes place in four to six weeks. In these, all that is needed is to protect the temporarily paralysed muscles by a splint, and to keep them healthy by electrical stimulation at intervals. If no recovery occurs, the nerve should be explored, and appropriate action taken (p. 19).

Delayed Ulnar Neuritis. Where evidence of late ulnar nerve irritation appears, it should be dissected free from its bed in the groove behind the medial epicondyle, and transplanted to lie in front of the humerus.

(iii) *Myositis Ossificans.* If the recovery of movement ceases, X-rays should be taken, and any evidence of the development of myositis ossificans is an indication for a further period of complete rest in a plaster-of-Paris cast for three or four weeks.

(b) *Anterior Displacement*

This is a much less common injury than supra-condylar fractures of the humerus with posterior displacement, and it is also an injury of adults rather than children. It results from a backward fall on to the point of the elbow, thereby driving the smaller fragment forwards, along with the forearm. Complications, other than residual joint stiffness, are uncommon.

Treatment

Reduction is stable in extension, but in view of the risk of stiffness this is impracticable, and usually some residual deformity must be accepted. The elbow is immobilised first below the right angle for two to three weeks, after which the arm is actively mobilised in a sling.

(ii) Y-shaped Fractures of the Lower End of the Humerus

These fractures are not very common. They occur in adults, and are due to a powerful blow striking the lower end of the humerus, splitting it longitudinally. Displacement may be severe, and in younger adults open reduction with internal fixation using screws or a bolt may be required.

(iii) Fractures of the Lateral Humeral Condyle (Fig. 34)

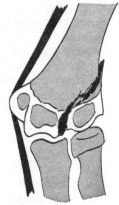

These fractures are due to lateral angulatory forces applied to the extended elbow. It is seen in both adults and children, but is commoner in the latter. In children the true extent of injury may not be appreciated from radiographs because of the amount of epiphyseal cartilage present.

Complications. (i) *Delayed Ulnar Neuritis.* Unless an almost perfect reduction is obtained, a residual valgus deformity will follow. As a result, delayed ulnar neuritis may occur.

(ii) *Non-union.* This is fairly common and may lead to later development of a valgus deformity.

FIG. 34. Fracture-separation of the epiphysis for the lateral humeral condyle—showing how the ulnar nerve may be stretched

Treatment

In order to ensure close bony apposition, open reduction is usually indicated. The detached condyle being secured either by sub-peristeal sutures or a small nail or screw.

(iv) Fracture of the Capitulum

In adults, the capitular portion of the lateral condyle may be fractured, the loose fragment being displaced upwards. As the fragment may be almost free in the joint, with only a small soft tissue attachment, a vascular necrosis often occurs.

Open operation is the best method of treatment. If there is a reasonable soft tissue attachment, the capitulum may be re-attached by sub periosteal sutures, but if it is almost free in the joint, excision may give the best results.

(v) Avulsion of the Epiphysis for the Medial Epicondyle (Fig. 35)

In severe lateral angulatory strains of the elbow, particularly when there is also powerful contraction of the wrist flexors attached to the medial epicondyle, this fragment may be avulsed. This can only occur in later childhood, when the epiphysis for the epicondyle is well developed, but not yet attached to the humerus itself. This injury in effect represents a tear of the medial joint capsule, and it is often associated with dislocation of the elbow, when the epicondyle becomes lodged between the joint surfaces, blocking reduction.

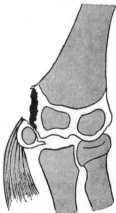

FIG. 35. Fracture separation of the epiphysis for the medial epicondyle

Fibrous union is the rule following avulsion of the medial epicondyle, but as the articular surfaces of the elbow joint are unaffected, this is of no significance.

Complication. Delayed ulnar neuritis, or immediate damage to the ulnar nerve are common, because the nerve is so closely related to the bone at this point. Delayed neuritis at this site is due to the nerve becoming strangled by scar tissue as it lies in its groove.

Treatment

Avulsion of the epicondyle indicates severe capsular damage to the elbow joint. A period of rest in a collar-and-cuff sling for two to three weeks is therefore required, followed by gentle active mobilisation.

If the epicondyle is trapped between the articular surfaces of the humerus and ulna, it may be possible to release it, if, under general anaesthetic, the joint is held in valgus angulation, and strong faradic stimulation is applied to the common flexor muscles, thereby pulling the fragment out. If this fails open reduction is indicated, in which case transplant of the ulnar nerve at the same time, to avoid the later onset of delayed neuritis is often worth while.

B. DISLOCATION OF THE ELBOW

This is a common injury occurring throughout adult life, and is due to a fall on the outstretched hand, with the elbow a little flexed. In a child a similar fall would cause a supra-condylar fracture. The elbow is normally a stable hinge joint, so that in order to produce a dislocation, extensive tearing of the joint capsule must take place, sometimes with avulsion of bony fragments (such as the medial epicondyle already described). Sometimes the radial head is fractured at the same time as the dislocation. Displacement is either backwards, or laterally, sometimes being a combination of both.

Complications. (i) *Nerve injuries.* Nerves related to the elbow joint are occasionally damaged, particularly the ulnar nerve because of its close relationship with the humerus. In most cases the injury is slight, and full recovery follows.

(ii) *Myositis ossificans* may occur later, affecting the anterior or medial joint capsule, where there has been extensive tearing, involving the periosteum.

(iii) *Recurrent dislocation* follows on rare occasions, if the coronoid process has been fractured.

Treatment

Manipulative reduction is usually simple. It is accomplished by gentle traction on the semi-flexed joint, the flexion being cautiously increased, while direct pressure is exerted over bony points to overcome the displacement. Open reduction is only required in cases where a loose bony fragment causes a block to manipulative reduction. After reduction, the joint should be immobilised at 90° in a plaster-of-Paris slab for two to three weeks to permit healing of the capsular tear. Active mobilisation is then permitted, with the protection of a collar-and-cuff sling for a further two weeks, so that flexion is regained initially. Full movement takes several months to return, and slight residual stiffness is common.

C. FRACTURES OF THE OLECRANON (Fig. 36)

Fracture of the olecranon usually results from sudden contraction of the triceps as the elbow is forcibly flexed, the olecranon thereby being snapped

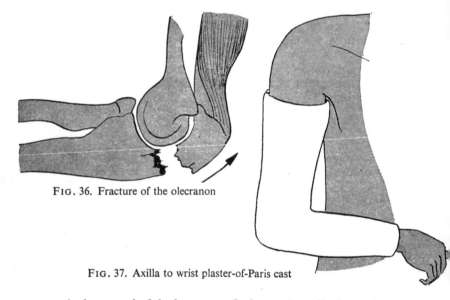

FIG. 36. Fracture of the olecranon

FIG. 37. Axilla to wrist plaster-of-Paris cast

over the lower end of the humerus. Owing to the pull of the triceps, some separation of the loose fragment invariably occurs. Occasionally the olecranon is fractured by a direct blow on the point of the elbow, when there is comminution without separation of the fragments because the periosteum is intact.

Treatment

Owing to the pull of the triceps, apposition of the fragments could only be achieved by splinting the elbow in full extension, which would certainly leave severe permanent limitation of flexion. For this reason, operative treatment is the rule. Where there is a single fragment, internal fixation, using a nail or lag-screw (Fig. 8) gives good results. If there is comminution the fragments should be excised and the triceps tendon re-attached to the stump of ulna.

Post-operatively a plaster-of-Paris cast (Fig. 37) from axilla to wrist is applied and retained for about four weeks, after which gentle active mobilisation is commenced.

D. FRACTURES OF THE HEAD OF THE RADIUS
(Fig. 38)

This injury is caused by a fall on the hand which drives the radial head against the capitellum. It is important to appreciate that a blow of sufficient severity to break the bone will also cause considerable bruising

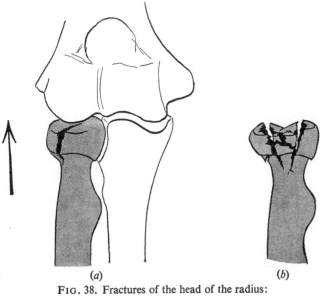

(a)   (b)

FIG. 38. Fractures of the head of the radius:

(a) Vertical crack   (b) Comminuted

to the articular cartilage on both surfaces. Radiologically there may merely be a vertical crack in the bone, or one fragment may be considerably displaced outwards and downwards, or the whole radial head may be comminuted. The head of the radius may be fractured at the same time as the elbow is dislocated.

Treatment

Where displacement is slight, treatment should be conservative, the arm being protected in a collar-and-cuff sling for two or three weeks, gentle active flexion in this being permitted. This is followed by increasing active movement, with the arm in a triangular sling worn outside the clothes until a reasonable range of movement has been regained.

If displacement is severe, then the head of the radius should be excised.

Fractures of the head of the radius complicating dislocation of the elbow are often comminuted, and require excision, but in these cases it is often better to wait several weeks until the reaction to the original trauma has subsided before exploring the injured joint.

E. FRACTURES OF THE NECK OF THE RADIUS (Fig. 39)

These are injuries of childhood, the fracture being of a greenstick nature. Slight displacement can be accepted, but an attempt should be made to correct angulation greater than about 30°. Often this can be done by pressure with the thumbs, but if much swelling is present it may be better to expose the annular ligament surgically and apply direction pressure on the bone.

FIG. 39. Fracture of the neck of the radius

F. 'PULLED ELBOW'

This is an injury of young children and is probably due to momentary subluxation of the radial head out of its annular ligament as a result of the infant being lifted up by its hand. Treatment consists of resting the arm in a sling under the clothes for a few days until the discomfort has subsided.

G. RUPTURE OF THE BICEPS INSERTION

Rarely, if there is sudden, forcible extension of an actively flexing elbow, the insertion of the biceps may be avulsed from the neck of the radius. This is demonstrated clinically by loss of active flexion and marked bruising in the antecubital fossa. Treatment consists of operative repair.

CHAPTER EIGHT

UPPER LIMB—FOREARM AND WRIST INJURIES

Summary

I. FOREARM

I. A. Fractures of Radial and Ulnar Shafts
B. Fracture of the Ulna, with dislocation of the Radial Head
C. Fracture of the Radius, with dislocation of the Lower End of the Ulna

II. LOWER ENDS RADIUS AND ULNA

A. Adults:

(i) Colles' Fracture
(ii) Smith's Fracture
(iii) Fracture of the Radial Styloid

B. Children

(i) Fracture-separation of the Lower Radial Epiphysis
(ii) Greenstick Fracture of the Lower Ends of the Radius and Ulna
(iii) Fracture of the Lower End of the Radius with Overlap

III. CARPUS

A. Fracture of the Waist of the Scaphoid
B. Fracture of the Tuberosity of the Scaphoid
C. Dislocation of the Lunate
D. Dislocation of the Carpus

(i) True Radio-carpal Dislocation
(ii) Peri-lunar Dislocation of the Carpus
(iii) Peri-lunar Trans-scaphoid Dislocation of the Carpus

E. 'Sprained Wrist'

I. FOREARM

In considering fractures of forearm bones it is necessary to appreciate that preservation of rotation at the wrist is very important, and this must be borne in mind during reduction and subsequent treatment. The elbow is basically a humero-ulnar joint, whereas the wrist is a radio-carpal joint. If therefore one bone only is fractured and displaced, there will be dislocation of the more mobile end of the other. With fractures of the ulnar shaft the head of the radius is dislocated, and with fractures of the radial shaft the lower end of the ulna is displaced.

A. FRACTURES OF RADIAL AND ULNAR SHAFTS

These may follow direct or indirect violence. In those due to *direct violence*, both bones will be broken at about the same level, and the fracture will be either comminuted or transverse. In these injuries there may also be considerable soft-tissue damage, with injury to the median, ulnar, or posterior interosseous nerves. In addition, if severe swelling is present, this may interfere with arterial circulation to the muscles, so that Volkmann's Ischaemic Contracture may occur.

Those due to *indirect violence* are rather commoner in children. In these, the ulnar fracture is spiral, but the radial fracture, while at a different level, is often transverse, because in the forceful twist it is snapped directly across the ulna. In children the radial fracture may be of greenstick type.

Complications

Apart from the soft tissue complications already mentioned, *non-union* of forearm fractures, especially those due to direct violence, is fairly common. Occasionally, usually where there has been a compound fracture with low grade infection *cross-union*, in which a bridge of bone joins the radius to the ulna, may occur. This is serious, because it completely prevents any rotation movement at the wrist.

Treatment

Perfect reduction of the radial fracture is required. If the injury is below mid-forearm level, the ulnar fracture usually falls into satisfactory alignment when the radius is reduced. In rotational injuries, especially in children, manipulative reduction is employed. Similarly, in injuries due to direct violence, if there is merely an angular deformity, manipulation only is necessary. After reduction, immobilisation is by a plaster-of-Paris cast, extending from the axilla above to the metacarpal heads below (Fig. 40), with the elbow at 90°. The position of rotation of the carpus will depend upon that which corrects the deformity.

Where there is overlap of the bone ends, open reduction is often required. Internal fixation, either consisting of plate and screws or an intra-medullary pin, is used. If both bones are plated, ideally the internal

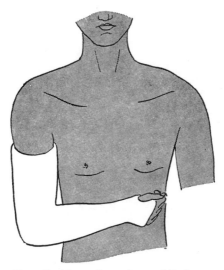

FIG. 40. Above-elbow plaster-of-Paris cast

fixation should be sufficiently secure to avoid the need of external splintage by a plaster-of-Paris cast.

B. FRACTURE OF THE ULNA WITH DISLOCATION OF THE RADIAL HEAD (MONTEGGIA)

Displacement may be either forward bowing of the ulnar shaft, with anterior dislocation of the radial head (Fig. 41(a)) or backward, with posterior displacement of the radial head (Fig. 41(b)). The former, which is commoner, results from a forced pronation twist, which extends the elbow at the same time. The less common backwardly displaced type is due to a flexion-supination force. In children the ulnar fracture may be of green-stick type, in which case its significance may not be appreciated, and in consequence the displacement of the radial head may be overlooked.

Treatment

In the more common type, with forward dislocation of the head of the radius, manipulative reduction should be employed in children. This consists of flexing the elbow and fully supinating the forearm. In adults, open reduction of the ulnar fracture is usually required, when the radial head normally becomes replaced. An intra-medullary nail provides very

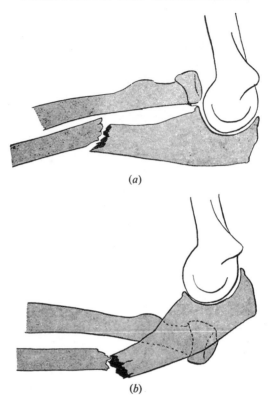

(a)

(b)

FIG. 41. Monteggia fracture of the ulnar shaft, with dislocation of the radial head:

(a) forward   (b) backward

satisfactory internal fixation. In the less common type, with backward displacement, as the fracture would only be stable with the elbow in full extension, open reduction with internal fixation of the ulna is always indicated.

C. FRACTURE OF THE RADIUS WITH DISLOCATION OF THE LOWER END OF THE ULNA (GALLEAZZI)

This injury, which is the reverse of the Monteggia type of fracture, consists of a displaced fracture of the lower half of the radial shaft, with dislocation of the lower end of the ulna (Fig. 42). It also follows a rotational strain, and the ulnar head is almost always displaced posteriorly. It is not seen in children, where greenstick fractures of both bones occur.

Treatment

Unless perfect reduction of the radial fracture is maintained, residual displacement at the inferior radio-ulnar joint will follow. Open reduction, with internal fixation of the radius, usually by a plate, is therefore indicated.

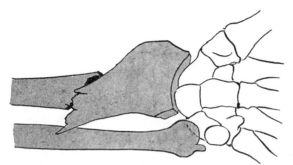

FIG. 42. Galleazzi fracture of the radial shaft with dislocation of the lower end of the ulna

II. LOWER ENDS OF RADIUS AND ULNA

Fractures of the lower end of the radius due to falls on the hand are very common in all age groups. In adults, the ulnar styloid process may be avulsed by its attachment to the fibro-cartilaginous disc. In children, however, greenstick fractures of the lower end of the ulna frequently occur.

A. ADULTS

Two forms of displacement may occur, depending upon the direction of the injury force. In falls with the hand outstretched, there is backward displacement of the lower end of the radius. When the wrist is flexed, there is forward displacement.

(i) Fracture of the Lower Radius with Posterior Displacement (Colles' Fracture)

Fractures of the lower end of the radius with posterior displacement, first described about 150 years ago by Benjamin Colles, a Dublin surgeon, are common throughout adult life, but particularly in the elderly. This is partly because the elderly are rather more liable to fall heavily, but also because their bones are more osteoporotic than in younger adults. As, at the moment of impact, the patient is usually moving forwards, supination is also a factor in producing the characteristic appearance.

Displacement of the lower end of the radius is threefold—it is both backwards, and tilted backwards, and in addition it is tilted in a radial direction (Fig. 43). Depending upon the degree of violence, some comminution may be present, particularly posteriorly. The ulnar styloid is also usually avulsed. Clinically the displacement causes what is described as a 'dinner-fork' deformity (Fig. 44).

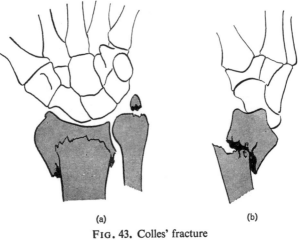

(a)   (b)

FIG. 43. Colles' fracture

(*a*) Antero-posterior view   (*b*) Lateral view

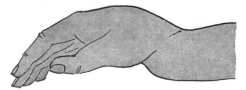

FIG. 44. The clinical appearance of a Colles' fracture

Complications. These may be early or late.

(a) *Early.* The *median nerve* may be irritated by pressure from the bone as it passes beneath the transverse carpal ligament. This causes parasthaesia in the thumb, index, and middle fingers. With accurate reduction symptoms usually improve as the swelling due to be injury subsides. Occasionally there is rupture of the tendon of *extensor pollicis longus*, due to bony disorganisation of the groove in the lower radius through which it passes.

(b) *Late.* Due to bony absorption at the fracture site, particularly in comminuted fractures, *residual subluxation of the inferior radio-ulnar joint* may remain, causing persistent discomfort over the lower end of the ulna, which is clinically more prominent than normal. *Sudek's Atrophy* (p. 20) leading to painful stiffness and swelling with trophic changes in the skin is seen more commonly after Colles' fracture than any other injury.

Treatment

Where there is significant displacement, manipulative reduction under general anaesthesia is required. This is achieved by direct pressure on the displaced lower fragment with the operator's thumbs, at the same time rotating the carpus into a position of pronation and ulnar deviation. After reduction, a 6-inch wide plaster-of-Paris slab is applied over the dorsum of the wrist, and moulded round its radial side to retain the ulnar deviation of the hand. As swelling may occur, for the first one or two days this is secured by a crêpe bandage, after which the cast is completed. It should extend from the metacarpal heads posteriorly, and the proximal palma

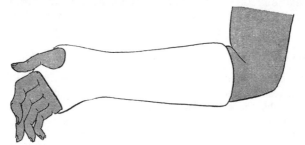

FIG. 45. Colles' type below-elbow plaster-of-Paris cast

crease anteriorly, to just below the elbow (Fig. 45), and is retained for five or six weeks.

As the majority of patients are elderly, it is important to encourage early use of the limb as a whole in the plaster, and especially of the fingers. Otherwise stiffness may be a problem later.

Treatment of Complications

(*a*) Residual Subluxation of the lower end of the ulna. Usually, after an interval of two to three months, symptoms subside without treatment. Occasionally excision of the lower end of the ulna is needed.

(*b*) Rupture of the extensor pollicis longus tendon requires surgical repair, and transplant of the extensor indicis into the distal end of the ruptured tendon gives best results.

(*c*) Median nerve symptoms usually disappear spontaneously. If they persist, relief can be obtained by division of the transverse carpal ligament.

(*d*) Sudek's Atrophy has been dealt with elsewhere (p. 20).

(ii) Fracture of the Lower Radius with Anterior Displacement (Smith's Fracture)

This fracture, which may also be described as a 'reversed Colles' fracture' follows a forcible flexion injury to the wrist. It is comparatively uncommon, and occurs in younger adults, sometimes resulting from accidents on bicycles or motorcycles, because of the position of the hands on the handlebars.

Treatment

Reduction is effected by the opposite manoeuvre to that employed in the reduction of a Colles' fracture—the hand being supinated and dorsiflexed, after which the wrist is splinted by a plaster cast in a slightly cocked-up position.

(iii) Fracture of the Radial Styloid

The radial styloid alone may be fractured by a fall which forces the hand in a radial direction. Displacement is not usually significant. Treatment consists of a below-elbow plaster cast, worn for three or four weeks.

B. CHILDREN

Fractures of the lower ends of the radius and ulna in children are very common, usually resulting from falls on the outstretched hand or blows which dorsiflex the wrist. They may take two forms, either a fracture of the lower shaft, or fracture separation of the epiphysis.

(i) Fracture-separation of the Lower Radial Epiphysis (Fig. 46 (*a*))

In this injury, there is backward displacement of the radial epiphysis, to which is attached a triangular fragment of variable size from the diaphysis. There is also, often, a greenstick fracture of the distal end of the ulna.

Treatment

Because of the natural tendency for the moulding out of deformities with growth, minor displacement can be accepted. When reduction is indicated, it is carried out by the same manoeuvre as that employed with a Colles' fracture. Immobilisation, by a below-elbow plaster cast is required for three weeks.

(ii) Greenstick Fractures of the Lower Ends of the Radius and Ulnar

These injuries are very common, particularly in minor degree in younger children. In this case, the radius alone is affected, usually about 1 inch proximal to the epiphysis. There is no actual break in bony continuity, the dorsal surface of the radius being merely buckled (Fig. 46 (*b*)). In more severe injuries there is an appreciable angular deformity with a break in continuity on the anterior surface of the bone (Fig. 46 (*c*)). Both bones are often involved in these cases.

Treatment

In 'buckle' fractures of the lower radius, protection only is required for two or three weeks by a below-elbow plaster cast. It is probable that many of these injuries are never referred for medical opinion, yet uneventful recovery always takes place.

In fractures where there is more marked displacement, with angular deformity which is visible clinically, manipulative reduction is required. In carrying this out, it is important to appreciate that unless the fracture is completed, by snapping through the angulated posterior radial cortex when the wrist is palmar-flexed, the normal resilience in children's bones will cause the deformity to reappear as soon as the operator's pressure is relaxed. Over-reduction is almost impossible because of the tough dorsal periosteum. After reduction, three weeks' immobilisation in a plaster cast is required.

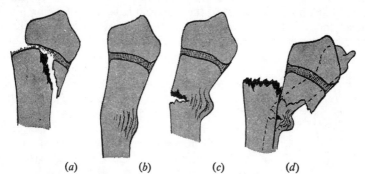

(a)   (b)   (c)   (d)

FIG. 46. Fractures of the lower radius in childhood

(a) Fracture separation of the lower radial epiphysis
(b) 'Buckle' fracture of the lower radius
(c) Greenstick fracture of the lower radius
(d) Fracture with overlap of the radius, with greenstick fracture of the ulna

(iii) Fracture of the Lower End of the Radius With Overlap (Fig. 46 (d))

These injuries follow more severe falls. There is usually an associated greenstick fracture of the lower end of the ulna, though sometimes there is a complete fracture in this bone also.

Treatment

It is necessary, first, to overcome the overlap of the fractured bone ends. Therefore, before any attempt is made to correct the dorsal displacement, longitudinal pressure down the shaft of the radius is exerted by the operator's thumbs. Often cautious slight increase in donal angulation may assist in 'hitching' the bone ends, after which the deformity is corrected by palmar flexion. In these cases, immobilisation in an above-elbow cast for three to four weeks is required.

III. CARPUS

The wrist is a radio-carpal joint. Significant injuries involving carpal bones, therefore, are almost restricted to the scaphoid and lunate.

A. FRACTURE OF THE WAIST OF THE SCAPHOID
(Fig. 47)

This type of fracture results from forcible radial deviation of the carpus, either due to a fall, or sudden twisting such as occurs when a car being cranked backfires. The waist of the scaphoid is broken by being pinched between the radial styloid and capitate bone. If violence is considerable some displacement occurs, and there may be an associated fracture of the tip of the radial styloid, but often there is merely a hairline crack which is

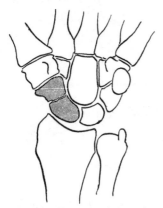

FIG. 47. Fracture of the waist of the scaphoid

difficult to detect radiologically. For this reason, the clinical features of a fractured scaphoid are important. There will be tenderness and some swelling in the 'anatomical snuff-box' bounded by the tendons of the extensor pollicis longus, abductor pollicis longus, and the radial styloid, and any attempt to move the hand in a radial direction will aggravate the pain. Fractures of the waist of the scaphoid are often more easily visualised on X-ray if oblique views are taken in addition to routine antero-posterior and lateral projections. Further, if the clinical features in any way suggest a fractured scaphoid, then the wrist should be immobilised, and fresh films taken two or three weeks later, when the absorption at the fracture line will make it more easily visible radiographically.

Complications. Most of the blood supply to the scaphoid enters at its distal end. Fractures through its waist, therefore, may largely cut off the circulation to the proximal fragment. Because of this anatomical arrangement, delayed union, non-union, and avascular necrosis may occur.

Avascular Necrosis. This state may be diagnosed six to eight weeks after the occurrence of the injury, when X-ray will show apparent increase in density of the proximal fragment. This in fact is because, having no blood supply, it cannot be affected by the normal hyperaemia and resulting osteoporosis which follows a fracture.

Later there is softening of the avascular fragment, so that it collapses, so that the shape is distorted, and *osteo-arthritis* of the wrist follows.

Treatment

Because of the poor blood supply to the proximal fragment, immobilisation must be complete. A plaster cast is used immobilising the wrist, but also including the metacarpophalangeal joint of the thumb. To allow use of the hand in the cast, it should be applied in the 'position of function', with the wrist slightly dorsiflexed, and the first metacarpal in some opposition (Fig. 48). Immobilisation must continue until union has occurred,

FIG. 48. Scaphoid plaster-of-Paris cast

usually about 12 weeks in all. To prevent stiffness and encourage the circulation, the patient should be encouraged to use his hand as normally as possible in the plaster, provided that he reports any cracks in it at once, before it gives way.

Treatment of Complications

(a) *Non-union.* Where this occurs, without distortion of the proximal fragment due to avascular necrosis, in most cases no treatment is required. Old, un-united fractures of the scaphoid, are sometimes discovered by chance in patients who have X-rays of the wrist taken for some other reason.

(b) *Avascular Necrosis.* Where this is diagnosed before collapse of the proximal fragment has occurred, immobilisation should be continued up to six months from the time of injury. In established cases, with pain in the wrist treatment may be either conservative or operative.

Conservative. The supply of a light polythene wrist support, for wear if painful, or when the patient has heavy work to do, may keep symptoms under control. This applies particularly to the elderly or infirm.

Operative. Excision of the radial styloid is a simple procedure which may be sufficient to control symptoms where changes are localised, but in younger patients, or where the whole radio-carpal joint is disorganised, arthrodesis of the wrist is required.

B. FRACTURE OF THE TUBEROSITY OF THE SCAPHOID (Fig. 49)

This is an injury which results from a direct blow on the thenar eminence. As there is normal blood supply to this segment of the bone, and the main articular surfaces are not involved, treatment need be symptomatic only. Often, supporting strapping for two weeks is sufficient.

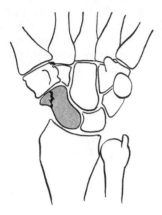

FIG. 49. Fracture of the tuberosity of the scaphoid

FIG. 50. Dislocation of the lunate—showing how the median nerve may be damaged

C. DISLOCATION OF THE LUNATE (Fig. 50)

If there is an injury to the carpus, which involves forced dorsi flexion, occasionally the joint between the capitate and lunate becomes dislocated. Then, as the wrist returns to the neutral position, the lunate becomes displaced forwards. Pressure on the median nerve by the dislocated lunate usually causes parasthaesia in the thumb, index, and middle fingers.

Complication. Apart from median nerve irritation, avascular necrosis in the displaced lunate commonly occurs, as the widespread capsular stripping may interfere with its blood supply.

Treatment

Manipulative reduction consisting of traction on the wrist which is then palmar flexed slowly, together with direct pressure on the lunate usually succeeds. If it fails, as open reduction almost inevitably leads to avascular necrosis, excision gives best results.

Treatment of avascular necrosis: when this is established, treatment will depend upon the degree of disability, and secondary changes in the surrounding bones. The choice lies between: firstly, a light supporting splint for wear as required, used where symptoms are mild, or where surgery is contra-indicated. Secondly, excision of the bone, possibly with replacement by an acrylic prosthesis. Thirdly, arthrodesis of the wrist.

D. DISLOCATIONS OF THE CARPUS

These are serious injuries, which are not very common and are due to considerable violence. They are only seen in fit young adults, as in children or older people, fractures will result. Three types may occur:

(i) True dislocation of the radio-carpal joint. These are the least common, usually a carpal bone remains articulating with the radius.

(ii) Peri-lunar dislocation of the carpus. In this, the lunate remains in place, and the carpus is dislocated round it.

(iii) Peri-lunar trans-scaphoid dislocation of the carpus. In this, not only does the lunate remain in contact with the radius, but there is a fracture of the scaphoid, the proximal pole remaining attached to the radius, and the distal pole being displaced with the carpus.

Treatment

In all cases, reduction is rarely difficult, but in trans-scaphoid perilunar dislocations—which are the least uncommon—avascular necrosis of the scaphoid fragment almost invariably follows.

E. 'SPRAINED WRIST'

This term is used to describe an injury in which the wrist is palmar flexed, thereby tearing the posterior capsule. An X-ray may show that a flake of bone has been avulsed from the dorsal surface of the triquetral.

Treatment is symptomatic, but usually the patient is more comfortable in a below-elbow plaster cast for two or three weeks.

UPPER LIMB—HAND INJURIES

INTRODUCTORY REMARKS

THE hand is perhaps man's most unique part. Phylogenetically it is very close to the basic primitive mammalian pattern, yet, because of the high tactile sensation it possesses, and the wide range of movement possible in the digits, it is, second to the human cerebral cortex, our most useful organ. Movements of the digits are concerned either with grasp or pinching. In the former, the fingers surround an object in one direction, with the thumb surrounding it in the opposite way, and considerable power may be exerted. In the latter, the tip of the thumb is brought into contact with that of the index and middle fingers. This is the position employed in doing finer work.

In considering the management of hand injuries, therefore, the preservation of movement is of great importance, and if any residual stiffness is anticipated the part must be in the position functionally most useful. The

FIG. 51. Position of function in the hand

fingers should, wherever possible, only be immobilised semiflexed at all their joints. The thumb should be placed with its metacarpal in 'opposition'—that is rotated through 90° to the plane in which the finger metacarpals lie. The wrist itself should ideally be held slightly dorsiflexed. When all these are combined the hand is said to be in the *position of function* (Fig. 51).

It is also important in the treatment of all hand injuries to encourage active mobilisation in all joints which do not specifically require to be immobilised. In all injuries, swelling should be discouraged, and where present, measures taken to reduce it, but this applies particularly to the hand for two reasons: firstly, because the resulting pain will prevent active movements by the patient, and secondly, the presence of either blood or oedema fluid in the tissue planes is liable to cause adhesions which in the hand would interfere with the free gliding of tendons.

Individual hand injuries will be dealt with in two parts—those involving bones and joints, and those affecting the soft tissues, but it must be emphasised that, more than elsewhere in the body, the management of bony and soft tissue injuries go together.

I. SKELETAL INJURIES

A. INJURIES OF THE METACARPUS

(i) Fractures of the Base of the First Metacarpal

These common injuries result from a longitudinal thrust down the metacarpal shaft. Two forms occur: a vertical fracture line through the base, with dislocation of the joint between the metacarpal and trapezium, and a fracture with a transverse line, involving the metacarpal alone.

(a) *Fracture Dislocation* ('*Bennett's Fracture*') (Fig 52 (*a*))

This is most frequently seen in young adult males, often due to injuries at sport. A large fragment of the base is sheared off the metacarpal shaft, which is adducted and displaced downwards.

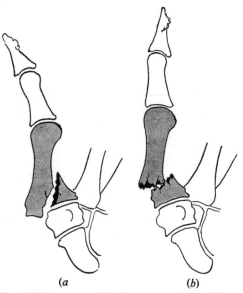

(*a*)   (*b*)

FIG. 52. Fractures of the base of the first metacarpa
(*a*) Bennett's fracture-dislocation
(*b*) Fracture throudgh the base of the metacarpal shaft

Treatment

If osteo-arthritis in the joint at the base of the first metacarpal is to be avoided in later life, perfect reduction is essential. Closed reduction is usually possible. Traction is exerted in the line of the thumb, which is then abducted while pressure is applied over the base of the bone (Fig. 53). A scaphoid type of plaster cast (Fig. 48) is then applied in this position, being carefully moulded at the base of the metacarpal. In order to maintain the metacarpal in full abduction, the metacarpo-phalangeal joint must be immobilised in a flexed position. The cast is maintained for four weeks, during which time frequent X-rays through the plaster are required to ensure that re-displacement does not occur. If any difficulty in closed reduction is experienced, open reduction with fixation either with a sub-periosteal stitch or a special small screw is indicated.

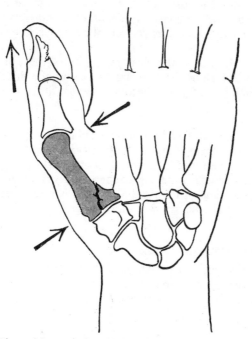

FIG. 53. Lines of force employed in the reduction of a Bennett's fracture

(b) *Fracture through the Proximal End of the First Metacarpal* (Fig. 52 (*b*))

In these injuries the fracture line is transverse, and the joint unaffected. There is some inward bowing in most cases. In children there may be a fracture separation of the epiphysis of the metacarpal, which in the case of the first, is situated at its base.

Treatment

As no joint is involved perfect reduction is not vital. If displacement is marked, the fracture may be reduced in the same way as a Bennett's fracture. Immobilisation is by a scaphoid type of plaster cast (Fig. 48) maintained for three or four weeks.

(ii) Fractures of the Bases of the Second to Fifth Metacarpals

These injuries follow direct blows on the dorsum of the hand, and may take all forms from minor cracks to comminuted fracture-dislocations of the carpo-metacarpal joints. Reduction, if required, is rarely difficult, and is followed by about three weeks in a below-elbow plaster cast.

(iii) Fractures of Metacarpal Shafts

These may be either oblique or transverse, depending upon the direction of force which caused the injury.

Oblique fractures lead to some shortening of the metacarpal shaft, but alignment is not often significantly disturbed. Transverse fractures are more liable to an angular deformity, and there may also be overlap of the fragments.

Complication. Owing to the close proximity of the extensor tendons, these may also be torn by the bone, or, as a result of a direct blow, unless the digit is mobilised, they may become adherent at the fracture site.

Treatment

Uneventful union invariably occurs in oblique fractures, which therefore merely require the protection of a plaster cast for two or three weeks until the pain has subsided. Transverse fractures do require reduction if displaced. Where there is overlap of the fragments, open operation and internal fixation using an intramedullary wire is often useful as external splintage may thereby be avoided, allowing greater mobility of the hand from the outset.

(iv) Fractures of Metacarpal Necks

These are common injuries resulting from a blow on the metacarpal head. In children this leads to a fracture separation of the epiphysis for the head. It occurs most commonly in the fifth metacarpal, followed by the

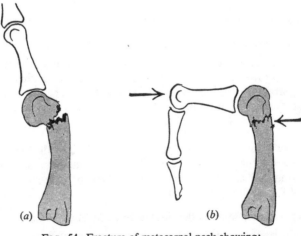

FIG. 54. Fracture of metacarpal neck showing:
(a) displacement   (b) method of reduction

fourth and second, being least common in the first. Displacement of the smaller fragment is forward (Fig. 54(*a*)).

Treatment

Manipulative reduction is achieved by flexing the finger fully at both the metacarpo-phalangeal and proximal inter-phalangeal joints, when pressure along the line of the proximal phalanx will push the displaced metacarpal head back into place (Fig. 54(*b*)). Following reduction, the finger is immobilised in this fully flexed position for two or three weeks, and then gently mobilised.

(v) Dislocation of the Metacarpo-phalangeal Joints

In this, the proximal phalanx is normally displaced backwards in relation to the metacarpal head (Fig. 55). It is commonest in the thumb, followed by the index finger. Occasionally, particularly in the thumb, the dislocation is associated with a vertical split in the joint capsule, which then becomes button-holed round the metacarpal neck, forming a block to reduction.

Treatment

Manipulative reduction is achieved by first hyperextending the proximal phalanx, and then, by direct pressure at its base, lowering it over the metacarpal head. If traction is applied reduction may be prevented by the metacarpal head being gripped between the flexor tendons, or, in the case of the thumb, the long flexor and the thenar muscles.

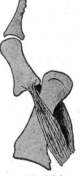

FIG. 55. Dislocation of metacarpo-phalangeal joint of the thumb

(vi) Sprains of the Metacarpo-phalangeal Joints

Side to side movement at metacarpo-phalangeal joints is prevented by the collateral ligaments, so that if a digit is subjected to a sideways stress, the ligament may be torn through, thus allowing the joint to become subluxed. This occurs most commonly in the thumb, followed by the fifth and index fingers. In the thumb, a flake of bone may be avulsed from the base of the proximal phalanx by the collateral ligament, and, when this is present, unless the fragment becomes reattached, residual laxity remains. This is most frequently seen on the ulnar side.

Treatment

In the thumb, supportive strapping for ten to fourteen days suffices in minor injuries. Where a bony flake has been avulsed, immobilisation in a scaphoid type of plaster cast is required for three or four weeks. Occasionally surgical repair is necessary. In fingers, the affected digit should be strapped to its healthy neighbour (Fig. 56) thereby permitting flexion and extension, but restricting lateral movement.

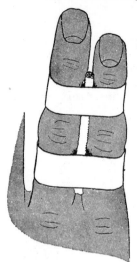

FIG. 56. Method of strapping an injured finger to its neighbour

FIG. 57. Fraction mid shaft phalanx to show relationship to the flexor tendons

B. DIGITAL INJURIES
(i) Fractures of Phalanges

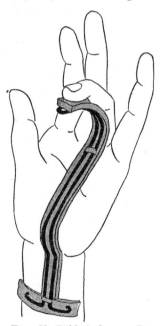

FIG. 58. Böhler's finger splint

Phalanges may be damaged either by direct violence from a blow or a crushing force in which case soft-tissue damage at the same time may well have occurred, or by indirect violence.

Fractures due to direct violence are usually transverse, at mid-shaft level, and owing to the combined pull of the flexor and extensor tendons, displacement consists of forward angulation (Fig. 57), in which case the bone ends will impinge upon the flexor tendons in their sheath.

Fractures due to indirect violence may be oblique, with some lateral displacement, or one of the articular condyles at the distal end may be sheared off.

In children, fracture dislocation of the epiphysis at the base occurs.

Treatment

Where there has been forward angulation reduction is achieved by traction and flexion of the finger. If interference with the gliding of the flexion tendons in their sheath is to be avoided, perfect reduction is essential. Occasionally an intramedullary wire is employed to provide internal fixation.

After reduction, the finger is splinted in a position of semiflexion at all joints, and a Böhlers finger splint (Fig. 58) provides a simple means of so doing.

(ii) Fractures of the Distal Phalanx

The end of the distal phalanx may be crushed as a result of a direct blow. The fracture here can be ignored, and the injury regarded as involving soft tissues only. A sub-ungual haematoma is often present and requires evacuation if the nail is to be preserved. In children, fracture separa-

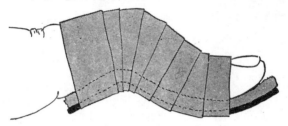

FIG. 59. Mallet finger splint

tion of the epiphysis may occur, and if displacement is severe, reduction may be required. A flake of bone may be avulsed from the base by the extensor tendon, this injury is treated as if there is a tendon rupture on a 'Mallet finger' splint (Fig. 59) for three or four weeks.

(iii) Dislocation of Inter-phalangeal Joints

These may be either in the antero-posterior or lateral planes. In the former reduction by traction will be required, after which the position is stable. In the latter, spontaneous reduction often takes place, but, because the collateral ligament on one side has been completely disrupted, recovery may be prolonged.

Treatment

After reduction, the finger is supported by strapping it to an unaffected neighbour for two to three weeks (Fig. 56). Active movement is encouraged.

II. SOFT TISSUE INJURIES

A. SKIN

In skin injuries of the hand, two points require to be considered—firstly the siting of scars, and secondly replacement of skin loss.

(i) Scars:

In accidental lacerations, the direction of the cut is entirely fortuitous, and the important consideration is to obtain rapid, uneventful healing with minimal reaction. Where surgical procedures of any kind are performed in the hand, however, the line of incision must be carefully planned, so that at no point is a natural crease line crossed directly by the cut. Figure 60 shows the standard lines for surgical incisions in the hand on its palmar aspect, which is the more important side.

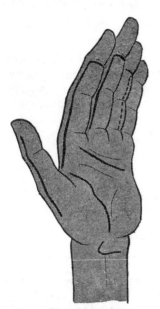

FIG. 60. Lines of incisions for use in hand surgery

(ii) Replacement of Skin Loss: (*see also* p. 10)

Manual skin may be lost in three ways: Firstly, an area may be cleanly sliced off by something sharp, such as a knife or piece of broken glass. Secondly, loss may be by a combination of crushing and sheering forces, which both lacerates and devitalises the skin. Finally, if the hand is caught in the moving parts of some machine, skin may be torn off. This is known as 'degloving'. In a finger, the skin may be avulsed in this way if a ring is accidentally violently pulled off.

In replacement of skin, at any part of the hand which is commonly subject to direct pressure, a full thickness graft must be employed. This may be achieved in several ways:

(i) Where there has been loss of skin from the pulp of a finger, it may be flexed to lie in contact with the thenar eminence, from which a flap of skin is raised and sutured over the raw area. The donor site is then covered by a split skin (Tiersch) graft taken either from a thigh or forearm.

(ii) Small areas of full thickness skin loss may be covered by free full thickness (Wolfe) grafts, taken from such sites as the chest wall. The resulting raw area is then, in turn, covered by split skin.

(iii) If skin loss has been extensive, as in degloving injuries, replacement may be effected by burying the raw area under a flap of skin raised from the abdominal wall. Then, about three weeks later, when the flap has obtained a new blood supply from the denuded area, the hand with its new skin cover may be released from the abdominal wall, the edges being trimmed and sutured.

B. NERVES

Peripheral nerve injuries are dealt with elsewhere (p. 19) but it is important to appreciate that sensory loss in the hand, particularly the finger-tips, is extremely disabling because it both impedes function, and also by removing a protective mechanism, makes injury more likely to occur. For this reason, divided digital nerves should be repaired where possible. Occasionally, partial sensation to the tip of the thumb or index finger may be restored by moving an island of skin, together with its neurovascular bundle, from some less vital site, such as the ulnar side of the ring finger.

C. TENDON INJURIES

In the hand itself, the flexor tendons differ greatly from the extensor tendons in both nature and method of operation, so that the two groups will be considered separately.

(i) Flexor Tendon Injuries

General Considerations. The flexor tendons to the fingers and thumb have wide excursions. In order to work efficiently, they must be able to glide freely, yet, whatever position the digit may occupy, they must not alter their relationship to surrounding structures. Where, therefore, they may have to move round corners, they pass through synovial sheaths, lubricated with synovial fluid, and these in turn are anchored by fibrous tissue.

In the fingers the synovial sheaths, in which the flexor tendons run, end opposite the distal inter-phalangeal joint. In the index, middle, and ring fingers, it commences proximally opposite the heads of the metacarpals, whereas in the little finger it is continuous with the general synovial sheath in which all the finger flexors run at the level of the wrist joint (Fig. 61). In the thumb the flexor pollicis longus tendon runs on its own, and its sheath extends from the wrist to the inter-phalangeal joint.

The flexor tendons in their synovial sheath at the wrist are held in place by the tough flexor retinaculum stretching from the scaphoid to the pisiform. In the fingers there is a fibrous sheath running the length of the synovial sheath. This is firmly attached to the sides of the

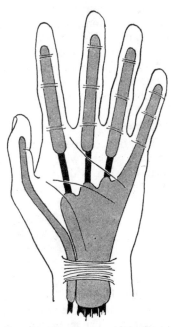

FIG. 61. The anatomy of the flexor synovial tendon sheaths in the hand

shafts of the proximal and middle phalanges, and their opposite joints. In the thumb the fibrous sheath commences at the metacarpal head extending only to the inter-phalangeal joint.

There are two sets of flexor tendons to each finger. The flexor digitorum profundus tendons run through to be inserted into the bases of the distal phalanges arising from their muscle belly which lies deep in the forearm. The tendons of flexor digitorum sublimus lie more superficially, and over the proximal phalanges each one splits so that the two parts pass on either side of the profundus tendon which lies beneath, to be inserted into the base of the middle phalanx.

Arising from the profundus tendons in the hand are the small lumbrial muscles which pass in the interdigital cleft, where each joins the tendon of one of the interossei to be attached to the extensor expansion on the dorsum

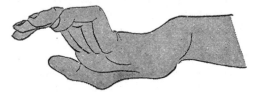

FIG. 62. Claw-hand deformity

of the proximal phalanx. This makes it possible to flex the metacarpo-phalangeal joint, while active extension of the inter-phalangeal joints is maintained. The lumbrials and interossei (together known as the intrinsic muscles) are all supplied by the deep branch of the ulnar nerve, so that an injury to this nerve permits hyperextension of the metacarpo-phalangeal joints with loss of active extension at the inter-phalangeal joints. The resulting deformity is known as a 'claw hand' (Fig. 62).

Treatment

Two factors govern the treatment of flexor tendon injuries. Firstly, because of their wide excursion and free movement, where there is complete division, wide retraction of the proximal end inevitably occurs, so that an extensive exposure may be necessary at the time of surgical repair.

FIG. 63. Bunnell's method of tendon suture

Secondly, if normal function is to be restored, there must be no adhesion formation within the synovial sheath which would prevent their free gliding movement. The method of repair therefore will depend upon the level of injury, and also the extent of trauma to surrounding structures which occurred at the time of division—a severe crushing injury, particularly if it has also caused a concomitant fracture at the same level may entirely preclude a successful result from direct tendon repair, and some alternative less satisfactory form of treatment may have to be adopted.

Clean incisions of the tendons will be considered first.

(i) *In the Palm.* At this level direct repair of the tendon is usually possible, using the Bunnell method of suture (Fig. 63) which is strong and yet minimises further scar formation at the actual site of the division.

(ii) *In the Finger.* Here, because the division is in the synovial sheath, direct tendon repair is doomed to failure owing to adhesion formation between the sheath and suture line. For this reason, where both tendons have been divided *tendon grafting* must be employed.

The tendon graft may be taken either from the palmaris longus, the plantaris, or the long extensor tendon of the third or fourth toes. No attempt is made to repair the flexor digitorum sublimis, which is excised, along with the stump of the flexor digitorum profundus tendon. The graft is then threaded through the empty synovial sheath, the distal end being secured to the base of the distal phalanx. The graft is then sutured under moderate tension, to the proximal end of the profundus tendon in the middle of the palm, using the Bunnell method, and the surplus of the tendon is discarded (Fig. 64).

After treatment consists of splinting the finger semiflexed for three weeks, to permit the suture lines to heal, after which active mobilisation is started.

The timing of the flexor tendon repair is important, in order to minimise scar formation, in clean incised wounds, immediate grafting may safely be carried out, but where the wound is in any way contaminated, or there has been an element of crushing in the original injury, surgery should be postponed until all tissue reaction has settled down and a full range of passive movement has been regained.

Fig. 64. Extent of tendon graft used to repair flexor digitorum profundus

Where the flexor digitorum profundus alone has been divided opposite the middle phalanx, satisfactory repair may often be obtained by excising the short distal stump of tendon, and bring the proximal end directly up to the base of the distal phalanx. This procedure is known as *tendon advancement.*

If there has been extensive soft tissue damage as well as flexor tendon division the prospects of a successful tendon repair by any means will be remote, in which case it may be better to accept a finger which is stiff in the position of function, by arthrodesing the inter-phalangeal joints in the semiflexed position. Occasionally, where there has been extensive damage to one finger alone, especially if sensation has also been impaired, best results will be obtained by amputation, usually through the metacarpo-phalangeal joint.

Flexor Tendon Injuries at Wrist Level

Here, all the finger flexor tendons run in one synovial sheath, with the median nerve in close proximity. Any laceration at the wrist which divides these tendons is very likely to divide the nerve as well. Surgical repair is a complicated procedure, and, in order to reduce scarring the flexor digitorum profundus tendons and median nerve only are repaired. The flexor sublimus tendons are sacrificed.

(ii) Extensor Tendon Injuries

Only at the level of the wrist do the extensor tendons run in synovial sheaths. In the fingers, the extensor apparatus ceases to be a true 'tendon' and is better described as the 'extensor aponeurosis'. For this reason, the problems of retraction of the severed ends, and free gliding of the tendons which are so important in the repair of flexor tendons do not exist.

Treatment

Direct suture of the divided tendon ends, followed by a suitable splint to maintain the tendon in a relaxed position for three weeks gives good re-sults.

Individual Extensor Tendon Injuries

(a) *Extensor Pollicis Longus*

As has been mentioned (p. 84), this tendon may suffer attrition rupture as it passes round the tubercle on the dorsum of the radius. This usually follows a Colles' fracture which has left some bony irregularity at this point. The rupture tendon may be either sutured directly or the tendon of extensor indicis may be transplanted into the distal end. Whichever procedure is adopted will depend upon the extent which the severed ends are frayed.

(b) *At the Proximal Inter-phalangeal Joint*

Here the extensor apparatus is in three slips. A central slip which is inserted into the base of the middle phalanx, and two side slips (into which are inserted the tendons of the intrinsic muscles) which unite together to be inserted into the base of the distal phalanx.

Injury at this level will divide the central slip alone, so that the proximal inter-phalangeal joint will assume a flexed position, while the two side slips become displaced forwards and hyper-extend the distal phalanx (Fig. 65 (*a*)). The resulting appearance is known as a '*Boutoniere Deformity*'.

Treatment

Rather than attempt repair to the central slip, which would be difficult, equally good results are obtained if the two lateral slips are sutured together longitudinally over the inter-phalangeal joint.

(c) *At the Distal Inter-phalangeal Joint ('Mallet Finger')*

This is a very common closed injury, in which the extensor is avulsed from its attachment to the base of the distal phalanx. Occasionally a small fragment of bone is pulled off with the extensor. The cause is usually forceful flexion of the actively extruded finger, as when it is stubbed against some fixed object.

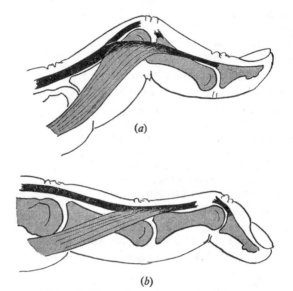

(a)

(b)

FIG. 65. Finger extensor expansion injuries

(a) Proximal inter-phalangeal joint ('Boutoniere' deformity)
(b) Distal inter-phalangeal joint ('Mallet finger' deformity)

The appearance is characteristic (Fig. 65 (b)), the distal inter-phalangea joint being flexed, while the proximal joint tends to assume a hyper-extended position.

Treatment

The finger should be splinted with the distal inter-phalangeal joint hyper-extended and the proximal joint semiflexed, thus allowing the torn ends to come together. This position is maintained for about six weeks. The splint may be made of plaster-of-Paris, on a strip of aluminium lined with felt, (Fig. 59) or some plastic material.

Results are often imperfect with some residual lag remaining; but, as functional disability is slight, and the risk of leaving permanent stiffness if surgical repair is attempted is great, this should be accepted.

CHAPTER TEN

LOWER LIMB—HIP AND THIGH

Summary

A. Dislocation of the Hip

   (i) Posterior Dislocation
   (ii) Anterior Dislocation
   (iii) 'Central' Dislocation

B. Fractures of the Upper End of the Femur

   (i) Sub-capital Fractures of the Femoral Neck

     (*a*) Impacted Abduction Fractures
     (*b*) Un-impacted Adduction Fractures

   (ii) Transcervical Fractures of the Femoral Neck
   (iii) Basal Fractures of the Femoral Neck
   (iv) Inter-trochanteric Fractures of the Femur
   (v) Sub-trochanteric Fracture of the Femur
   (vi) Isolated Fractures of the Trochanters

C. Fractures of the Shaft of the Femur

   (i) Fractures of the Femoral Shaft in Adults
   (ii) Fractures of the Femoral Shaft in Infancy and Childhood

D. Fractures of the Lower End of the Femur

   (i) Supra-condylar Fractures
   (ii) Fractures of the Femoral Condyles

A. DISLOCATION OF THE HIP

Traumatic dislocation of a normal hip can only follow considerable violence, because, unlike the glenoid in the shoulder, the acetabulum is a deep cavity into which the femoral head fits snugly. The head of the femur may be displaced either forwards (anterior dislocation) or backwards (posterior dislocation) of which the latter is considerably more common. In addition, a direct thrust along the line of the femoral neck occasionally shatters the acetabulum, so that the femoral head is displaced into the pelvic cavity. This amounts to a fracture-dislocation of the hip, and is often described as a 'central dislocation'.

(i) Posterior Dislocation of the Hip

The head of the femur can be driven out of the acetabulum backwards, if a longitudinal thrust is applied along the shaft of the femur when the hip is flexed, and also slightly adducted. It is therefore an injury commonly due to road accidents, in which the patient was sitting in a moving vehicle which came to a sudden halt.

The clinical appearance is characteristic (Fig. 66) the affected leg being internally rotated, adducted, and shortened.

Complications. Two important complications may occur:

(i) *Immediate.* The sciatic nerve may be stretched as it runs round the back of the femoral neck. Damage varies from mild neuropraxia to a severe traction injury causing permanent total paralysis. Usually, however, damage is not severe, the lateral popliteal division of the nerve being most vulnerable, causing foot drop and numbness over the outside of the calf.

(ii) *Late.* The rent in the capsule of the joint which occurs, coupled with the inevitable complete avulsion of the ligamentum teres from the acetabulum, may cut off the blood supply to the femoral head, leading to avascular necrosis. This will cause an apparent increase in density of the femoral head on X-ray because interference with blood flow to the head will prevent the normal osteoporosis associated with the hyperaemia which follows a severe injury.

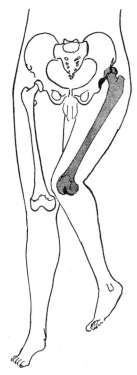

FIG. 66. The clinical appearance of posterior dislocation of the hip

Later, the head will collapse, and severe osteo-arthritis changes will follow.

Treatment

Manipulative reduction is usually successful. The anaesthetised patient is laid on his back, with an assistant anchoring the pelvis by pressure on the iliac crests. The operator flexes the hip to 90°, so that the displaced femoral head comes to lie directly behind the acetabulum, then by traction combined with slight adduction of the hip, the dislocation is reduced (Fig. 67).

FIG. 67. Method of reducing posterior dislocation of the hip

After treatment consists of maintaining the leg in traction for about four weeks, to permit healing of the capsular tear, after which weight bearing is permitted. Radiographs should be taken at monthly intervals for the first three or four months, so that avascular necrosis of the femoral head may be detected early before collapse has occurred.

Occasionally manipulative reduction fails, or if the posterior tip of the acetabulum has been fractured, redisplacement occurs. In such cases, open reduction, using a posterior approach is necessary. The lip of the acetabulum, if fractured, may be held in place by a screw.

Treatment of Complications

Sciatic nerve injuries are treated initially by protective splinting, with care to avoid pressure sores developing in anaesthetic areas of skin. Residual permanent paralysis is treated either by the supply of a suitable supportive appliance or by surgical measures, such as muscle transplants or arthrodesis of flail joints (p. 284).

Avascular necrosis is treated in its early stages by the rigid avoidance of weight bearing until radiographs show that the bony texture of the femoral head has returned to normal. In practise this may take many months, and as the patients with traumatic dislocation of the hip are usually young, fit adults, arthrodesis often provides the best solution.

(ii) Anterior Dislocation of the Hip

This rather uncommon injury results from an injury which forcibly abducts the extended hip, causing the femoral head to lie below and in front of the acetabulum. The leg assumes a characteristic position of abduction and external rotation.

Complications are less common than in posterior dislocation of the hip.

Treatment

Reduction is effected by a combination of adduction, internal rotation, and flexion of the hip. This is followed by about three weeks traction to allow repair of the soft tissue damage.

(iii) 'Central Dislocation' of the Hip

This injury is due to direct violence, which drives the femoral head through the floor of the acetabulum. The articular surfaces of both are therefore extensively damaged.

Treatment

Where the central displacement is marked, in view of the extensive articular damage, best results may be obtained by accepting the position, thereby leaving the patient with a stiff, but stable and relatively painless hip. If reduction is attempted, painful osteo-arthritis will inevitably follow. Where displacement is not marked, reduction by traction on the limb is indicated. Occasionally operative reconstruction of the acetabulum floor may be employed.

B. FRACTURES OF THE UPPER END OF THE FEMUR

Because of the angle formed between the neck and shaft of the femur, fractures of the upper end are very common. They usually result from an indirect twisting force, and are most often seen in the elderly, where senile osteoporotic changes are present. The fractures may be grouped according to the level at which they occur:

(i) Sub-capital fractures, where the neck joins the head, are the highest.

(ii) Transcervical fractures occur through the middle of the femoral neck.

(iii) Basal fractures of the neck are just above the level of the trochanters.

(iv) Inter-trochanteric fractures, often comminuted, occur through the trochanters.

(v) Sub-trochanteric fractures—which are least common, are in fact fractures transversely through the upper femoral shaft.

In addition, occasionally, the lesser trochanter may be avulsed by a sudden pull by the psoas muscle inserted into it, and the tip of the greater trochanter may be cracked by a direct blow over it.

(i) Sub-capital Fractures of the Femoral Neck

These are common injuries of elderly women, due to a combination of senile osteoporosis, which tends to be more marked in post-menopausal females, and the fact that the angle between the neck and shaft of the femur is sharper in women, thereby throwing more severe strains upon the femoral neck. The fracture may present in two ways—it may be *impacted*, when the head of the femur is driven into the neck, or *unimpacted*, where the head is free.

(a) *Impacted Abduction Fractures of the Femoral Neck*

In these, the head of the femur is in an abducted position, so that it rests on top of the neck, where as a result of muscle pull they become impacted together (Fig. 68).

Clinically there may be little beyond pain in the hip following an injury, often fairly trivial, to suggest a fracture. There is no shortening and active movement is possible.

FIG. 68. Impacted abduction fracture of the femoral neck

Treatment

Many of these fractures unite without treatment, often because they are never diagnosed. As, however, if they become disimpacted at a later stage, treatment may be difficult, internal fixation with a Smith-Petersen nail followed by early ambulation gives the most satisfactory results.

(b) *Unimpacted Adduction Fractures of the Femoral Neck*

These form the larger and more important group.

The femoral head is in an adducted position,

lying below the stump of the femoral neck, which lies pointing forward (Fig. 69).

The clinical picture is characteristic. An elderly woman sustains a minor rotational injury to her leg and falls to the ground. She is then unable to rise, or move the affected limb, and complains of severe pain in the hip. On examination the injured leg is shortened, and lies with the foot fully externally rotated (Fig. 70). No active movements at the hip are possible.

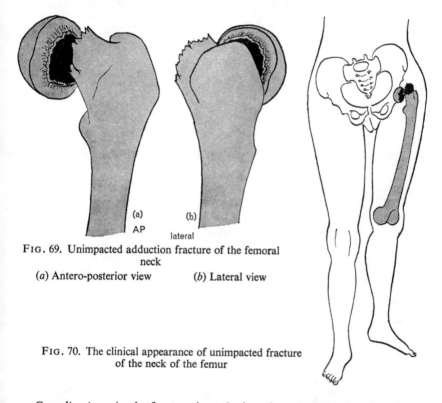

FIG. 69. Unimpacted adduction fracture of the femoral neck

(a) Antero-posterior view   (b) Lateral view

FIG. 70. The clinical appearance of unimpacted fracture of the neck of the femur

Complication. As the fracture is at the junction of the head and neck of the femur, the blood supply to the capital fragment is often cut off, so that *avascular necrosis* very commonly follows.

Treatment

Because of the poor blood supply to the head fragment, perfect immobilisation is desirable. Any form of external splintage is unlikely to hold the small, hemispherical femoral head firmly, so internal fixation is necessary to secure union.

Another reason why external splintage cannot be employed is that the risks to life of hypostatic pneumonia, pressure sores, urinary infection, and

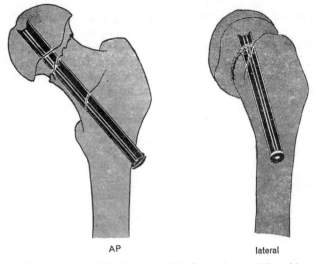

AP   lateral

FIG. 71. Smith–Petersen nail for fracture of the femoral neck (AP and lateral views)

pulmonary embolism which accompany immobilisation in an elderly per
son are much greater than the operative mortality.

In practice two measures are available, the choice often depending upon the individual surgeon. Either, the fracture may be reduced and fixed by a

FIG. 72. Austin–Moore prosthesis replacing femoral head

trifin (Smith–Petersen) nail, inserted under X-ray control (Fig. 71), or the loose femoral head may be excised and replaced by a 'Vitallium' prosthesis (Austin–Moore, Fig. 72).

The advantage of nail fixation is that, providing uneventful union takes place, the hip is virtually restored to normal. The great disadvantage, however, is that if the head has been rendered avascular, either the fracture fails to unite, in which case the nail is extruded, or the head will collapse, often causing the nail to protrude into the acetabulum.

A prosthesis usually gives a good early result, but a few years later it is liable to become loosened, but in elderly patients with a short expectation of life, this may not matter.

Whichever method is employed, operation should not be delayed to avoid the dangers of immobilisation.

(ii) Transcervical Fractures of the Femoral Neck

These are fractures through the middle of the femoral neck. At this level, the capsular attachment to the femoral head, which carries its main blood supply, is therefore usually undamaged, so that avascular necrosis is much less common than in sub-capital fractures.

Treatment

As the danger of avascular necrosis is not marked, internal fixation by a trifin nail usually gives good results.

(iii) Basal Fractures of the Femoral Neck

Fractures at this site—where the neck joins the femoral shaft, but not involving the trochanters—are not very common. It is at this level that the occasional fracture of the upper end of the femur in younger patients usually occurs.

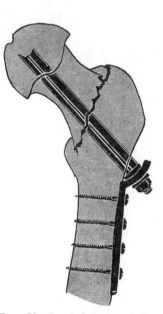

Treatment

Internal fixation usually gives results. To gain a secure hold on both fragments a combined nail and plate (Fig. 73) is required. The nail obtains good fixation on the smaller proximal fragment, and this is fixed to the femoral shaft by means of the plate, and screws. On the rare occasion when this fracture occurs in late childhood, immobilisation of the limb in a well fitting plaster-of-Paris hip spica (Fig. 74) is perfectly satisfactory.

FIG. 73. Basal fracture of the femoral neck treated by nail and plate fixation

(iv) Inter-trochanteric Fractures of the Femur

These fractures, with subcapital fractures are a very common injury of elderly people. At this level, however, they occur with equal frequency in both men and women. They are often comminuted, the lesser trochanter is frequently avulsed and pulled upwards by the ilio-psoas muscle which is inserted into it (Fig. 75).

Treatment

Union of these fractures rarely presents a problem, so that simple traction on the injured leg allows the fracture to unite in a reasonably satisfactory position. However, the patient who sustains such an injury is almost always elderly, and the risks of semi-immobility that this entails are considerable. For this reason internal fixation using a nail-and-plate is to be preferred in most cases, as the patient can be mobilised freely in bed immediately, and, if a secure hold on both main fragments has been obtained, ambulation may commence within three to four weeks of operation (Fig. 73).

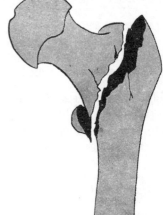

FIG. 75. Inter-trochanteric fracture of the upper end of the femur

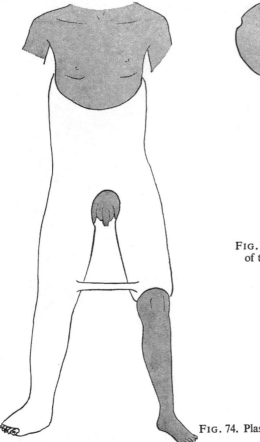

FIG. 74. Plaster-of-Paris hip spica

(v) Sub-trochanteric Fractures of the Femur

Fractures at this level are really through the upper femoral shaft. They are comparatively uncommon unless the bone at this site is abnormal. Metastatic carcinomatous deposits are common in the upper end of the femur, leading to pathological fractures. The bone at this site may also be weakened through the changes of Paget's disease (p. 294).

Treatment

Owing to the pull of the psoas muscle, the small proximal fragment tends to be flexed, making the maintenance of reduction difficult unless internal fixation with either a nail-and-plate, or an intra-medullary nail, is employed. If the fracture is pathological, the causal lesion must also be treated.

(vi) Isolated Fractures of the Trochanters

Occasionally the tip of the greater trochanter is cracked as a result of a direct blow. This is rarely of importance, and beyond protecting the limb by avoiding weight bearing for a few weeks until the reaction to the trauma has settled down, no specific treatment is required.

The lesser trochanter may be avulsed by the pull of the psoas muscle. In itself this is of no importance, but sometimes this occurs because the bone at this level is weakened through pathological change, particularly a secondary neoplastic deposit. This possibility must therefore always be borne in mind, and if necessary a biopsy should be taken. If a neoplastic deposit is present, a primary should be sought, and usually a course of radiotherapy is administered.

C. FRACTURES OF THE SHAFT OF THE FEMUR

This is a common, severe injury which may occur at any level. They usually are due to considerable direct violence, and are therefore often associated with injuries elsewhere, and frequently result from road accidents.

Secondary carcinomatous deposits are common in the femur, particularly in its upper shaft, so that pathological fractures are common. Oblique fractures of the femoral shaft also frequently occur in infants and young children due to indirect rotational strains on the bone. The femur is also sometimes fractured during birth, especially in cases of breach delivery with extended legs.

(i) Fractures of the Femoral Shaft in Adults

The degree of trauma necessary to fracture a normal femoral shaft is considerable. The patient therefore is liable to be severely shocked, and even in closed fractures the blood loss into the surrounding tissues may amount to one to two pints. The fracture line may be transverse or comminuted, and displacement, which will depend upon the direction of the causative force, may be severe.

Complications. Fat embolus is commoner in fractures of the femoral shaft than in other bones. This is dealt with elsewhere (p. 164). Because the bone is surrounded by muscle, injuries to the femoral vessels or sciatic nerve are not very common. Residual stiffness of the knee due to scarring in the quadriceps muscle binding, anchoring it to the bone at the level of the fracture, may be a problem.

Non-union sometimes occurs, especially in compound fractures, but because the femoral shaft has a good blood supply, it is not often seen.

Treatment

This may be conservative or operative, and is governed by the general condition of the patient, the level of the fracture, and the presence of injuries elsewhere.

FIG. 76. Thomas's splint, using 'fixed' skin traction

(a) *Conservative:* Because, in most cases, union does not present a problem, perfect immobilisation is unnecessary, and a good position can be maintained by traction. This is best carried out by the use of a Thomas splint, and may be either 'fixed' or 'balanced'. In *fixed traction* (Fig. 76) the leg is attached directly to the end of the splint, whose ring obtains counter pressure against the ischial tuberosity. In most cases, the leg is secured to the splint by adhesive extension strapping ('skin extension').

In *balanced traction* (Fig. 77), weights are attached directly to the limb, which merely rests on the Thomas splint. Traction is obtained by a Steinmann's pin inserted through the tibial tubercle ('skeletal traction'). With this method knee flexion can be practised while traction is maintained by the use of an addition to the Thomas splint which hinges at the knee joint.

In practice fixed (skin) traction is employed mainly in the early stages, particularly if the patient has to be moved.

Where the fracture is clinically and radiologically united, which in a normal adult takes about twelve weeks, traction is dismantled. It is often wiser to equip the patient with a protective weight relieving caliper for a month or so when he starts to walk, as in the event of falling considerable angulatory strains may be thrown upon the bone.

(b) *Operative.* The femoral shaft is one of the fracture sites most suitable for internal fixation, using an intramedullary (*Küntscher*) nail. In most cases the nail can be driven upwards through the proximal fragment making a second small incision over the region of the Great trochanter to allow it to extrude. The fracture is then reduced under direct vision and the nail driven downwards into the distal fragment. The alternative is that a wire could be inserted from an incision made over the Great trochanter down the shaft of the femur and then that is used to reduce the fracture and the nail is then driven along it, across the fracture site, and the wire is then removed.

Post-operatively, the patient can be allowed free in bed, but, to avoid bending the nail, weight bearing should be deferred until there is radiological evidence of union.

The three indications for internal fixation of femoral shaft fractures are:

(i) *Local.* The nature of the fracture may make reduction difficult to achieve and difficult to retain. This applies particularly to fractures of the upper femoral shaft, where the pull of the psoas tendon and the glutei tend to abduct and flex the small proximal fragment. Occasionally some muscle may become lodged between the two fragments and make satisfactory reduction difficult.

(ii) *General.* Where there are multiple injuries, as, for example, fractures of both legs, internal fixation of the femoral fracture may make the overall management of the patient much easier.

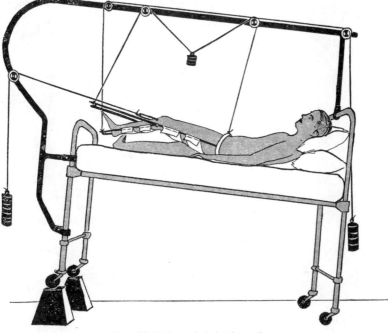

FIG. 77. Balanced skeletal traction

(iii) *Pathological Fractures.* Internal fixation by intramedullary nailing is usually fairly simple in fractures through secondary metastatic deposits, and makes the patient's management both easier and more comfortable. These often occur in advanced cases, where union cannot occur. Nailing may be combined with radiotherapy.

(ii) Fractures of the Femoral Shaft in Infancy and Childhood

Unlike femoral shaft fractures in adults, those occurring in children are often due to indirect rotatory twisting strains, having oblique fracture lines. A baby's femur is also sometimes fractured during a difficult delivery, especially in breach presentations with extended legs.

Treatment

Rapid union is the rule, and, as residual joint stiffness is very uncommon in children, three to four weeks 'fixed' traction on a Thomas' splint is all that is required.

In infants and children under three years of age 'gallows traction' (Fig. 79) provides a simple and effective method of management.

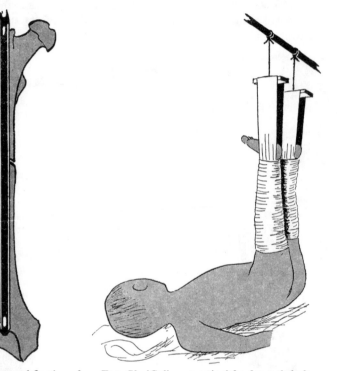

FIG. 78. Internal fixation of femoral shaft fracture using an intramedullary Künts-cher) nail

FIG. 79. 'Gallows traction' for femoral shaft fractures in early childhood

D. FRACTURES OF THE LOWER END OF THE FEMUR

Two groups of fractures occur in the lower end of the femur—fractures through the lower end (supra-condylar fractures), and fractures of the femoral condyles.

(i) Supra-condylar Fractures

The lower end of the femur has no muscle attachments anteriorly, whereas the two heads of the gastrocnemius have their origin posteriorly.

As a result, in supra-condylar fractures there is a characteristic flexion deformity of the lower fragment (Fig. 80). Because of this the medial or lateral popliteal nerves or the femoral vessels may also be injured.

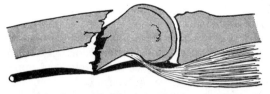

FIG. 80. Supra-condylar femoral fracture, showing how the femoral artery may be damaged

Treatment

Reduction can only be maintained if the flexing force of the muscles is relaxed by holding the joint bent, in a Thomas' splint with a knee flexion piece on traction. The angle of the splint being opposite the fracture site, rather than the knee joint (Fig. 81). Occasionally internal fixation with two curved intramedullary pins (Rush nails) may be employed.

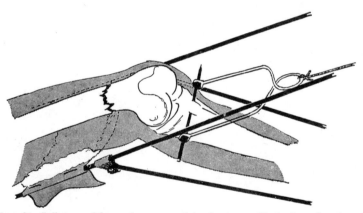

FIG. 81. Splintage of femoral supra-condylar fracture, with the knee flexed, and support just proximal to fracture site

In children a fracture separation of the lower femoral epiphysis may occur, with similar displacement to that seen in supra-condylar fractures in adults. As there is no risk of stiffness developing, reduction may be maintained by holding the knee flexed to a right angle in a plaster-of-Paris cast.

(ii) Fractures of the Femoral Condyles

These injuries are comparatively uncommon. They may take two forms, either one condyle alone may be fractured, as a result of a sideways blow just above the knee or both condyles may be fractured in a Y pattern, due to a direct blow on the femoral condyles when the knee is fully flexed.

Treatment

This is difficult, because with an intra articular injury early mobilisation is desirable, but maintenance of a reasonable reduction to avoid residual angular deformity is also important. Fortunately union of the fracture rarely presents a problem

The simplest way of treating these fractures consists of the application of a plaster-of-Paris cylinder (Fig. 83) after reduction. This is maintained for three or four weeks, after which the cast is split, and mobilisation commenced. Weight bearing is not permitted for eight to ten weeks.

Alternatively, when one condyle only is involved, the fracture may be reduced by open operation and secured by a bolt passing transversely across both condyles.

CHAPTER ELEVEN

LOWER LIMB—KNEE INJURIES

Summary

Introductory Remarks

A. Injuries of the Extensor Apparatus

(i) Rupture of the Quadriceps Insertion
(ii) Fractures of the Patella
(iii) Rupture of the Ligamentum Patellae
(iv) Avulsion of the Tibial Tubercle
(v) Dislocation of the Patella

B. Injuries in the Lateral Plane

(i) Fracture of the Lateral Tibial Condyle
(ii) Ligamentous Injuries
(iii) Combined Ligamentous and Bony Injuries
(iv) Dislocation of the Knee

C. Rotational Injuries

(i) Injuries of the Medial Semilunar Cartilage
(ii) Injuries of the Lateral Semilunar Cartilage
(iii) Minor Rotational Strains

D. Injuries in the Antero-Posterior Plane

INTRODUCTORY REMARKS

The knee is the largest joint in the body, and, because the femur and tibia are also the longest bones, it is subjected to very powerful strains in all directions. It is very dependent for stability upon the supporting soft-tissue structures—tendons, muscles, and ligaments.

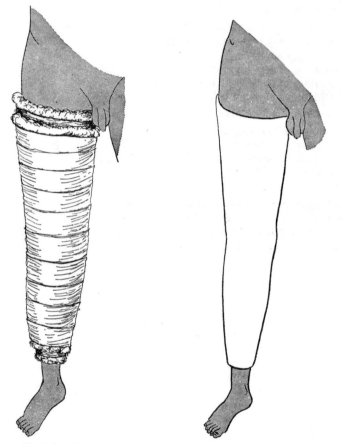

FIG. 82. Robert-Jones pressure bandage

FIG. 83. Plaster-of-Paris cylinder

Anatomically, the knee is classified as a 'hinge joint', but in fact the upper end of the tibia consists of two very shallow saucer-like depressions, and the femoral condyles are eliptical in shape so that on movement the femur rolls across the tibia. Also, when the joint is relaxed in flexion, a small amount of rotation is possible, but on full extension, which tightens the cruciate ligaments in the inter-condylar notch, the joint becomes locked straight. This property is important from the functional aspect, as when standing with the knees straight, it becomes possible to relax the thigh musculature. Any loss of full extension thus imposes a strain upon the patient when standing.

Of the muscles which assist in providing stability, the quadriceps is the most important because active extension is essential for both standing and walking. Therefore, after any significant knee injury active *quadriceps exercises* must be instituted.

Also, because the knee is so dependent upon the surrounding soft tissues for stability and any sizeable effusion should be *aspirated* to prevent the lining capsule from being stretched, thus leading to slight generalised laxity. Aspiration also provides a useful guide to the severity of the injury. If the fluid is clear yellow, this indicates that there has been no actual tearing of the joint lining at the time of injury, whereas if it is blood-stained this can only be due to an intra capsular injury, or a fracture involving the articular surfaces.

Whenever the knee has been subject to sufficient trauma to cause an effusion, a Robert-Jones *pressure bandage* should be applied. This consists of two layers of wool, each covered by a wide domette bandage firmly applied, extending from mid-calf to mid-thigh (Fig. 82). Not only does this help to control swelling, but it also provides a firm support for the injured joint and protects it from minor twists and angulatory strains.

In more severe injuries, such as any in which the effusion in the joint is pure blood (*haemarthrosis*), a plaster-of-Paris cylinder (Fig. 83) should be applied.

Classification of Knee Injuries

Knee injuries may be subdivided into four groups, depending upon the structures injured, and the direction of the causative force:

(*a*) Injuries to the extensor apparatus.
(*b*) Injuries resulting from forces acting in a lateral plane.
(*c*) Injuries caused by rotational strains.
(*d*) Injuries resulting from forces acting in the antero-posterior plane.

A. INJURIES TO THE EXTENSOR APPARATUS
(Fig. 84)

With the exception of injuries to the patella due to direct blows, the extensor apparatus is liable to damage when the knee is forcefully flexed at a moment when the quadriceps muscle is actively contracting. The injuries occur in five ways to some extent, depending upon the age of the patient. These are:

(i) Rupture of the quadriceps at its insertion.
(ii) Fractures of the patella.

(iii) Rupture of the ligamentum patellae.
(iv) Avulsion of the tibial tubercle.
(v) Dislocation of the patella.

(i) Rupture of the Quadriceps Insertion

This usually occurs in middle-aged individuals, in whom the muscles are beginning to lose some of their elasticity. Clinically there is a sudden pain above the patella and the patient is unable actively to extend the knee. At first, a gap may be felt above the patella, but soon this becomes filled by haematoma.

Treatment

Operative repair is essential, often a strip of fascia lata is employed for the suture. Surgery is followed by six weeks immobilisation in a plaster-of-Paris cylinder.

(ii) Fractures of the Patella

These take two forms. Where there has been a direct blow on the knee-cap, the patella breaks into several pieces, but, as the quadriceps expansion remains intact, separation of the fragments is uncommon. This type is known as a *stellate fracture*, and may occur at any age. Radiologically this should not be confused with a bipartite patella, in which the bone has developed from two centres of ossification.

In the second type, the patella is fractured transversely by indirect violence being cracked across the femoral condyles by a sudden contracture of the quadriceps muscle. In these *transverse fractures*, there will usually be wide separation of the fragments as the quadriceps expansion is also torn on either side. These injuries are commonest in fit adults.

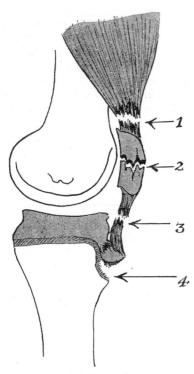

FIG. 84. Injuries to the extensor apparatus
(1) Rupture of quadriceps insertion
(2) Fracture of the patella
(3) Rupture of the ligamentum patellae
(4) Avulsion of the tibial tubercle

Treatment

In stellate fractures, the patella should be excised, the fragments of bone being shelled out, which does not interfere with the quadriceps mechanism so that mobilisation of the knee may be commenced two to three weeks post-operatively.

In transverse fractures, if the fracture is clean, it may be possible to repair the patella either by wire or a circumferential suture. The quadriceps expansion must be repaired at the same time. If, however, there is any comminution at the fracture line, patellectomy should be carried out, with careful repair of the quadriceps mechanism as any irregularity in the articular surface of the patella will lead to later osteo-arthritis. Transverse fractures require about six weeks post-operative splintage in a plaster-of-Paris cylinder in which ambulation should be encouraged.

In the occasional case where there is an undisplaced crack in the patella, no specific treatment is required—treatment being along the general lines already described.

(iii) Rupture of the Ligamentum Patellae

Like rupture of the quadriceps insertion, this injury usually occurs in middle-aged individuals. There is tenderness and a palpable gap below the patella, with loss of active extension. Occasionally, in younger individuals, a small fragment of the lower pole of the patella is also avulsed.

Treatment

This is surgical by repair of the ligament. Where the lower pole of the patella has been avulsed, this is exercised, and the tendon sutured to the main portion which is drilled so that the sutures may be firmly attached. Post-operatively, six weeks splintage is required.

(iv) Avulsion of the Tibial Tubercle

This is an uncommon injury of late childhood, in which the tongue-like extension of the upper tibial epiphysis to which the ligamentum patellae is attached becomes pulled upwards. Significant displacement is rare, so that no specific treatment is usually required.

(v) Dislocation of the Patella

The patella may be displaced laterally. This is an injury which may result from a direct blow from the medial side. Usually, however, it results from a sudden contraction of the quadriceps, and is associated with several minor anomalies. These are: firstly, a small, high patella. Secondly, the lateral femoral condyle is a little less prominent than normal. Thirdly there may be a degree of genu valgum present, so that the line of force taken by the extensor apparatus lies towards the lateral side of the joint. Lastly, it is commoner in females—usually adolescent girls, because of the extra width of their pelvis (Fig. 85).

Clinically, the dislocation is usually obvious, and reduction often takes place spontaneously when the joint is extended.

In most patients, owing to the various predisposing factors in the joint, recurrent dislocation occurs. Osteo-arthritis is then a common sequel. In these cases, the history may suggest a torn medial semilunar cartilage (p. 131) with repeated incidents of the knee 'giving way' when the patella displaces, with momentary 'locking' of the joint in a flexed position, becoming suddenly 'unlocked' when the patella clicks back into place.

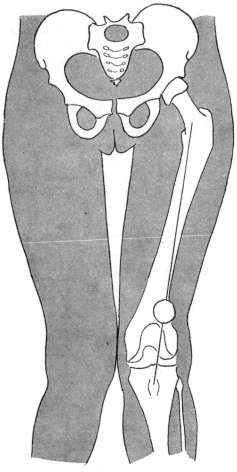

FIG. 85. Causation of recurrent dislocation of the patella

Because the medial joint capsule is stretched, pain is mainly on the inner side. Examination, however, is characteristic. The tenderness is above the joint line on the inner side of the patella, and if the patella is pushed laterally as the knee is gently flexed, the patient becomes typically apprehensive, as she feels an incident is liable to be precipitated.

Treatment

After the first episode, a trial of conservative treatment is justifiable, and the limb is put in a plaster-of-Paris cylinder which is moulded on the outer side of the knee-cap while setting, to encourage healing of any rent in the medial joint capsule. This is retained for three to four weeks, after which an intensive course of exercises to strengthen, particularly the vastus medialis portion of the quadriceps, are prescribed.

When recurrence occurs, operation is indicated. This consists of transposing the tibial tubercle, and thereby the patellar ligament, to a more medial position, releasing the lateral joint capsule, and taking a tuck in the inner side at the same time.

If osteo-arthritis changes are present, the patella may also be excised, but simple patellectomy is ineffective, as the quadriceps tendon of patellar ligament are still able to dislocate laterally.

B. INJURIES IN THE LATERAL PLANE

Angulatory strains on the knee result in three types of injury (Fig. 86):

(i) Entirely bony—where the bone is crushed, usually the tibia, more rarely the femoral condyle.

(ii) Entirely ligamentous—where the whole joint is opened up by complete rupture of the collateral ligament, and both cruciate ligaments.

(iii) Combination of bony and ligamentous, where the tibial condyle is crushed on one side and the collateral ligament is torn on the opposite side.

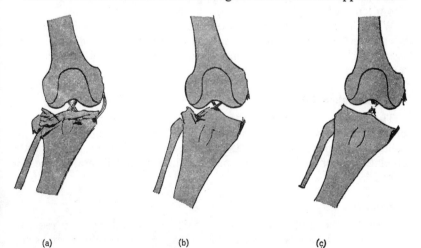

(a)   (b)   (c)

FIG. 86. Angulatory injuries to the knee

(a) Crush of the tibial condyles
(b) Crush of the lateral tibial condyle and rupture of the medial ligament
(c) Rupture of the medial and cruciate ligaments

In all these the force usually acts on the outer side of the joint, causing crushing of the lateral tibial condyle and tearing of the medial collateral ligament.

Rarely in very severe injuries the knee joint may be completely dislocated.

(i) Fracture of the Lateral Tibial Condyle

Where these occur alone, the injury is often due to a direct blow on the outer side of the knee—it is commonly known as a 'bumper fracture'. The condyle as a whole may be crushed, or it may be split, with a central portion driven downwards, with the lateral semi-lunar cartilage becoming wedged between the fragments.

Treatment

This is dependent upon two factors: firstly, the age and general condition of the patient, as in the elderly early ambulation is important.

Secondly, the nature of the fracture. Where displacement is slight, rapid mobilisation is desirable, though weight bearing cannot be permitted for about eight weeks. In such cases, the effusion is aspirated and a pressure bandage, incorporating a plaster-of-Paris backsplint is applied. A few days later, when the initial reaction has subsided, the bandage is removed and active mobilisation commenced.

When there is considerable comminution, leading to an angular deformity, some correction may be achieved by moulding the leg under a general anaesthetic, after which a plaster-of-Paris cylinder is required for about six weeks, the patient remaining non-weight bearing for a total of about ten weeks.

When there is one large depressed fragment, usually in a younger patient, open reduction, which also often involves excision of the semi-lunar cartilage, may be employed. This may be followed by internal fixation using a screw or bolt.

(ii) Ligamentous Injuries

These occur in younger adults in whom the bony texture is tough. In order to permit displacement, not only will there be a complete tear of the collateral ligament, but also of the capsule on the affected side, and of the cruciate ligaments. In the large majority the medial collateral ligament is affected.

Treatment

Operative repair of the medial collateral ligament and capsule is required as usually the lower flap is inverted into the joint. Often the medial semi-lunar cartilage is also torn, and requires removal. Surgical repair of the cruciate ligaments is technically not easy, requiring a fairly extensive exposure, so that it is not often undertaken. Post-operatively, protection by a plaster-of-Paris cylinder is necessary for about six weeks.

Occasionally a few fibres of the medial ligament are torn from its femoral attachment. These may raise a small flap of periosteum, so that some calcification may occur, and be visible radiologically. This condition, known as *Pelligrini–Steida* syndrome may cause persistent pain in one localised spot. Treatment consists of mobilisation. If pain persists a local injection of hydro-cortisone suspension may be employed.

(iii) Combined Ligamentous and Bony Injuries

In these cases, where the usual lateral angulatory strain takes place, the medial collateral ligament is torn on the inner side, and the lateral tibial condyle is crushed on the outer side, the central inter-condylar eminence remaining undamaged.

Treatment

Operative repair of the torn ligament is rarely required, but open reduction of the tibial condyle may be indicated, depending upon the degree of comminution present.

(iv) Dislocation of the Knee

This is a very severe injury, which is fortunately rare, resulting from a violent shearing force applied to the knee. Because the popliteal vessels are anchored by deep fascia, these are often damaged as are the main nerve trunks. Reduction by manipulation usually succeeds. Occasionally surgical intervention is required.

C. ROTATIONAL INJURIES

Rotational strains applied to the knee, particularly when it is semiflexed at the time, are liable to cause injury to the semilunar cartilages.

Anatomy. Owing to the width of the pelvis, the femur normally makes a slight angle with the tibia in the antero-posterior plane. For this reason most weight is taken through the lateral compartment of the joint, and as a result on rotation, the medial femoral condyle moves across the tibia, as it pivots on the outer side.

The semilunar cartilages (menisci) are remains of the complete cartilaginous discs which in foetal life separate the articular surfaces of the femur and tibia. They differ on the two sides. On the medial side it is attached to the medial collateral ligament, so that it cannot move with the femoral condyle. On the lateral side, the cartilage has no attachment to the lateral ligament, which is a cord-like structure extending from the femoral condyle to the head of the fibula. On this side also, the cartilage is a much more bulky structure, the two limbs almost meeting where they are attached to the tibial spine. Consequently the medial cartilage is that more liable to be injured as a result of rotational movements, whereas the lateral cartilage is subject to more direct compression.

(i) Injuries of the Medial Semilunar Cartilage

These occur if, in the course of an external rotational twist to the knee, part of the meniscus gets trapped between the femur and tibia, thereby causing it to be split. Depending upon the degree of flexion at the moment of injury, the meniscus may be split in one of three ways (Fig. 87):

(*a*) A tag may be split from the anterior horn.

(*b*) A central split may occur, with its two ends still attached, the detached portion being displaced to lie in the inter-condylar notch—a 'bucket-handle' tear.

(*c*) A tag may be split from the posterior horn.

Clinical Features

Meniscus injuries are rare in childhood, being most common in young adults. When the normal degenerative changes appear in later life, the meniscus is worn away by attrition, so that tearing becomes less common.

FIG. 87. Tears of the medial meniscus

(*a*) Anterior horn tear
(*b*) 'Bucket handle' central tear
(*c*) Posterior horn tear

The usual history is one of a fall in which the semiflexed knee is violently externally rotated. There is severe pain, and often a 'tearing' sensation, on the inner side of the joint. The patient then is unable to rise from the ground because the knee cannot be extended. Within a few hours the joint fills with fluid. Later it may suddenly free itself ('unlock'), or it may remain 'locked' in semiflexion until 'unlocked' by manipulation under an anaesthetic.

Subsequently the condition may appear to settle down, but later further incidents either of locking, or of the joint suddenly giving way—particularly when going down steps—will follow.

Tears of the posterior horn of the cartilage occur as a result of a twisting injury when the knee is almost fully flexed—i.e. when the patient is squatting. They are, therefore, common among coal miners.

On examination, there is tenderness in the line of the joint, and, if seen soon after the injury, an effusion may be present. While the torn fragment of cartilage is still displaced, a block to full extension of the knee will be found. Often, if the knee is flexed, and then slowly extended while at the same time it is also abducted and externally rotated, a characteristic 'click' may be heard or felt as the torn portion momentarily catches between the femoral and tibial condyles. This is known as 'McMurray's Sign'.

When the knee is seen between incidents, however, while a typical history may be obtained, little in the way of abnormality may be found upon clinical examination.

Treatment

Because the semilunar cartilages are devoid of blood supply, once a tear has taken place, healing cannot occur. Excision of the torn semilunar cartilage (*meniscectomy*) is therefore the only satisfactory method of treatment. This must be followed by a course of quadriceps exercises of increasing intensity.

If a patient reports with the knee 'locked' because the torn portion is jammed between the articular surfaces, manipulation under anaesthetic is required to release it. In 'bucket-handle' tears the displaced portion does not return to its normal place, but comes to lie across the middle of the joint in the inter-condylar notch.

(ii) Injuries of the Lateral Semi-lunar Cartilage

These are not as common as injuries of the medial cartilage, partly because severe internal rotational twists on the semiflexed knee occur less frequently than external rotational twists, and partly, for anatomical reasons, the lateral meniscus is less likely to be subjected to shearing forces. But, due to the fact that the lateral meniscus is more bulky, the primitive foetal state of a complete disc interposed between the lateral femoral and tibial condyles is not uncommon. This condition is known as a *discoid cartilage*. Where such a state exists, the central portion is almost bound to be torn sooner or later, and at an earlier age than normal, often in late childhood.

In addition, because the lateral cartilage is subjected to greater compression forces than the medial, degenerative changes are more common on this side, leading to *cyst* formation.

Clinical Features

The clinical picture of a torn lateral meniscus is similar to that of the medial meniscus injuries, except that true 'locking' is less frequently seen on the outer side. The possibility of a congenital *discoid* cartilage should be suspected in a child who presents with a knee which regularly gives a marked click as it extends. This is due to the fact that the meniscus is swept backwards as the joint extends, and then when a certain tension is reached, it suddenly clicks forward into its normal position again.

The presence of a *cyst* is shown by a tense swelling in the line of the joint on its outer side. They most commonly occur in the anterior portion of the meniscus.

Treatment

Meniscetomy is the only satisfactory method of treatment. The opera
tion on the lateral side is technically a little harder to do because the semilunar cartilage is more centrally placed, and the ilio-tibial tract on this
side makes exposure more difficult. For this reason many surgeons like to
splint the joint with a plaster-of-Paris slab in the early post-operative
phase.

(iii) Minor Rotational Strains

Injuries resulting from rotational strains which are not sufficient to tear
a meniscus are common. In these there is either a strain of the capsular
attachments of the meniscus ('*coronary ligament strain*') or one of the fatty
pads below the patella becomes nipped between the femur and tibia.

Clinically, the immediate picture of sudden acute pain in the affected
side of the joint, possibly followed by an effusion, may be suggestive of
damage to a semilunar cartilage. However, there is no locking, and full
recovery follows.

Treatment

This consists of aspiration of any effusion, the application of a pressure
bandage for a few days, and quadriceps exercises.

D. INJURIES IN THE ANTERO-POSTERIOR PLANE

Forces causing injury in this plane may act either by forcing the tibia
backwards on the femur, usually when the knee is flexed, or they may
hyperextend the joint. They cause damage to the cruciate ligaments. In
the former, the posterior cruciate ligament is injured, while in hyper-
extension the anterior cruciate ligament is affected.

Occasionally, the tibial spine, or in children the whole inter-condylar
eminence is fractured.

Treatment

This is usually along conservative lines. The effusion is aspirated, and a
plaster-of-Paris cylinder applied for a few weeks, after which an intensive
course of quadriceps exercises is instituted. Some residual antero-posterior
laxity in the joint will persist, but good quadriceps muscles can compensate
for this. Rarely, in fractures of the tibial spine, open operation and fixation by a small pin or bone peg is employed.

CHAPTER TWELVE

LOWER LIMB—FRACTURES OF THE TIBIA AND FIBULA

Summary

A. Fractures of Both Bones

(i) Due to Direct Violence
(ii) Due to Indirect Violence

B. Fractures of the Tibia Alone
C. Fractures of the Fibula Alone
D. Fractures of the Upper End of the Tibia
E. Fractures of the Tibia and Fibula in Childhood

(This section is not concerned with fractures which involve the knee or ankle joints.)

FRACTURES of the tibia and fibula may result from either direct or indirect violence. Because the tibia has a large subcutaneous surface, it is one of the commonest bones in which compound fractures occur. In addition, the tibial shaft, particularly in its lower half, does not possess a very abundant blood supply, so that union of fractures often presents a problem.

A. FRACTURES OF BOTH BONES

(i) Due to Direct Violence (Fig. 88)

These follow a direct blow or angulatory force applied to the leg. They are usually due to considerable violence and are often associated with injuries elsewhere. The tibial fracture line may be transverse, at the same level as the fibular fracture, or it may be comminuted. Occasionally the tibia is broken at two different levels, with the fibular fracture lying some-

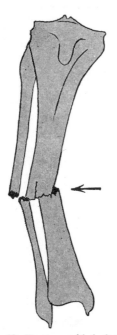

FIG. 88. Fracture mid-shaft tibia and fibula due to direct violence

FIG. 89. Fracture mid-shaft tibia and fibula due to indirect violence

where between them. The amount of displacement varies considerably, depending upon the direction and strength of the injuring force.

(ii) Fractures Due to Indirect Violence

These injuries result from a rotational strain. The fracture line, therefore, is oblique or spiral (Fig. 89) with the fibular fracture at a different level, but running in approximately the same direction as the tibial fracture. Angular displacement may not be marked, but some shortening due to overlap, and rotation of the foot, are almost inevitable.

Treatment

Both because of the importance of maintaining a good position, and because of the risk of difficulty in obtaining union, immobilisation of the fracture must be as perfect as possible.

Reduction may be by open or closed methods. After closed reduction, an above-knee plaster cast (Fig. 90) is employed. This extends from just below the groin, to the base of the toes. The foot should be held at right angles to the tibia in both planes, and the knee is fixed in a few degrees of flexion to prevent rotatory movements at the fracture site. Minor degrees of residual angulation may be corrected by wedging the plaster at the fracture site (Fig. 91). For the first ten to fourteen days after injury, the leg should be kept elevated, after which depending upon the stability of the fracture in the plaster cast, either a walking heel may be added to the plaster, and the patient can start bearing weight on the leg, or he can be got up and become ambulant on crutches non-weight bearing. In adults, immobilisation can rarely be discontinued under twelve weeks from the time of injury.

Open reduction, which almost always includes internal fixation, is indicated when it is not possible to obtain a good position by closed means, or where redisplacement occurs. It is also sometimes required in cases with multiple injuries to make the overall management of the patient easier. With the sole exception of the compound fracture, where reduction

FIG. 90. Above-knee walking plaster-of-Paris cast

can be carried out under direct vision through the skin wound, internal fixation is employed. Three methods of internal fixation are possible:

(i) In unstable oblique fractures, one or two screws may be inserted at right angles to the fracture line (Fig. 92). This is a comparatively small operative procedure, but as complete immobilisation of the fracture is not obtained, an above-knee plaster cast is also required.

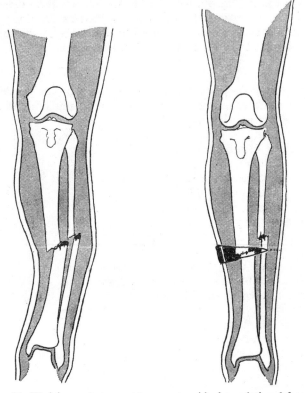

FIG. 91. Wedging a plaster cast to correct residual angulation deformity

(ii) In most cases a plate and screws (Fig. 93) provides the most satisfactory method. If really firm fixation with at least three screws above and below the fracture site, external splintage with a plaster cast may be deferred for two or three weeks. By this time the operative wound will have healed and a useful range of movement in the knee and ankle will have returned. This means that, when the plaster cast is added, the limb will have recovered from the initial trauma, and residual problems due to stiffness after the cast is ultimately removed will be minimised.

(iii) An intra-medullary nail may be employed. This has the advantage that, occasionally, external splintage by plaster-of-Paris may be avoided, though the actual insertion is sometimes technically difficult.

Whatever method of treatment has been employed, after the fracture has united and external splintage has been discarded, a period of rehabilitation is usually required to overcome residual stiffness and swelling and also to regain the patient's confidence and restore full function in the limb.

Occasionally, either where there is an unstable compound fracture, or gross comminution is present, open reduction is not possible, and it is not

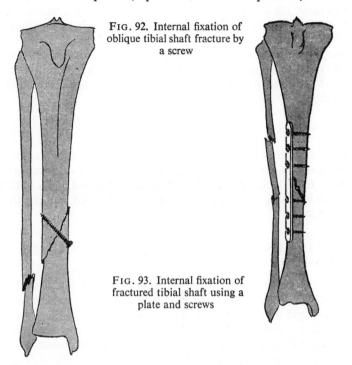

FIG. 92. Internal fixation of oblique tibial shaft fracture by a screw

FIG. 93. Internal fixation of fractured tibial shaft using a plate and screws

possible to retain length by plaster-of-Paris alone. In these cases about four weeks of traction with a Steinmann's pin through the calcaneum, incorporated in the plaster cast, may be employed until the risk of redisplacement has passed.

B. FRACTURES OF THE TIBIA ALONE

These are invariably due to direct violence from a blow, such as a kick at football. Displacement is rarely significant, as the fibula will maintain position, but also because the fibula is intact, the normal 'take up' between the fractured bone ends is not possible, so that union may be slow.

Treatment

As the fracture is stable an above-knee walking plaster cast is used until the fracture has united.

C. FRACTURES OF THE FIBULA ALONE

If the outer side of the calf is subject to a severe blow, the fibula may be cracked. The fracture is of no significance, as the fibular shaft takes no part in weight bearing, and supportive treatment by strapping from the toes to the knee alone is required.

Occasionally the lower fibular shaft may be the site of a 'stress' fracture (see p. 17) following repetitive strains, as may occur in occupations such as professional ballet dancing.

Where, after an injury, a fracture of the fibular shaft is discovered, the possibility that this is associated with a diastasis of the inferior tibio-fibular joint must be borne in mind (p. 144), and the ankle region should also be examined.

D. FRACTURES OF THE UPPER END OF THE TIBIA

Fractures of the upper end of the tibia which do not involve the knee joint are not very common. They are important, however, because at this level the anterior tibial vessels pass between the tibia and fibula so that the main vascular trunks are anchored and may be injured, causing them to go into spasm.

E. FRACTURES OF THE TIBIA AND FIBULA IN CHILDHOOD

As the inferior tibio-fibular joint is rather more mobile in childhood, spiral fractures of the tibia alone are common. Significant displacement is rare and rapid union is the rule. Greenstick fractures of the lower tibial shaft are also common. Treatment in most cases merely consists of an above-knee walking plaster cast, worn for three or four weeks.

CHAPTER THIRTEEN

LOWER LIMB—ANKLE INJURIES

Summary

BECAUSE the ankle takes all the body's weight indirect rotational injuries are very common, as the foot is fixed on the ground while the body continues to move forward. Those associated with internal rotation tend to be mainly ligamentous ('*sprains*'), whereas those due to external rotations are bony.

Injuries resulting from direct abduction or adduction forces are less common, because they are not associated with forward body movement. These are due either to falls from a height on to the side of the foot, or to sideways blows when the body is stationary.

Lastly, the ankle may occasionally be injured by a direct upward thrust.

A. INJURIES DUE TO INTERNAL ROTATION

(i) Sprained Ankle

Because, in the foot and ankle, there is normally a greater natural range of inversion than eversion movement, the lateral ligaments of the ankle suffer first in internal rotational injuries.

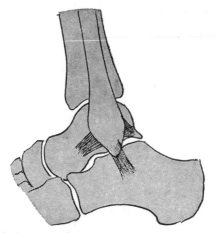

FIG. 94. Anatomy of the lateral ligament of the ankle joint

Associated with this, the styloid process of the fifth metatarsal may be avulsed (p. 152).

The lateral ligament of the ankle is in three parts (Fig. 94): The anterior talo-fibular segment, running horizontally forwards from the lateral malleolus, the middle calcaneo-fibular portion, running vertically downwards, and the posterior talo-fibular segment, running horizontally backwards.

The first, and commonest, portion of the ligament to be torn, therefore, will be the anterior talo-fibular segment. This is what usually occurs in a '*sprained ankle*'.

Clinically, there will be swelling and bruising over the outer side of the ankle, with tenderness most marked just in front of the tip of the lateral malleolus. The inner side of the joint will appear normal. Radiologically no bony injury is usually seen, but sometimes a small flake may be avulsed from the malleolus.

If the injury has been more severe, then the whole ligament will be torn, in which case tenderness is marked below as well as in front of the malleolus. Also, because the talus itself will have been tilted at the moment of injury, there will have been a fairly extensive tear of the joint capsule, so that some bruising and swelling will probably be present over the inner side in addition. Radiologically, there will be no bony injury beyond an occasional flake avulsed from the tip of the lateral malleolus, though if the ankle is gently inverted at the time the film is taken, a tilt of the talus may be demonstrated.

Treatment

Where the anterior portion of the ligament alone has been torn, support by adhesive strapping for ten to fourteen days is indicated. This should extend from the base of the toes to below the knee. The direction of the strapping as it is applied being such that the foot tends to be everted.

If the clinical picture suggests that the entire ligament has been torn through, a below-knee walking plaster-of-Paris cast (Fig. 97) which extends from the tibial tubercle to the base of the toes, with the foot at right angles to the leg in both the antero-posterior and lateral planes should be worn for about six weeks. Occasionally direct surgical repair of the torn ligament is undertaken in these cases.

(ii) Recurrent Sprains of the Ankle

Where there has been a tear of the central cal-caneo-fibular portion of the lateral ligament which has been inadequately treated, some residual laxity will persist. In such cases there will be instability of the joint, so that the patient will complain of the ankle constantly giving way and 'letting him down'. On clinical examination little abnormal may be found, though sometimes it may be possible to detect clinically that there is some tilt of the talus on passive inversion of the foot. Radiologically the abnormal opening of the outer side of the ankle joint may be demonstrated in an antero-posterior film taken with the foot forcibly inverted (Fig. 95).

Treatment

The tendency to repeated inversion may be controlled to some extent if the heel of the shoe is

Fig. 95. Talus tilt associated with lateral ligamentous disruption and laxity

'floated-out' on its outer side, coupled with a course of exercises to strengthen the peroneal muscles. Often, however, surgery is required to reconstitute the ligament, by using the tendon of peroneus brevis which is detached proximally from its muscle belly, and threaded through a hole drilled in the lateral malleolus.

B. INJURIES DUE TO EXTERNAL ROTATION (POTT'S FRACTURES)

Because external rotation of the foot is limited by bones in contact with each other, injuries cause fractures. As, however, any displacement also

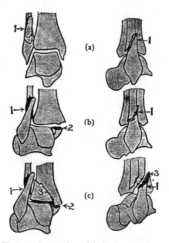

FIG. 96. External rotational injuries to the ankle joint
(a) First-degree Pott's fracture
(b) Second-degree Pott's fracture
(c) Third-degree Pott's fracture

involves the ankle joint a fracture-dislocation is produced. The first time an injury of this nature was described was in 1769, by Percival Pott, after whom they are called.

External rotation injuries are subdivided into three categories, according to the amount of damage caused (Fig. 96).

(i) First-degree Pott's Fracture

Where a *single* structure, the lateral malleolus, is damaged. This consists of an oblique fracture line extending upwards and backwards without displacement.

(ii) Second-degree Pott's Fracture

In this *two* structures are damaged because the talus is displaced laterally and externally rotated. On the outer side, therefore, the lateral malleolus is obliquely fractured, and displaced outwards. On the inner side, either the medial malleolus is fractured traversely, and has moved laterally with the talus, or, less commonly, the medial ligament of the ankle joint has been torn through completely.

(iii) Third-degree Pott's Fracture

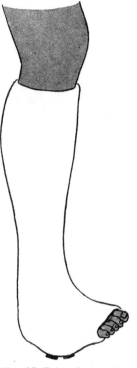

Here, the talus is displaced both outwards, and backwards, in addition to being externally rotated, and *three* structures are injured. The lateral malleolus is obliquely fractured, and displaced both outwards and backwards. Either the medial malleolus is fractured and displaced with the talus, or the medial collateral ligament torn through. In addition, there is a vertical fracture through the tibial articular surface, the small fragment so formed also being displaced backwards with the talus.

Treatment

In first-degree Pott's fractures there is no displacement, so that treatment consists simply of a protective below-knee walking plaster-of-Paris cast (Fig. 97), worn for three weeks.

In second and third degree fractures, reduction is required. This may be either by closed manipulation, or open operation. In *closed* reduction,

FIG. 97. Below-knee walking plaster-of-Paris cast

the injured limb of the anaesthetised patient is hung over the end of the operating table, thereby relaxing the muscles. The surgeon is seated, and with the foot maintained at a right angle upon his knee, he uses his hands to reverse the displacement by simultaneously pulling the heel forward, as he internally rotates and adducts the ankle joint (Fig. 98). A below knee plaster cast is then applied. Weight bearing is deferred until the swelling and reaction to injury have subsided—usually four to six weeks later. Splintage is maintained for ten to twelve weeks, after which, as swelling and stiffness may be troublesome, a period of active mobilisation, using a supporting bandage is usually required.

Open reduction is indicated in all cases where a perfect anatomical position is not achieved by closed means, or where redisplacement occurs. Manipulative reduction may be impossible because of the interposition of soft tissues between the fragments. On the inner side this consists of a flap of periosteum, while on the outer side the peroneal tendons may be displaced between the bone fragments. After reduction one, or more commonly, both malleoli are fixed by obliquely placed screws which should pass through to pierce the bone cortex on the opposite side. The posterior fragment in a third-degree fracture usually returns to normal position when

FIG. 98. Method of reducing fracture dislocations of the ankle joint

the malleoli are reduced, but sometimes this too must be secured at the time of operation. Post-operative management is the same as where closed reduction has been employed.

C. INJURIES DUE TO DIRECT ABDUCTION (Fig. 99)

In these injuries the talus is displaced directly laterally. Two forms occur —either both malleoli may be fractured, or there is rupture of the interosseous ligament at the inferior tibio–fibular joint, with separation (*diastasis of the inferior tibio–fibular joint*).

In the latter case, to permit displacement, the fibular shaft must also be fractured, sometimes at quite a high level. On the medial side, either the malleolus is fractured transversely, or the medial collateral ligament is torn through, in which case, if the ankle only is X-rayed, no bony damage may be visible as the fibular fracture may not be included in the films.

Similarly, where an isolated fracture of the fibular shaft is found (p. 138) the ankle joint should always be inspected for evidence of injury on its medial side.

Treatment

Both types of injury are often better treated by open reduction and internal fixation, as closed reduction tends to be unstable. This applies particularly to diastasis of the inferior tibio–fibular joint, where a screw should be passed transversely from the fibula across through the tibia.

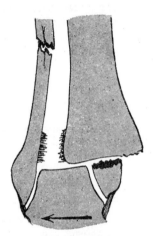 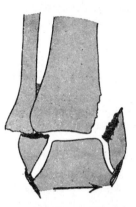

FIG. 99. Diastasis of the inferior tibio–fibular joint, with fracture of the medial malleolus

FIG. 100 Direct adduction injury of the ankle joint

D. INJURIES DUE TO DIRECT ADDUCTION (Fig. 100)

In these injuries, which are comparatively uncommon, the talus is displaced medially, and in order to do so both malleoli are fractured. The lateral malleolus has a transverse fracture line, whereas the medial malleolus runs obliquely upwards.

Treatment

Manipulative reduction is usually successful, occasionally open operation, and internal fixation of the malleoli by screws is required. In either case a below-knee plaster-of-Paris cast is then applied and maintained for ten to twelve weeks.

E. INJURIES DUE TO VERTICAL COMPRESSION

In falls from a height, when the patient lands on his feet, the calcaneum usually sustains a crush fracture (p. 149) but occasionally, if for some reason the heel is not directly involved, the talus may be driven directly upwards against the lower end of the tibia, thereby causing a crushing injury to the articular surface. As the patient is likely to twist, or fall sideways upon landing, some lateral or rotational displacement also is usual.

As the articular cartilage is extensively crushed, damage is more extensive than the radiological appearance suggests, and severe osteo-arthritic changes commonly follow.

Treatment

Manipulative reduction should be attempted, internal fixation is contra-indicated as it can only cause further damage to the injured bone. Weight bearing must be deferred until the fracture has united. Often, owing to joint disorganisation, arthrodesis of the ankle is required.

G. ANKLE INJURIES IN CHILDHOOD

Owing to the increased mobility in children's feet, ankle injuries are rather less common than in adults. Similarly, because the ligaments are strong and elastic, 'sprained ankles' are not often seen.

(i) External Rotation Injuries

The usual effect of external rotational strains applied to the foot in childhood will be to cause a fracture-separation of the lower tibial epiphysis, together with a greenstick fracture of the lower end of the fibula. As such injuries usually occur when the child is running, some backward displacement is also present.

Treatment

Where there is a significant degree of displacement, manipulative reduction, similar to that already described for Pott's Fractures of the ankle in adults is employed (p. 142). This is followed by a below-knee plaster-of-Paris cast, in which weight bearing can usually be permitted, worn for four to six weeks.

(ii) Internal Rotation Injuries

Because ligamentous tearing is unlikely to occur, the usual result of an internal rotation twist to a child's ankle is also a fracture-separation of the lower tibial epiphysis which is displaced backwards. The fibula often remains undamaged, acting as the axis of rotation for the tibial epiphysis.

Treatment

This consists of manipulative reduction rotating the foot in the opposite direction to the displacement, followed by a below-knee plaster cast, as described.

(iii) Direct Adduction Injuries

These injuries are important, because if displacement occurs a crushing force is applied to the inner side of the tibial epiphysis. This may cause *premature fusion* of the epiphysis on this side of the bone, whereas normal growth continues in the lower end of the fibula, and also on the outer side of the tibial epiphysis. As a result a *varus* deformity of the ankle follows as normal growth proceeds. (As this injury frequently followed children catching their foot if they fell when climbing fences, this is often known as a '*railings fracture*'.)

Treatment

Immediate treatment is the same as for other ankle injuries, consisting of reduction where significant displacement has occurred, followed by a below-knee plaster cast. But, where this type of injury is suspected, the patient must be reviewed from time to time for several years, and if deformity occurs suitable supports, including where severe an inside iron and outside T-strap should be worn until growth has ceased, when a corrective osteotomy of the lower tibia may be carried out if necessary.

CHAPTER FOURTEEN

LOWER LIMB—INJURIES OF THE FOOT

Summary

A. Injuries of the Tarsus

  (i) Rupture of the Tendo Achillis

    (*a*) Partial
    (*b*) Complete

  (ii) Fractures of the Calcaneum
  (iii) Injuries to the Talus
  (iv) Mid-tarsal Dislocation
  (v) Other Mid-tarsal Injuries

B. Injuries of the Forefoot

  (i) Fractures of Metatarsal Bases
  (ii) Fractures of Metatarsal Shafts

      (Stress Fracture of Metatarsals)

  (iii) Injuries of the Toes

A. INJURIES OF THE TARSUS

The bones concerned in this region are the talus and calcaneum. To the latter is attached the powerful calf muscles, via the tendo-Achillis.

(i) Rupture of the Tendo Achillis

This may be partial or complete, and follows a sudden contracture of the calf muscles.

(a) *Partial Ruptures*

This occurs at the musculo-tendinous junction—about half way up the calf. They are associated with sudden sharp pain in this region, after which bruising appears. No active treatment is required beyond a supporting bandage worn for two to three weeks, and full recovery is the rule. If, clinically, there is a lot of bruising and a palpable gap when this area is pressed upon, then a plaster-of-Paris case should be applied to provide protection.

(b) *Complete Rupture*

This occurs through the tendon itself, usually about 2 inches above its insertion into the calcaneum.

The clinical picture is characteristic. The patient is usually a fit middle-aged individual in whom the muscles are well developed, but whose elastic tissues are beginning to show early signs of degenerative changes. He will give a history of a sudden very sharp pain behind the ankle, as he makes a springing movement. This may be during some athletic activity such as tennis, or when jumping down two or more steps. The pain feels so much like a direct blow, that the patient often states he turned to see what had struck him. Following the injury, while some active plantar-flexion of the foot is possible by the long toe flexors, there is complete inability to raise the heel from the ground.

Examination at an early stage will reveal a palpable gap in the tendon at the site of rupture, but after 24 hours this fills with organising bloodclot so that it may no longer be evident in cases not seen early.

Treatment

Operative repair is required in all cases, and this is followed by six weeks in an above-knee plaster cast, in which the knee is held in about 40° of flexion, to relax the gastrocnemius muscle, and the ankle is fixed in about 30° of plantar-flexion (*equinus*).

(ii) Fractures of the Calcaneum (Fig. 101)

These follow falls from a height on to the feet. They are therefore quite commonly bilateral. They are often accompanied by injuries elsewhere associated with an upward compression thrust, such as crush fractures of vertebral bodies, notably in the upper lumbar region, or fractures of the base of the skull. For this region the condition of the lumbar spine should always be checked in patients with calcaneal fractures, and both the heels and spine should be inspected in patients brought in unconscious with basal fractures of the skull.

The clinical appearance is characteristic. There is obvious widening of the heel, with flattening of the longitudinal arch (*traumatic flatfoot*). In addition, because the plantar fascial attachments to the calcaneum are torn, bruising arising from the fracture haematoma can be seen in the sole of the foot. Radiologically, the bone is crushed, and the disorganisation of the subtalar joint can be seen. There is diminution of an angle made by a line which runs along the upper border of the bone, having its apex at the sub-talar articular surface (Fig. 101). The fracture line often extends forwards to the mid-tarsal joint.

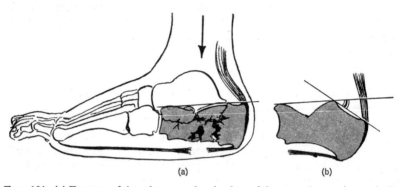

(a)   (b)

FIG. 101. (a) Fracture of the calcaneum showing loss of the normal posterior angle (b)

Later, when the reaction to injury has settled down, an excessive range of passive dorsiflexion of the foot may be demonstrated, because the flattening of the bone has caused some laxity in the tendo-Achillis. Marked residual stiffness in the sub-talar joint is a usual feature.

Treatment

As the injury consists of a crush to a bone which is mainly cancellous, reduction of the fracture is rarely feasible. The main aim of treatment must be to minimise the residual stiffness in the sub-talar and mid-tarsal joints. The patient therefore is kept in a bed with its foot raised on blocks and early active and passive mobilisation carried out. Weight bearing is not permitted for eight to ten weeks. Later, an insole to compensate for the flattening of the longitudinal arch may be required. If severe pain persists in the sub-talar region, this joint may be arthrodesed.

Very occasionally the bone is not grossly crushed, and it may be possible to restore congruity of the sub-talar articular surface by surgical means.

Minor Fractures of the Calcaneum

Occasionally only the posterior part of the bone is injured—the sub-talar joint not being involved. Such cases respond very well to a period of three to four weeks in a below-knee walking plaster cast.

The anterior margin of the calcaneum may be avulsed when the tarsus sustains a forced inversion twist. This, also, is not an important injury, and requires merely a fairly brief period in a below-knee plaster cast.

(iii) Injuries of the Talus (Fig. 102)

Major injuries are fortunately not very common, because the talus, like the carpal scaphoid (p. 88), receives most of its blood supply from its distal end, the blood entering through the sinus tarsi near its neck. For this reason avascular necrosis of the body of the talus is a common complication.

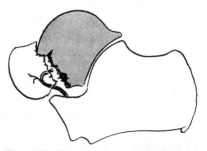

FIG. 102. Fracture through the neck of the talus, to show how the blood supply to its body may be cut off

The usual fracture site is through the neck of the talus as a result of a forced dorsi-flexion injury to the foot. More rarely, as a result of a violent twisting injury the talus may be dislocated. Most commonly the body retains its relationship to the tibia, but the tarsus is displaced from it at the sub-talar and talo-navicular joints (*pan-talar dislocation of the tarsus*). Sometimes when the neck is fractured, the body of the bone is displaced backwards from both the ankle and sub-talar joints.

Treatment

Fractures of the neck of the talus are reduced by putting the foot into plantar flexion (equinus), and this position must be maintained until union has occurred. Dislocations should be reduced by closed manipulation if possible, as open operation will involve further division of blood vessels to the bone. If avascular necrosis occurs (shown either by non-union of the fracture, or increased bony density of the body radiologically) a good result cannot be anticipated, and arthrodesis of both the ankle and sub talar joints is indicated.

Minor injuries of the talus are common, consisting of flakes of bone avulsed at ligamentous attachments. Treatment merely consists in protection of the painful area until the reaction to trauma has resolved.

(iv) Mid-tarsal dislocation

This injury results from a violent rotational twist applied to the forefoot, when the heel is fixed. Reduction is rarely difficult, but as, in addition to extensive soft tissue disruption, some damage to the articular surfaces is almost inevitable, later osteo-arthritic changes are common. After reduction, a below-knee plaster cast is worn for about six weeks, following which a period of intensive active mobilisation is usually needed.

(v) Other Mid-tarsal Injuries

Injuries to the mid-tarsal bones may follow direct crushing blows on the tarsus itself, or wrenching forces applied to the foot. They may affect either the inner or outer side but rarely involve the whole tarsus. Of these a severe adduction injury which fractures the navicula causing the medial fragment to subluxate is the most serious. In this case primary arthrodesis of the talo-naviculo-cuneiform joints usually gives best long-term results.

Dislocation of the tarso-metatarsal joints also occurs. Rarely this requires urgent reduction as irritation of the dorsalis pedis vessels as they pass between the bases of the first and second metatarsals may cause vascular spasm, and circulatory insufficiency in the forefoot.

B. INJURIES OF THE FOREFOOT

These consist of injuries to the metatarsals and toes.

(i) Fractures of the Metatarsal Bases

These, like mid tarsal injuries, may follow a wrench or crushing force. They are rarely serious, and often only require a period of supporting strapping applied from the base of the toes to the knee, with a felt pad under the longitudinal arch.

Fracture of the Fifth Metatarsal Base

This is a common injury, and is due to an inversion twist of the forefoot, the base of the metatarsal being avulsed by the tendon of peroneus brevis which is inverted into it. As has been described, it is often associated with a 'sprained ankle' (p. 140).

Treatment

This consists of either supporting strapping or a below-knee plaster cast worn for two to three weeks, depending upon the amount of discomfort and soft tissue damage which is present.

(ii) Fractures of Metatarsal Shafts

These are common injuries, often occurring when some heavy object is dropped on the foot. In the central metatarsals displacement is rarely gross, and can usually be accepted. In the *first metatarsal* good alignment is essential.

Treatment

In the case of the second to fifth metatarsals, a below-knee walking plaster cast, with a toe-platform (Fig. 103) gives symptomatic relief and should be worn for three weeks.

In the case of the first metatarsal acceptable alignment can usually be obtained by moulding under anaesthetic, after which a below-knee plaster cast with a toe-platform is worn for six weeks. The first three weeks should be non-weight bearing as any minor softening of the plaster cast may permit re-displacement at the fracture site.

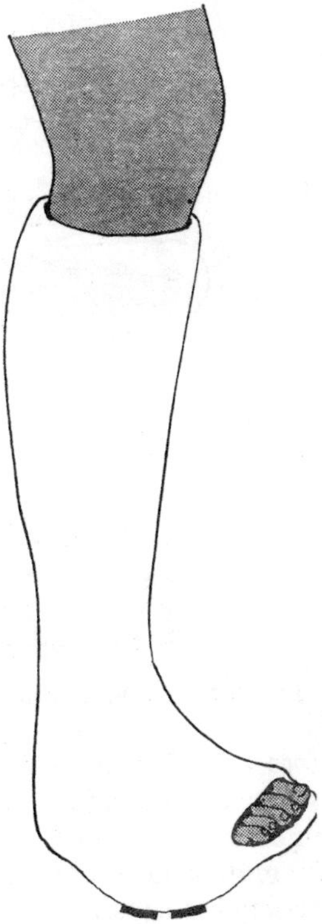

Stress Fractures of the Middle Metatarsals

The second, and occasionally the third, metatarsal bones are the commonest sites for stress fractures to occur. They were first described among recruits to the Imperial German Army in the First World War, and are therefore known as '*march fractures*'. They occur in young adults in whom there is flattening of the metatarsal arch (p. 190) so that the heads of the second and third metatarsals take an excessive amount of weight. Usually the patient is an individual who normally leads a semi-sedentary life, and who suddenly becomes more active (such as an office worker who takes a hiking holiday).

Symptoms consist of sudden pain in the forefoot, with slight swelling, aggravated by weight bearing. X-rays at first are often negative, though usually a hair-line crack through the distal metatarsal shaft can be seen if carefully sought. After a few days callus formation can be seen.

FIG. 103. Below-knee walking plaster-of-Paris cast, with toe platform

Treatment

This consists of a plaster cast worn until the main discomfort has subsided (10–14 days), followed by a metatarsal support worn in the shoes (Fig. 104) and a period of physiotherapy aimed at improving the function of the small intrinsic muscles in the feet.

(iii) Injuries of the Toes

Dislocation of the metatarso-phalangeal and inter-phalangeal joints of the toes occur, but they are much less common than the equivalent injuries in the hand. Manipulative reduction is usually successful and is followed either by a period of two to three weeks in a below-knee plaster cast, with toe-platform, or by strapping the injured member to its healthy neighbour.

Fractures, due to heavy objects falling on the toes, are common. Several

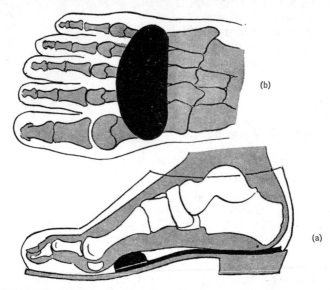

(b)

(a)

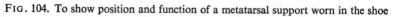

FIG. 104. To show position and function of a metatarsal support worn in the shoe

toes are often injured simultaneously. Treatment, depending upon the severity of the injury, will consist of either a plaster-cast or strapping the injured toe to an uninjured neighbour. In the latter case, the patient will be more comfortable initially wearing shoes with tough leather soles, and roomy toe caps.

CHAPTER FIFTEEN

AMPUTATIONS

Summary

GENERAL REMARKS

Where a limb or portion of a limb is functionally useless, or contains a disease process which may endanger life, amputation is required.

When amputation is considered as a deliberate 'cold' procedure, several factors must be taken into consideration. In the lower limb, where stability is the major requirement a good artificial limb may give extremely good functional results. In the upper limb where tactile sensibility and grasp are most useful, an artificial limb cannot be as useful as a natural limb.

In deciding upon the level of operation, this must be governed by the type of artificial limb available to replace it. In emergencies, amputations may have to be carried out at any level, but the final stump must be at *the site of election*. The situation of the final scar will also be governed by the ultimate artificial limb to be supplied.

INDICATIONS

(i) Trauma

The part may be so obviously damaged that survival is impossible, in which case immediate amputation cannot be avoided. Alternatively, after attempt to save the limb, it may become clear that a useful part cannot be achieved and the patient will be better off with an artificial limb.

(ii) Vascular Insufficiency

Where there is severe peripheral vascular disease with gangrene, amputations at a site above the level where reasonable circulation is still present may be necessary both to save life and to enable the patient to lead a more normal life with an artificial limb.

(iii) Malignant New Growths

Amputation for many primary neoplastic conditions may be the only hope of saving the patient's life.

(iv) Other Indications

Where a patient has a useless limb either as a result of gross congenital deformities or muscle paralysis, occasionally an amputation at a carefully planned site may enable the patient to be supplied with an artificial limb which is more use to him than his own limb was.

OPERATIVE TECHNIQUE

Occasionally in an emergency following trauma a '*guillotine amputation*' may be carried out, leaving as much of the part as possible, so that later, when the extent of damage can be more accurately assessed, and the local area is surgically clean, further amputation at the site of election may be carried out.

In formal amputations skin flaps should always be of full thickness, including deep fascia, and should be under no tension where they cross the bone. It is usually also desirable to suture divided muscle over the bone ends. Great care must be taken in the ligature of main vessels. Nerves, in an attempt to regenerate, develop a lump at the divided end (*amputation neuroma*). As these are always rather hypersensitive, the level of division should be such that they will not be irritated subsequently by the socket of the artificial limb.

Post-operatively, bandaging must be carefully carried out, to mould the stump into conical shape so that it will fit easily into the socket of the prosthesis.

COMPLICATIONS

The divided nerve end may cause pain apparently projected into the limb which has been removed. This is known as a *phantom limb*. In minor degree this always occurs, and is useful in assisting the patient to learn to control the artificial limb. Sometimes, however, the pain is very severe, the patient feeling as if the toe or finger-nails are digging into the flesh of the limb which is no longer there. In these cases, spells of percussion over the tender neuromata sometimes relieve symptoms. In resistant cases, occasionally, division of the nerves at a higher level is required.

Sometimes, where the bone end has been extensively stripped of periosteum, particularly if low grade sepsis has occurred, the end may separate forming a '*ring sequestrum*'.

In conclusion, therefore, when an amputation is considered as a 'cold' procedure, it may be profitable to send the patient to a Limb Fitting Centre before operation so that preliminary steps may be taken for the ultimate supply of the artificial limb, and in addition where a major part of a limb requires removal, as it is a very final procedure, the support of another surgical colleague is helpful both for the patient, and also for the surgeon himself.

A. LOWER LIMB AMPUTATIONS

(i) Hind-quarter Amputation

This is a most drastic operation in which not only is the whole lower limb removed, but in addition the ilium, ischium, and pubis on the affected side. It is carried out only in the treatment of primary malignant disease involving the upper femur or pelvic bones. The fitting of an artificial limb is difficult, because the only bony points upon which weight can be taken are the stump of the pubic symphasis anteriorly and the ala of the sacrum on the affected side posteriorly.

(ii) Disarticulation of the Hip

In this operation, the lower limb is removed through the hip joint. It also leaves considerable disability because the prosthetic limb must contain both an artificial hip and knee. Weight is transmitted to the artificial limb through the ischial tuberosity, the patient in effect sitting in the socket of the limb on the affected side.

(iii) High Above-knee Amputation

Amputation at this level is performed 3 to 4 inches below the great trochanter. As a result, the femoral stump flexes up to a right angle, owing to the unopposed action of the psoas muscle. This gives a broader area upon which the artificial limb can take weight, though an artificial hip is still necessary. Such a prosthesis is known as *'tilting table prosthesis'*.

(iv) Standard Above-knee Amputation

At this level, the aim is to provide a conical stump, having good muscle power, which can be inserted into the socket of the artificial limb, thereby providing motive power to move the limb, though weight is borne at the top, through the ischial tuberosity. Because weight is not taken directly by the stump, equal skin flaps are cut, leaving a scar across its end. To be efficient, the femur should be divided between 10 and 11 inches from the top of the trochanter.

(v) Through-knee Amputations

In these amputations, weight is taken upon the end of the stump directly. They are, therefore, much easier for elderly patients, such as those in whom amputation is required for peripheral vascular disease, to manage. The operation may be performed in two ways: either the knee may be disarticulated, a large anterior flap being turned across the femoral condyles, or the femoral condyles may be divided transversely and the articular surface then removed from the patella, which is turned to lie on the raw lower femur, to which it eventually fuses. A long anterior flap is again employed. This is known as a *Stokes–Gritti* amputation.

(vi) Standard Below-knee Amputation

This is the commonest major amputation. The length of the stump governed by the prosthesis. If it is too short it may be liable to slip out of the socket when the knee is actively flexed. If it is too long, because the tibia is subcutaneous, an adherent, painful scar may remain. The ideal length is five and a half inches from the knee joint, though somewhat shorter stumps may be effective if this length is impossible to obtain. In order to obtain a conical stump, the fibula should be divided about 1 inch higher than the tibia. Equal skin flaps are employed, the weight being taken by the tibial tubercle and upper end of the tibia. Recently a light prosthesis, with a strap which crosses above the patella has been employed (*patellar tendon bearing prosthesis*). This avoids the use of the heavy thigh corset which is normally fitted.

(vii) Syme's Amputation

This is amputation of the feet through the ankle joint, the lower margin of the tibia and fibula being excised. The tough skin at the back of the calcaneum is brought forward thus providing an end-bearing stump. This has the advantage that it is easier for the patient to learn to control, but as the prosthesis is bulky round the ankle, it is ugly in women, and pressure effects on the stump may occur.

(viii) Tarsal Amputations

Where the forefoot has been severely crushed, a useful stump, which, with a suitable sponge rubber insert, can be fitted into an ordinary lace-up shoe may be obtained by amputation through the base of the metatarsals. A large plantar skin flap is used, so that the suture line is not in a weight-bearing area.

For severe toe deformities, disarticulation of all toes may be sometimes employed.

B. UPPER LIMB AMPUTATIONS

(i) Fore-quarter Amputation

This is a very radical procedure in which the whole upper limb is removed, including the clavicle and scapula. It is employed only in the treatment of malignant disease. The fitting of a prosthesis after operation, even for cosmetic appearances alone, is almost impossible, and usually a pad to replace the scapula, so that clothing remains in place, is the only practical solution.

(ii) Disarticulation through the Shoulder

This also is usually reserved for the treatment of malignant disease. Where possible the humeral head is retained *in situ*, and amputation performed at the level of the surgical neck, to give a rounded contour upon which to suspend the prosthesis. In the case of primary malignant disease of the humerus itself, however, this is not possible as it is desirable to remove the whole bone (p. 270).

(iii) Above-elbow Amputation

While it is not so important in the arm as the leg to adhere to fixed length for the amputation stumps, as the prosthesis is not used for weight bearing, better final results are obtained in the case of the upper arm if the humeral stump is about 8 inches long.

In the case of complete traumatic brachial plexus injuries, often a better functional and cosmetic result is obtained if the shoulder is arthrodesed and the flail limb amputated above the elbow.

(iv) Below-elbow Amputation

Amputation through the elbow has no place, as it is essential for the prosthesis to be able to bend at elbow level. In below-elbow amputation, the stump must be long enough to move the artificial hand. Occasionally, as if double amputation following trauma has been necessary, reconstructive surgery may be employed at the same time. In this the radius and ulna are separated, leaving a 'V' with which the patient may be trained to grasp objects, this having the advantage that tactile sensation is preserved ('*Krukenberg claw*').

(v) Amputations through the Hand

Because the preservation of tactile sensibility is most important, amputations through the hand should be as conservative as possible, preserving any portion of a digit that can be salvaged. This applies particularly to the thumb, and for this reason no standard procedure is described.

(vi) Amputations of Digits

Amputations of stiff, painful fingers may be carried out at any level, but in the case of the middle, ring, and little fingers, if the whole digit must be sacrificed, removal of the metacarpal bone as well, but obviating a gap, improves both the cosmetic and functional results.

In the case of the thumb, any portion should be preserved. If the whole thumb must be removed, then it may be possible by dividing the second metacarpal near its base, deepening the cleft between it and the third metacarpal and then rotating it through 90°, to replace the lost part (*pollicisation of the index finger*).

CHAPTER SIXTEEN

HEAD INJURIES
(by R. Campbell Connolly)

Summary

Pathology of Clinical Findings

(*a*) Concussion
(*b*) Cerebral Contusion or Laceration
(*c*) Compression

Management

(*a*) General Principles
(*b*) Care of the Unconscious Patient
(*c*) Cerebro-spinal Fluid Rhinorrhoea and Otorrhoea
(*d*) Depressed Fractures
(*e*) Epilepsy

IN any group of patients involved in severe accidents a high proportion will suffer head injuries either alone or complicating other injuries. In order to manage these cases satisfactorily a clear understanding of the pathology of the brain injury in relation to the clinical state is essential.

PATHOLOGY AND CLINICAL FINDINGS

Injuries to the head may be open or closed and the skull may or may not be fractured, but the underlying injury to the brain may be similar in any event and can be classified as follows:

(a) *Concussion*

This is essentially a transient paralysis of function of the cerebrum occurring at the moment of injury. The patient is therefore immediately unconscious but there is a strong tendency to rapid spontaneous recovery. He will always have a period of amnesia and the duration of the post-traumatic amnesia is the best guide to the severity of the concussion.

(b) *Cerebral Contusion or Laceration.*

In these cases damage may be confined to quite a small area of the cortex such as one of the poles of the cerebral hemisphere or in more severe cases may be widespread. Even in the more minor lesions there is usually immediate loss of consciousness and often clinical evidence of local dysfunction of the brain, such as hemiparesis or dysphasia, except when only silent areas are involved. The unconsciousness and neurological signs will be maximal immediately following the injury and will tend to recover slowly. In very severe cases, deep unconsciousness will persist for long periods and the patient's condition may deteriorate as respiratory and cardiovascular complications begin to occur.

(c) *Compression*

This occurs nearly always as a result of haemorrhage into the middle or anterior fossae of the skull and rarely into the posterior fossa. Much less commonly it is caused by aerocoeles or encysted collections of cerebro-spinal fluid in the subdural or subarachnoid spaces.

Acute extra dural haemorrhage occurs from meningial arteries torn by an overlying fracture. Subdural haematomas may form acutely from rupture of a single vein, or from cortical veins or arteries torn in a cerebral laceration. Chronic subdural haematomas are commonest in the older age groups, often following a trivial injury, and particularly when there is some cerebral atrophy; the source of bleeding is usually a cortical vein close to the superior sagittal sinus and a slowly expanding blood cyst forms over one or both cerebral hemispheres.

As any haematoma increases in size the brain becomes progressively.

compressed and displacement of the cerebral hemispheres distorts and damages the brain stem. These changes result in deterioration of consciousness and in most cases a third cranial nerve palsy on the side of the lesion with a contra-lateral hemiparesis.

MANAGEMENT

(a) *General Principles*

Quickly increasing compression of the brain demands urgent operation to prevent both death and permanent severe neurological disability. It is therefore essential that compression should be recognised as early as possible, but this can only be achieved by a period of observation. Thus having dealt with emergencies, such as obstruction of the airway or severe haemorrhage, which might immediately endanger life it is important to make an accurate neurological assessment as soon as possible. This must include the state of consciousness, pupilary size and reactions, and movement and tone in the limbs; when possible a history of the patient's state of consciousness prior to admission to hospital should be obtained. In the acute phase these observations together with recordings of temperature, pulse, respiration, and blood pressure should be repeated every 15 to 30 minutes.

Except in very severely injured cases where there is deep unconsciousness and often marked neurological signs from the moment of injury, patients suffering cerebral concussion, contusion or laceration should improve steadily, the signs being maximal at the onset.

On the contrary, in cerebral compression, after a variable period, deterioration of consciousness occurs steadily with or without neurological signs such as progressive inequality of the pupils and hemiparesis. In the intervening period, usually not lasting more than a few hours, the patient may have regained consciousness (the 'lucid interval'). Occasionally the temporal muscle on the side of the lesion becomes swollen owing to haemorrhage into it from an extradural haematoma through a fracture line in the temporal plate (a 'safety valve haematoma'). Additional evidence of intracranial haematoma may sometimes be seen in good quality antero-posterior X-rays of the skull when the pineal body is calcified and shown to be displaced across the midline.

All cases who deteriorate in this way should be operated upon immediately by the surgeon at hand. Delay in transfer or awaiting outside help greatly increases morbidity and mortality. In extra-dural haemorrhage the haematoma nearly always lies beneath a fracture so that when one is seen on X-ray a burr hole should be made immediately beside it and then enlarged with nibbling forceps following the fracture line downwards towards the base of the skull until the haematoma is discovered.

In patients, often elderly, who only deteriorate slowly over a period of days following the injury, special investigations such as angiography may be desirable and transfer to a neurosurgical centre should be possible.

Causes of deterioration not requiring surgery to the head include epilepsy, fat embolism, respiratory embarrassment and hyperthermia.

Epilepsy, when an actual fit has not been observed, may be recognised by the suddenness of alteration of consciousness followed by spontaneous improvement.

In fat embolism deterioration of consciousness is usually slow and focal neurological signs are absent.

(b) Care of the Unconscious Patient

In addition to the regular observations noted above an unconscious patient requires special care particularly from the point of view of respira-ation, temperature control, and nourishment.

A clear airway is essential and in many cases this can be achieved by posturing, sucking away excessive bronchial secretions, and, perhaps for a short time, the use of an ordinary anaesthetic airway. As a temporary measure endotracheal intubation may be valuable, but temporary trache-otomy is the most effective and often a life-saving procedure so that when there is doubt about its need it should be undertaken earlier rather than later.

Body temperature has a strong tendency to rise above normal and this should always be prevented by removing bed-clothes, fanning, and cold sponging. Chlorpromazine is rarely necessary and there is probably little to be gained by lowering body temperature below normal.

When blood loss has been replaced by an intravenous drip, further fluids and nourishment are best given by a Ryle's tube.

(c) Cerebro-spinal Fluid Rhinorrhoea and Otorrhoea

Most cases of cerebro-spinal fluid rhinorrhoea and all cases of cerebro-spinal fluid otorrhoea cease spontaneously within a few days, but while they last Sulphadimidine and anti-biotics should be given prophylactically to prevent meningitis. Aerocoeles sometimes complicate cerebro-spinal fluid rhinorrhoea and should be excluded by lateral X-rays of the skull in the supine position taken at weekly intervals while the leakage of fluid persists. Fascial repair of a dural defect in relation to the nasal air sinuses should be considered by a neurosurgeon in cases of cerebro-spinal fluid rhinorrhoea lasting more than seven to ten days.

(d) Depressed Fractures

Closed depressed fractures of the skull do not call for urgent treatment unless there is evidence of cerebral compression. In infants spontaneous elevation will nearly always take place within a few months. In older patients the need for elevation will depend upon the size and degree of the depression.

Open depressed fractures should be carefully debrided and closed within forty-eight hours.

(e) *Epilepsy*

There is a risk of post-traumatic epilepsy in patients suffering severe head injuries involving cerebral contusion, laceration, or compression. These should therefore be treated prophylactically with an anti-convulsant drug for two years when, in the absence of fits, it may be discontinued gradually. Phenobarbitone 30–60 mg. twice daily is effective in adults.

ORTHOPAEDICS

CHAPTER ONE

ORTHOPAEDICS—INTRODUCTION

Summary

Descriptive Terms
  (i) **To Describe Operations**
 (ii) **To Describe Movements and General Deformities**
(iii) **To Describe Individual Parts (including specific deformities)**

THE branch of medicine referred to as 'Orthopaedics' is primarily concerned with the locomotor system of the body. This consists primarily of the bones, joints, muscles, and peripheral nervous system as they affect the limbs and spine.

In considering orthopaedics, it is important for the student to appreciate that, firstly, while a localised lesion is the presenting feature it usually affects the mechanics of the body as a whole and this must constantly be borne in mind. Secondly, if any operation is contemplated, this is merely the first incident (albeit a major one) in a course of treatment. The success of any surgical measure is very intimately bound up with the after care, and this, in turn is greatly dependant upon the efforts of the patient himself.

DESCRIPTIVE TERMS

Various specialist words are employed in orthopaedics, and it may be helpful if they are mentioned at the outset.

(i) Operations

In operations upon joints, *arthrodesis* means that the joint is fused. This in practice implies that an artificial fracture has been made, and it must therefore be splinted, either internally or externally until it has united, and the two bones concerned have become one. Where a diseased joint fuses spontaneously, this is *ankylosis*, which can be either bony—a natural arthrodesis—or fibrous, where a jog of movement still remains.

Arthroplasty means that the joint has been re-made, often by the employment of a metallic implant (*prosthesis*) to replace one or more of the joint components.

Arthrotomy implies merely that the joint has been opened and, probably, explored.

In operations upon bones, *osteotomy* is division of a bone—that is the creation of an artificial fracture. This is usually employed either to correct a deformity, or in the lower limb, to alter the line of weight-bearing thrust.

Tenotomy is used to describe simple operative division of a tendon. *Tenodesis* is an operation to anchor a tendon at a new site. Tendons may also be *transplanted*. This is employed where one group of muscles cannot function, either because they are paralysed, or as a result of previous injury. *Tenolysis* means freeing a tendon from adhesions, usually due either to earlier trauma or infection.

(ii) Movements and Deformities

Flexion implies bending a joint, in the case of the shoulder this is used to describe elevation of the arm in the forward plane. *Extension* describes straightening the joint out. *Hyper-extension* means that the joint is extended beyond the straight line. *Abduction* is the movement away from the mid-line—of the body in the case of the hip and shoulder, and of the individual limb in the case of fingers or toes. *Adduction* is the opposite, meaning movement towards the mid-line of the body or the limb, depending upon the joint concerned. *Circumduction* is a combination of all four movements, permitting the limb to be moved in a circular direction. *Rotation*, which may be *internal* or *external* also takes place in many joints.

In addition, if there is limitation of movement in a joint, so that it cannot reach the neutral position, an adduction, abduction, flexion, or rotational deformity is said to be present. If there is an angular deformity, so that the part points towards the mid-line of the body, this is described as *varus*, whereas if it is directed away from the mid-line, this is described as *valgus*.

(iii) Individual Parts

These are often given their latin names—thus *cubitus* is used to describe the elbow, *coxa* the hip, *genu* the knee, and *pes* the foot.

In the case of the spine, *kyphosis* is used to describe a flexion deformity at one level. *Lordosis* means the spine is extended. A lateral curve is described as *scoliosis*.

In the foot, an *equinus*—i.e. 'horse-like'—deformity is said to be present when the heel cannot be brought down to the ground easily. There is excessive dorsi-flexion present, so that the heel reaches the ground before the rest of the foot.

CHAPTER TWO

CONDITIONS ASSOCIATED WITH POSTURE

Summary

I. SPINAL CONDITIONS ASSOCIATED WITH POSTURE

A. Back-strain

(i) Due to Muscular Inefficiency
(ii) Due to Structural Abnormalities

   (a) Acute Back-strain
   (b) Chronic Back-strain

B. Prolapsed Inter-vertebral Disc

(i) Lumbar
(ii) Cervical

C. Spondylolisthesis

D. Scoliosis

(i) Postural
(ii) Structural

   (a) Congenital
   (b) Paralytic
   (c) Idiopathic

E. Coccydynia

II. LOWER LIMB CONDITIONS ASSOCIATED WITH POSTURE

A. Knees

(i) Genu Valgum
(ii) Genu Varum

B. Feet

(1) Lesions Affecting the Arches

   (i) 'Foot Strain'
   (ii) Flat Foot

      (a) Pes Planus
      (b) Pes Valgus
      (c) Spasmodic Flat Foot

   (iii) Pes Cavus
   (iv) Abnormalities of the Anterior Arch
   (v) Morton's Metatarsalgia

(2) **Lesions of the Toes**

  (i) **The Big Toe—General Remarks**

    (*a*) Hallux Valgus
    (*b*) Hallux Rigidus

  (ii) **The Lesser Toes**

    (*a*) Hammer Toe
    (*b*) Mallet Toe
    (*c*) Adducted Fifth Toe
    (*d*) Subungual Exostosis

HOMO SAPIENS is unique among vertebrates in adopting a vertically upright position. He therefore places mechanical strains upon his spine and lower limbs which are different to those affecting other species of animal, and for this reason, minor anomalies which, as far as is known, cause no symptoms in creatures who walk on all their four limbs, can be severely disabling in human beings.

I. SPINAL CONDITIONS ASSOCIATED WITH POSTURE

A. BACK-STRAIN

Back-ache is a very common complaint. In a large number of instances some specific cause can be shown, but often no definite abnormality is to be found. Such cases are labelled 'back-strain'. Two main factors make a back mechanically weak, and therefore more liable to cause such symptoms—these are:

(i) Muscular inefficiency.
(ii) Structural abnormalities.

(i) Muscular Inefficiency

Actual muscle paralysis cannot be included in this category, because, in such cases, the patient is disabled and requires some form of external support. Two causes of back-ache due purely to inefficiency in muscles are, firstly, when an individual who normally uses his muscles very little, suddenly makes greater demands upon them, as if a clerical worker starts doing heavy manual labour. Secondly, if the muscles are out of tone due to a febrile illness, general fatigue, or some similar cause.

In both such instances, a patient is liable to a sudden attack of back-ache.

(ii) Structural Abnormalities

Minor asymmetry in the bony structure of the spine, particularly in the lumbo-sacral region are very common, and if present, by adding slight constant extra strains upon the musculature and small inter-vertebral joints, increases the liability to 'back-strain'.

Typical examples are, if a transverse process of one side of the fifth lumbar vertebra actually articulates with the sacrum (known as *sacralisation*), or when the plane in which the inter-vertebral joints lie differs on the two sides. Often in a true antero-posterior radiograph the articular surfaces of a joint are clearly outlined on one side, and cannot be distinguished on the other.

Clinically, back-strain may be acute or chronic.

(a) *Acute Back-strain*

Acute lumbar back-ache ('lumbago') may be the presenting symptom of some specific condition, such as prolapse of an inter-vertebral disc (p. 176), but often no definite cause can be established, and the actual underlying pathology must remain obscure. Possibly, a fringe of synovial membrane is nipped between the articular surfaces of one of the small inter-vertebral joints, thereby causing sudden pain, and precipitating the acute muscle spasm which is the dominant feature of 'lumbago'. Alternatively a few fibres of one of the spinal ligaments may be torn, leading to the same chain of events. Whatever the cause, acute lumbago is commoner in patients who have either some minor structural anomaly or muscular inefficiency.

The clinical picture is one of acute back-ache of sudden onset in the lumbar spine, usually apparently caused by some sudden unguarded movement. The pain may be in the mid-line, or to one side usually in the sacro-iliac region. It is aggravated by any movement, and relieved by rest, usually lying flat on the back. Sitting often increases the discomfort, but when the pain is in the upper lumbar region, it may afford relief. If there is radiation away from the back, this indicates irritation of a nerve root at the site of the causal lesion, suggesting a prolapse of an inter-vertebral disc is the cause of the condition.

On examination, there is marked spasm in the muscles, often holding the spine slightly tilted to one side, with tenderness localised to one area. Elevation of the leg with the knee extended ('straight leg raising') is very limited because of the pain it causes in the back (as opposed to in the limb itself, where there is irritation of one of the sciatic nerve roots due to a prolapsed inter-vertebral disc).

In dealing with cases of back-ache, extra-spinal causes of pain in the back must always be excluded, particularly those arising from the renal tract in both sexes, and intra-pelvic organs in females. Almost always some localising symptoms or signs will be present, such as pain or frequency of micturition in the case of the kidneys or ureters, or a relationship to menstruation in the female genital organs. In addition, back-ache due to some local spinal or muscular lesion always has a 'mechanical' aspect, and therefore will be aggravated by certain positions and relieved by others.

Treatment

Acute back-strain commonly responds to a few days strict bed rest, on a firm flat mattress, as this allows the muscle spasm to relax. This is followed by a course of physiotherapy, consisting of heat and massage to relieve pain and relax the muscles, followed by exercises to improve their tone and efficiency. The latter should be slowly increased in tempo as the symptoms subside, and are usually better carried out when several patients are together in a 'class'. Providing all other causes of back ache have been excluded, acute back-strain often responds very well to manipulation, though as this carries a risk of increasing the prolapse of an inter-vertebral disc, it is probably better reserved for cases which fail to respond to an initial period of strict rest, and is completely excluded if there are any signs suggestive of nerve root irritation.

(b) *Chronic Back-strain*

This commonly follows an episode of acute back-strain, which, after an initial improvement then remains as a nagging ache, worse after any strenuous activity, particularly if this involves stooping, or lifting. It may affect any level of the back, but because stresses are greatest in the lumbo-sacral region, this is the most frequent site.

In these cases it is most important that other more serious causes of back pain are excluded—both those referred from elsewhere, and those due to local pathological changes. Radiographs are useful not only to demonstrate the minor structural changes already mentioned, but also to show evidence of degenerative changes (osteo-arthritis), neoplastic deposits, infective conditions (such as tuberculosis or osteomyelitis), metabolic disorders (such as senile osteoporosis), or other bony pathology. Often soft tissue swellings or calcification can be seen in good quality films. Blood investigations are also often indicated. A raised erythrocyte sedimentation rate, while not pointing to any specific condition, is suggestive of an active disease process somewhere in the body. If the white blood cell count is raised, it suggests an infective condition. A high alkaline phosphatase level in the blood points to osteoblastic activity and a high acid phosphatase level is specifically indicative of a carcinoma of the prostate gland.

In certain cases other investigations are indicated, such as radiographs of the chest or skeleton elsewhere, tests of the urine or sputum, or a lumbar puncture, possibly including the injection of radio-opaque material (*myelography*) to outline the contents of the spinal canal.

Treatment

Initially this is directed towards improving the tone of the spinal musculature, thereby affording protection to the site of weakness. A graduated course of exercises is therefore prescribed.

If these fail, then external support, in the form of a surgical corset, should be supplied. Sometimes this can be discarded after a few months wear, but usually it is required permanently.

B. PROLAPSED INTER-VERTEBRAL DISC

Anatomy. Inter-vertebral discs are elastic structures placed between the bodies of vertebrae to provide both firm support and yet allow a small range of movement. They consist of an outer ring of fibrous tissue—*The Annulus Fibrosus*—surrounding a central mass of thick gelatinous material —*The Nucleus Pulposus*.

Inter-vertebral discs are more liable to give trouble in those parts of the spine which are mobile and also subject to the greatest strains—the lower cervical and lower lumbar regions. They are least commonly involved in the thoracic spine, where the rib cage gives support and limits movement.

When a disc prolapse occurs, initially there is rupture of the annulus fibrosus, which causes acute pain and muscle spasm in the neck or back. Then, through the rupture, a protrusion of the nucleus pulposus takes place and enters the spinal canal. The central part of the disc posteriorly is protected by the strong posterior spinal ligament, so that a prolapse much more commonly occurs to one side. This, therefore, is very liable to

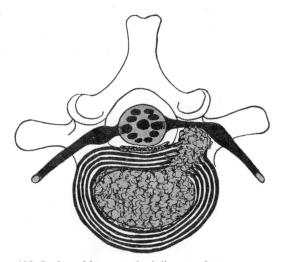

FIG. 105. Prolapsed inter-vertebral disc, pressing on a nerve root

impinge against a nerve root causing pain, sensory impairment, and muscle weakness in the area supplied by that segment (Fig. 105).

Central prolapse is fortunately rare, as this may cause spinal cord irritation in the cervical spine, or retention of urine by irritation of the canda equina.

The clinical pattern differs in the two areas most commonly affected, and these will be considered separately.

(i) Lumbar Disc Lesions

The most frequent level for a disc prolapse is the lumbo-sacral, because here the mobile lumbar spine joins the rigid sacrum and pelvis. After this, in order of frequency are prolapses of the discs between the fourth and fifth and third and fourth lumbar vertebrae respectively.

In the lumbar region, as the inter-vertebral articulations are well behind the bodies, on flexion the discs are compressed, so that prolapse will be due to some sudden forward bending when the muscles are relaxed.

Clinically, the patient—usually a young adult—complains of sudden very severe low back pain (lumbago), which may completely immobilise him, following a flexion movement. After an interval of a few days some improvement is noticed, but when activity is increased the nature of the pain changes and begins to spread down the leg, in an area depending upon which nerve root is being irritated. The back pain (due to tearing of the annulus fibrosus) and nerve root irritation (due to pressure from the protruding nucleus pulposus), usually follow each other, but may occur almost simultaneously.

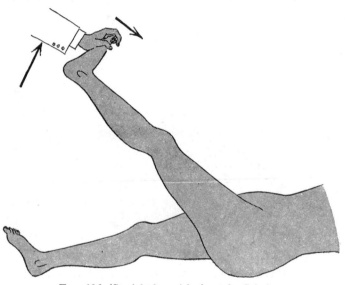

FIG. 106. 'Straight-leg raising' test for Sciatica

The pain is aggravated by any flexion movement of the spine, or by coughing, sneezing, and straining on defecation. This is partly because muscle tension is increased, but mainly because of increase in intrathecal pressure. It is relieved by recumbency on some flat, firm surface.

On examination, there is obvious muscular spasm in the spine, which is often tilted to one side. There is marked tenderness at the level of the disc prolapse on palpation.

Signs in the legs will depend upon the nerve root involved. At the lumbo-sacral level (L5—S1), pain will radiate down the back of the leg, from the ischial tuberosity to the calf, spreading to the outer side of the ankle to the outer toes, where there may be parasthaesia and some blunting of sensation to pin-prick (*sciatica*).

There may be some weakness present—affecting usually the extensor hallucis longus muscle. The ankle jerk will be diminished or absent. On raising the leg with the knee straight, acute pain will be caused radiating down the limb (as opposed to back-pain in 'acute back-strain'). This leads to muscle spasm which markedly restricts elevation (Fig. 106). This is because 'straight leg raising' pulls on the sciatic nerve, and therefore increases pressure of the nerve root on the disc prolapse.

At the fourth-fifth lumbar level, the pain will radiate more down the front of the shin to the dorsum of the foot, and the ankle jerk will be present. As this root is part of the sciatic nerve, straight-leg raising is also limited. At the third–fourth lumbar disc, the femoral nerve is affected, pain is therefore in front of the thigh radiating to the inner side of the calf, and often causing some weakness and wasting of the quadriceps. The knee-jerk will be diminished. Straight-leg raising will be full, but flexion of the knee, with the hip extended—thereby stretching the femoral nerve—will aggravate the pain in the front of the leg. Such patients are more comfortable with the hip flexed, and therefore usually prefer sitting in an upright chair to standing erect, or lying absolutely flat.

Investigations. In an acute disc prolapse occurring for the first time, the radiograph will appear normal. Later, because the disc material is no longer present, some narrowing of the affected disc space will be visible in the lateral view. Occasionally a lumbar puncture or myelogram are indicated.

Treatment

In the initial, acute phase, treament consists of rest. This aims at allowing the rent in the annulus to heal, and the actual prolapse to shrink by a process of absorption of its fluid content and fibrosis.

The patient is laid on a firm mattress with boards beneath to provide firm support, and he remains recumbent for ten to fourteen days. Continuous traction by means of a pelvic corset attached to a weight over the end of the bed may be added if improvement is delayed. As symptoms subside, exercises are added. At first these are purely in extension, carried out in bed, later increasing in tempo and range.

Where there have been several attacks, or if there is radiological evidence of narrowing of the disc space which indicates early degenerative change, a supporting corset should be prescribed.

Fig. 107. Plaster-of-Paris jacket

Sometimes after initial improvement, the condition becomes static, in which case a plaster-of-Paris jacket (Fig. 107) can be applied and is worn for eight to ten weeks, followed by a corset.

Where there is unequivocal evidence of nerve root pressure, and rapid improvement does not take place, to avoid permanent damage to the root, operative removal of the prolapsed disc should be employed.

(ii) Cervical Disc Lesions.

In the neck, disc lesions are commonest at the lower three spaces, between the fifth and sixth, sixth and seventh cervical vertibrae, that is where the mobile part of the cervical spine joins the more rigid thoracic spine. Here the inter-vertebral joints are more laterally placed and do not lie so far behind the bodies as in the lumbar spine, so that some sudden rotational movement commonly is the causal factor.

Degenerative changes in the lower inter-vertebral discs of the cervical spine invariably occur but they are increased where cervical disc lesions have occurred earlier.

Clinically, following a sudden movement, the patient is seized with acute pain in the neck, which is then held rigid (*acute 'stiff-neck'*). Often the head is tilted and slightly rotated to one side (*torticollis*). Associated with this are pains radiating down the arm corresponding to the skin area supplied by the irritated nerve root. Thus, at the fifth–sixth level the pain spreads from below the shoulder down the outer side of the arm to the thumb, in the sixth–seventh level it radiates down the back of the arm, to the middle fingers, and at the seventh cervical–first thoracic the fifth finger and ulnar side of the forearm are affected.

The pain characteristically wakes the patient at night, because when the neck extends, with the muscles relaxed out of their protective spasm, the nerve root irritation increases.

Treatment

Cervical disc lesions usually respond well to a course of physiotherapy in the form of traction, applied with the neck slightly flexed, coupled with heat to overcome the spasm. Between treatments, and particularly at night, a protective collar made of either sorbo-rubber or polythene should be worn. Operative excision of the disc itself is hardly ever employed, but occasionally, where there are marked radiological changes, fusion of the two affected vertebrae bodies through the front of the neck gives good results.

C. SPONDYLOLISTHESIS (Fig. 108)

This is a condition, probably of congenital origin, due to failure of fusion of the lamina and body of a vertebra, whereby one vertebra, with the spine above, becomes displaced forwards on the next one below. It is included in the postural section because while the basic abnormality might be present, it is doubtful if the displacement would occur in the absence of an upright posture. The lower lumbar vertebrae are those usually affected.

Clinically, the history of a chronic low back-ache, usually in a young adult. The onset is often insidious, but sometimes there is a history of

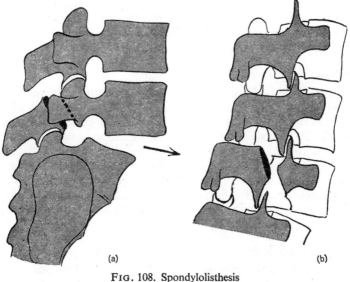

(a)   (b)

FIG. 108. Spondylolisthesis
(a) Lateral view   (b) Oblique view

some predisposing injury to the spine which was probably the cause of displacement in a pre-existing structural abnormality.

On examination, spinal movements will be rather restricted, but the characteristic feature is prominence of the spinous process of the vertebra below that affected, often with skin creases on either side if displacement is marked.

Treatment

In young, fit individuals, spinal fusion is indicated. This can, ideally, be done through an anterior intra-abdominal approach, fusing the two affected vertebral bodies using a block of bone taken from the iliac crest (Fig. 109).

In older patients, or where major surgery is otherwise contra-indicated, a spinal support should be supplied.

D. SCOLIOSIS

Lateral curvature of the spine may be due to some abnormality in the spine itself (*structural*) or because the spine is held

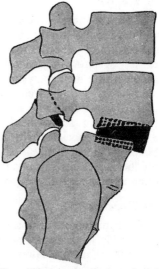

FIG. 109. Anterior 'body-to-body' fusion for spondylolisthesis

tilted (*postural*). Curves are of two types: *primary*, that resulting from the causal pathology, and *secondary*, of which there may be two—one above and one below the primary—to compensate for the main curve. Scoliosis, from whatever cause, rarely progresses after growth has ceased.

(i) Postural Scoliosis

This may be caused in a number of ways. The tilt in the lumbar spine resulting from the muscle spasm associated with an acute disc prolapse, already described (p. 178) is an example of this. The commonest cause of a permanent postural scoliosis is that due to the natural attempt to compensate for an inequality in leg lengths. In the latter case, in all but minor differences in leg lengths, structural alteration in the shape of the vertebrae follows, so that what was at first postural becomes structural. When a postural curve is present, if the patient can hang by his hands, the spine will completely straighten itself. This should therefore be done frequently and the patient must be taught to do it daily.

(ii) Structural Scoliosis

In these cases, causes may be subdivided into several groups.

(a) *Congenital*

The cause in these cases is some gross structural abnormality, such as the congenital absence of half a vertebra (*hemi-vertebra*) or fusion of several ribs on one side. The deformity is usually obvious at birth, and tends, if anything, to decrease with growth as the child compensates spontaneously.

(b) *Paralytic*

When the muscles on one side of the spine are paralysed, then a curve will develop. Naturally, if the paralysis occurs before growth has ceased, the deformity will be more marked than if it occurs in adult life. Common causes of paralytic scoliosis are Anterior Poliomyelitis, severe Spina Bifida with a menigomyelocele (p. 198), and, less commonly, neurofibromatosis and syringomyelia. Paralytic curves are characterised by the fact that a large number of vertebrae are involved in the primary curve. If the paralysis is severe the deformity may be gross.

Scoliosis associated with neurofibromatosis is probably due to a combination of local paralysis of the small muscles of the spine, and the tumour on the nerves forcing open the inter-vertebral foraminae. These curves often appear very sharply angulated.

(c) *Idiopathic*

The commonest example of scoliosis developing in childhood is labelled 'idiopathic' as the causal pathology remains obscure. In the primary curve not only is there a lateral bend, but also the vertebrae themselves are rotated, the bodies being displaced further to the side than the neural arches. This, in the thoracic region, results in the ribs in the concave side being very prominent posteriorly, the resulting '*rib hump*' thereby exaggerating the deformity. On the other hand, if the primary curve is in the lumbar region it is much less noticeable, and may pass unobserved until secondary degenerative osteo-arthritis causes back-ache in middle-life.

Treatment

This may be conservative or operative.

Conservative treatment is preferable during active growth. In mild cases, regular observation only is necessary. In more severe cases in children, particularly in the thoracic region, some corrective appliance may be used. This may be a plaster cast, usually incorporating the neck or one upper limb, applied in maximal correction. This is then cut and hinged at the apex of the primary curve, and a turnbuckle is added, so that the curve may be progressively straightened. Alternatively, a jacket is constructed, which, by obtaining purchase on the occiput and mandible above and the iliac crests below, using a turnbuckle, gradual distraction in the vertical plane is obtained (Milwaukee Brace).

Operative measures consist of fusion of the primary curve. Surgery is usually carried out in adolescence, after maximal correction in a jacket has been obtained. Attempts are being made to correct the primary curve by active surgical means, but so far they are still in the experimental stage.

E. COCCYDYNIA

This term describes pain in the region of the coccyx, but its use should be restricted to cases in which no other abnormal pathology can be found. It often results from a fall on the buttocks, and it is commoner in women, because of the increased width of their pelvic outlet. The pain is worse when sitting, and on rising from the sitting position.

Treatment

The large majority of cases settle down after some months on their own. Treatment is unsatisfactory, occasionally improvement is obtained by manipulation or the local injection of hydro-cortisone. Rarely excision of the coccyx is required.

II. LOWER LIMB CONDITIONS ASSOCIATED WITH POSTURE

Degenerative joint changes (osteo-arthritis) are dealt with elsewhere (p. 223), but it does mainly affect the weight-bearing joints of the lower limbs in man because of his upright posture. Apart from this, the knees and feet are considerably affected by posture.

A. THE KNEES

Normally, in the antero-posterior plane, the hips are separated by the width of the pelvis, whereas the knees are in contact, so that there is an angle formed between the line of the femur and the line of the tibia. Alterations in this angle are common, and are described as *genu valgum* ('knock knee') or *genu varum* ('bow-leg').

Because the femora and tibiae are the longest bones in the body any condition which affects their growth, or weakens their structure tends to alter the angle they make with each other at the knee, and body weight exaggerates this tendency. Examples are rickets (p. 289), osteomalacia (p. 289), renal osteodystrophy (p. 290), hyperparathyroidism (p. 293), and Paget's disease. If a deformity, in mild degree, is present the normal degenerative changes (osteo-arthritis, p. 223) will be increased on the side which takes more weight—the lateral compartment in Genu Valgum, and the medial compartment in Genu Varum—so that, with the erosion of the articular cartilage that results, some increase of the deformity in later life occurs.

(i) Genu Valgum

In mild degree, this is very common in young children, and tends to correct itself with normal growth. Often, it is associated with some degree of flat-foot deformity (p. 186).

In older children, a significant deformity requires active correction.

Treatment

In young children, with a fairly marked deformity, wedging of the shoe heels by adding one-sixth of an inch to the inner side is employed, and in severe cases corrective splints worn at night are also prescribed. In older children, surgery is the only means of achieving correction. Before epiphyseal growth has ceased, the lower femoral epiphysis on the inner side may either be fused (epiphysiodesis) or growth retarded by the insertion of metal staples, one arm of which goes into the epiphysis, and the other the metaphysis. Later, a corrective, supra-condylar osteotomy of the lower femur may be employed.

(ii) Genu Varum

Most young babies have a slight bowing of their tibiae. This is normal and corrects spontaneously. Very rarely, if the deformity persists, night-splints may be required.

In adults, bow-legs are occasionally associated with certain occupations, such as horse riding. Treatment is only required if symptoms arise. Wedging of the outer side of the shoe heels will increase the weight taken by the lateral compartment of the knee and sometimes helps. Otherwise a corrective osteotomy is needed.

B. THE FEET

Apart from his brain, man's feet are his most highly developed parts, and, because all the weight is taken by a small area, any quite minor variation in shape or structure may be significant.

The weight of the body when standing is taken primarily on the heels, but, to a lesser extent, also along the outer border of the feet and under the metatarsal heads, particularly the first and fifth. The toes do not take much weight, but are also on the ground. On walking, the body's centre of gravity moves forward over the forefoot, while the heel is raised. Further contraction of the calf muscles and small muscles in the foot then propels the body forward, and this movement is completed by pressure of the toes on the ground, thereby raising the metatarsal heads.

Foot disorders, therefore, fall into two groups: those affecting the mechanics of the arches of the foot, and those related to the toes.

(1) Lesions Affecting the Arches

Anatomy

There are two 'arches' in the normal foot—a longitudinal and an anterior.

The longitudinal arch runs from the calcaneum to the metatarsal heads and is better developed on the medial side. Structures which maintain the arch fall into three groups (Fig. 110): Firstly, there are the components of the individual tarsal joints, notably their ligaments, of which the long and

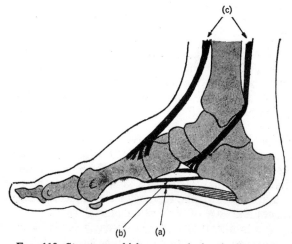

FIG. 110. Structures which support the longitudinal arch

(a) Short muscles in the foot
(b) Plantar ligaments
(c) Tendons of tibiales anterior and posterior

short plantar ligaments are the most important. Secondly, there are the short muscles of the foot, and plantar fascia which bow-string across from the heel to the metatarsal heads. Lastly, there are the tendons of the muscles in the leg which raise the apex of the arch from above—the long toe flexors, and tibiales anterior and posterior.

The anterior arch is formed by the metatarsal heads. The actual 'arch' is present only at rest, on weight bearing all five metatarsal heads are on the ground, but weight is normally taken mainly through the first and fifth. It is maintained by the transverse head of the adductor hallucis muscle, and the ligaments between the metatarsal heads.

(i) 'Foot-strain'

If the small intrinsic muscles of the foot lose their efficiency, the tarsal ligaments are liable to be strained.

The clinical picture is one of pain in the feet, worse on standing, and it is often associated either with some minor pre-existing structural abnormality which impairs the function of the small muscles, or to generalised fatigue. It is therefore common among individuals who normally lead a sedentary life, and then suddenly begin prolonged standing or walking, or in those convalescing from febrile illnesses. Examination will be negative, and blood tests and radiological investigations all normal.

Treatment

Initially a spell of rest is indicated, after which the intrinsic foot muscles are built up by a course of foot exercises. Electrical stimulation by means of faradic foot-baths may be employed to assist these, though they must not be allowed to replace the exercises.

(ii) 'Flat foot'

Flattening of the longitudinal arch occurs in two ways. It may be due to genuine loss of the longitudinal arch—true flat foot, or *pes planus*. Alternatively, it may be due to the fact that on weight bearing the foot rolls inwards, so that its medial border comes in contact with the ground, because the hind part of the foot is in a valgoid position—*pes valgus*.

(a) *Pes Planus*

These cases are often associated with some minor structural anomaly in the bony skeleton of the foot, so that the shape of the tarsal bones is slightly altered. This may take place at any one of three joints—that between the talus and navicula, the navicula and medial cuneiform bone, or the cuneiform and base of the first metatarsal.

Flattening due to alterations at the talo-navicular joint usually results from the head of the talus pointing in a rather more medial direction than normal. In extreme degree, there is in effect a congenital dislocation of the navicula on to the dorsum of the neck of the talus, which therefore appears to point directly downwards (*congenital vertical talus*). This deformity is noticeable at birth, as the head of the talus makes a smooth round bulge, and the arch is obviously reversed.

At the naviculo-cuneiform joint, flattening is often due to the presence of a minor accessory ossicle (*os tibiale externum*) in the tendon of tibialis posterior as it turns under the foot to spread out in its insertion. Not only does this cause an apparent flattening of the longitudinal arch, but also, by impairing the efficiency of the tibialis posterior muscle, it allows the foot to sag at this point.

At the metatarso-cuneiform level, loss of the normal slight downward alignment of the first metatarsal is a common cause of flattening of the longitudinal arch. More important, however, is the fact that the first metatarsal head does not take its normal share of the weight, the anterior arch being reversed, and as a result the big toe is maintained in an abnormal degree of flexion, causing osteo-arthritis at the metatarso-phalangeal joint (Hallux Rigidus)—this is dealt with later.

Treatment

In the large majority of cases, the slight structural abnormality is accepted, and treatment is aimed at preventing or controlling the symptoms

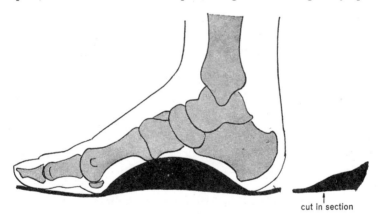

cut in section

FIG. 111. Longitudinal arch support

which may arise. This is achieved either by an intensive course of exercises to build up the foot musculature so that it is sufficiently powerful to cope with the extra strains thrown upon it, or by means of a longitudinal arch support made of moulded leather (Fig. 111). The former is usually advised for children and young adults in the first instance.

Very occasionally surgery, in the form of arthrodesis, is employed where the cause is localised to one joint in younger individuals.

(b) *Pes Valgus*

In this, the commoner type of 'flat foot', there is no actual structural abnormality in the foot itself, the foot merely rolls inwards when bearing weight. Often there is slight tightness of the tendo-Achillis, so that the foot, when inverted, cannot be passively dorsiflexed to a right angle, and only by eversion can the heel be brought down to the ground, ('*pes valgus-ex-equino*'). For the same reason, a marked valgus deformity of the foot on weight bearing is associated with neurological lesions which cause spasticity in the lower limbs. In at least 50% of cases, however, no such cause can be found, the shape of the foot on weight bearing being due to mild muscular and ligamentous laxity.

Clinically, in children, valgoid feet are often noticed by chance, in the course of a routine medical inspection. Attention may be drawn to the condition by excessive wear in shoes, which bulge on their inner side. Otherwise symptoms are those of aching in the feet, similar to those due to 'foot-strain', and occasionally painful callosities occur due to rubbing on footwear.

Treatment

In most cases this consists of exercises to build up the intrinsic muscles and the use of moulded leather arch supports. Surgery is very rarely necessary.

(c) *Spasmodic Flat Foot*

Occasionally, in young people, when there is some irritative focus in the tarsus, the peroneal muscles go into a state of continuous spasm,

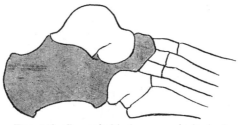

FIG. 112. Congenital 'calcaneo-navicular bar'

thereby pulling the foot into marked rigid valgus. The cause may be some chronic infective focus, such as tuberculosis or low grade osteitis of some tarsal bones, but it is most frequently seen where there is a congenital fusion between the calcaneum and navicula ('*calcaneo-navicular bar*', Fig. 112). This is often only visible on oblique radiographs.

Treatment

Sometimes the spasm may be overcome by relaxing the muscles under anaesthesia, after which a walking plaster cast in an over-corrected position is worn for several weeks. Afterwards a valgus insole should be prescribed. Often, however, the condition rapidly recurs, when triple arthrodesis (p. 206) is required.

(iii) Raised Longitudinal Arch (Pes Cavus)

This is the reverse of flat foot, and is usually associated with a varying degree of flexion deformity of the toes (*claw toes*). While, in most cases, no definite cause can be demonstrated, it is probably usually due to some degree of muscle imbalance. It is often seen in neurological conditions which affect the lower limbs.

Clinically, pes cavus can be subdivided into two types: In the first, and more benign, the high arch appears to be due to a degree of flexion deformity ('dropping') of the forefoot upon the hind foot which appears normal. As a result, some valgus of the heel occurs when the foot is brought to the ground.

In the second, and more severe type, the whole foot is affected, so that there is a relative calcaneus deformity of the heel, which is also often slightly inverted. It is in this type that clawing of the toes is most marked, with hyper-extension of the metatarso-phalangeal joints so that the phalanges may be dislocated on to the dorsum of the metatarsal necks. This is often due to partial or complete paralysis of the interosseous muscles, and is similar to the claw hand deformity resulting from intrinsic paralysis due to ulnar nerve division (p. 102).

Where no neurological underlying cause can be demonstrated the condition is often labelled 'Idiopathic Pes Cavus'.

Clinically, pes cavus is rarely seen in early infancy. It usually appears in childhood, and progresses until growth ceases. The incidence of spina bifida occultor (p. 198) discovered on routine X-ray is greater than in the population at large, and it has been suggested that tethering of the spinal cord, which normally does not grow in length to the same degree as the vertebral column may be an aetiological factor explained by the usual period of growth when it is first seen.

Symptoms are mainly due to the abnormal pressure on the metatarsal heads due partly to the shape of the forefoot, but mainly because the clawing of the toes prevents their performing their normal function of raising the forefoot from the ground in walking.

Treatment

This may be Conservative or Operative.

Conservative treatment is indicated during the period of active growth, and to control symptoms in the elderly. In the young, exercises for the intrinsics, and stretching of the toes to prevent fixed deformity may be useful in reducing the rate of progression and preventing symptoms developing later. In the elderly, very carefully made supports are useful in relieving pressure. They are made to distribute the body weight evenly under the soles of the feet, and away from the prominent metatarsal heads. Often, to avoid corns on the dorsally displaced claw toes, surgical shoes made to measure are necessary.

Operative treatment has two aims—the first to correct the high arch, and the second to straighten the toes and bring them down so that they can perform their function as levers to push the body forward in walking. Of the two, improvement in toe mechanics is probably the more important. This may be achieved by arthrodesing the inter-phalangeal joints so that the toes are straight, coupled with division of the extensor tendons, so that the metatarso-phalangeal joints can be flexed (*Lambrinudi's operation*). Alternatively, where passive correction is still possible, the flexor tendons may be divided opposite the proximal inter-phalangeal joint, and are then re-inserted into the extensor expansion on the dorsum of the toe, so that all their action is exerted into flexing the metatarso-phalangeal joint and extending the inter-phalangeal. With the big toe, the inter-phalangeal joint should be fused and the extensor tendon transplanted to the first metatarsal neck. Post-operatively a below-knee plaster cast, including the toes is worn for six weeks.

In older patients, palliative relief from severe pain under the anterior arch can be given if the metatarsal heads are excised through a transverse dorsal incision.

To correct the high arch, division of the posterior attachments of the plantar fascia and short toe flexors is sometimes successful, if done before growth has ceased. At a later period, the tarsus may be arthrodesed, taking a wedge out of the dorsum of the mid-tarsal region (*wedge tarsectomy*).

(iv) Abnormalities of the Anterior Arch.

Reversal of the anterior arch, so that excessive weight is taken on the middle metatarsal heads causes a characteristic pain on weight bearing, which the patient often describes as like 'walking on pebbles'. This is known as *metatarsalgia*. With it callosities at the site of abnormal pressure also develop. The cause may be structural, as when the first metatarsal lies at a more horizontal level than normal, or it may be associated with some generalised joint disease, such as rheumatoid arthritis (p. 231) which causes the toes to subluxate dorsally, thereby pressing the middle metatarsal heads downwards.

'Stress' fractures of the metatarsal shafts (p. 153) are liable to occur in individuals who have reversed metatarsal arches.

Treatment

In most cases symptoms can be controlled by the employment of meta-tarsal supports worn in the shoes (Fig. 104). These consist of sponge-rubber pads, fitted on insoles, which come to lie just behind the metatarsal heads, thereby distributing the weight away from the tendon area. As a temporary measure, a leather 'metatarsal bar' may be fitted across the sole of the shoe, also lying behind the metatarsal heads. Occasionally, operative treatment along the lines described for claw toes is required.

(v) Digital Neuroma (Morton's Metatarsalgia)

This is a specific condition occurring in middle-aged people, in which the digital nerve gets enlarged where it lies between two metatarsal heads. As a result it gets irritated, and causes severe pain localised to one inter-digital cleft, usually that between the third and fourth metatarsals. Less commonly between the second and third. This pain is constantly present, and is aggravated if the forefoot is squeezed from side to side. It often radiates down the sides of the affected toes.

Treatment

Conservative treatment is ineffective, and excision of the enlarged seg-ment of digital nerve ('neuroma') is required.

(2) The Toes

(i) The Big Toe (Hallux)

Of the toes, the big toe is the most important, because the weight is largely taken on the first metatarsal head, when standing, and on walking,

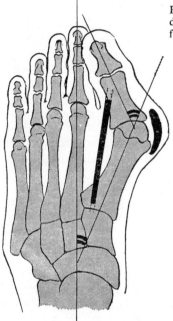

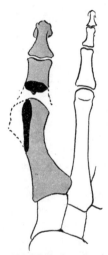

FIG. 113. Mechanism of pro-duction of hallux valgus de-formity

FIG. 114. Keller's operation for Hallux valgus

the thrust of the big toe is the most powerful in driving the body forwards.

Most abnormalities of the big toe result from mal-alignment of the first metatarsal, which may take two forms. Firstly, it may tend to resemble the first metacarpal in the hand, and to point medially (*metatarsus primus varus*). As a result the toe is deviated laterally, leading to the condition known as *hallux valgus*. This deformity is increased by the bow-string affect of the tendons (Fig. 113). Associated with this, the metatarsal head does not take full weight, so that the anterior arch is reversed.

Secondly, as already described when discussing pes planus (p. 186), it may assume a more horizontal line than the other metatarsals (*metatarsus primus elevatus*). As a result of this, the big toe is held slightly flexed, so that it can take weight, and this, in turn, increases the stresses upon the first metatarso-phalangeal joint so that osteo-arthritic changes occur, and the joint becomes stiffer, known as *hallux rigidus*.

(a) *Hallux Valgus*.

The presenting symptom in hallux valgus is usually pain over the prominent metatarsal head. This is due to rubbing from shoes, and leads to an adventitious bursa ('*bunion*'), which may become inflamed, or go frankly septic. In addition, metatarsalgia may be troublesome, and, if the big toe is markedly deviated, it may cause symptoms from deformity of the second toe, which tends to override the first.

Treatment

This depends upon the age and general condition of the patient. In the elderly and those with poor circulation, treatment is symptomatic. Surgical shoes, made to accommodate the deformed toes, and incorporating metatarsal supports, usually help. In the middle aged, comprising the largest presenting group, surgery is indicated to deal with the bunion and correct the valgus deformity of the toe, though it is not possible to restore normality. The usual operative procedure (*Keller's operation*) consists of excision of the base of the proximal phalanx, and of the prominent metatarsal head on the medial side (Fig. 114). This relieves pressure symptoms, but leaves the toe as an inefficient lever, so that, if metatarsal pain is to be avoided, metatarsal supports must be supplied.

In younger adults and adolescents it may be possible to correct the basic deformity by osteotomy of the distal metatarsal shaft, the head being moved medially, and rotated to correct the valgus deformity in the toe itself.

In addition the resulting 'hammer toe' deformity in the second toe has often to be treated surgically (see p. 193).

Often the second and third toes may be cocked up because of the subluxation at the metatarso-phalangeal joint, in which case the metatarsal head of the affected bone is better excised at the same time. This is sometimes the cause of a 'hammer toe' type deformity, in which case a 'spike arthrodesis' (see p. 193) is not indicated.

(b) *Hallux Rigidus*

This is osteo-arthritis of the first metatarso-phalangeal joint. Symptoms are due to pain on movement of the joint, particularly dorsiflexion, and exostosis formation on the dorsum of the metatarsal heads, which in turn leads to adventitious bursa formation similar to, but at a different site from that occurring in hallux valgus.

Treatment

As with hallux valgus, Keller's operation gives good results in relief of pain in the joint itself, but by impeding the toe's function as a lever, increases the liability to metatarsal pain. It is therefore a useful operation in the middle aged, but in younger patients an attempt to preserve toe function is also desirable. This can be achieved by arthrodesis of the metatarso-phalangeal joint, thereby in effect, increasing the length of the metatarsal, and leaving the patient with a short, single-jointed toe.

(ii) The Lesser Toes

The toes are liable to develop very similar deformities to those occurring in the fingers. In the latter, however, these result from definite injuries to the extensor apparatus (p. 104) whereas in toes they appear to develop spontaneously, possibly being aggravated by footwear.

(a) *Hammer Toe*

This deformity, which most frequently involves the second toe, because this is often the longest, consists of fixed flexion at the proximal inter-phalangeal joint, with hyper-extension at the distal inter-phalangeal and metacarpo-phalangeal joints. It is often seen in conjunction with a hallux valgus.

Clinically, presenting symptoms are due to a painful corn over the prominent head of the proximal phalanx. In addition, owing to dorsal subluxation at the metatarso-phalangeal joint, there may be a painful callosity under the metatarsal head.

Treatment

A felt pad applied behind the corn may relieve some of the pressure from shoes, and help from a chiropodist is also often useful, but surgery provides the only satisfactory answer. Best results are obtained by fusion of

FIG. 115. 'Spike arthrodesis' of proximal phalanx of a toe

the joint in an extended position, which can be done by converting the head of the proximal phalanx into a peg, and fitting this into a hole bored into the base of the middle phalanx ('*spike arthrodesis*', Fig. 115). Alternatively, the prominent head of the proximal phalanx may be excised.

(b) *Mallet Toe*

This is a flexion deformity of the terminal joint, similar in appearance to a mallet finger (p. 105). The cause is not clear, sometimes several toes are affected. Pressure from shoes causes painful corns to develop over the prominent head of the middle phalanx. Sometimes corns also appear on the tip of the toe.

Treatment

Chiropodist's padding may help to control a painful corn, but if really troublesome, excision of the head of the offending middle phalanx or amputation of the tip of the toe gives good results.

(c) *Adducted Fifth Toe*

In this deformity, often present since infancy, the fifth toe has adducted over the fourth toe, and as a result pressure symptoms usually follow.

Treatment

In children and young adults the deformity may be corrected by division of the tight dorsal capsule of the metatarso-phalangeal joint and extensor tendon, coupled with a '*v-y plasty*' which enables the skin to be elongated. In older patients the toe should be amputated.

(d) *Sub-ungual exostosis*

This is an outgrowth of bone from the tip of the terminal phalanx, which pushes the nail upwards, and causes reactive thickening in the surrounding skin. The big toe nail is that most commonly affected.

Treatment

This consists of gouging the bony lump, if necessary trimming back the nail in order to provide adequate exposure.

CHAPTER THREE

CONGENITAL DISORDERS

Summary

A. Generalised Congenital Abnormalities

B. Local Congenital Abnormalities

THESE may conveniently be considered in two groups. Firstly, there are those due to some generalised abnormality in development of some mesenchymal structure. Secondly, there are abnormalities in certain parts. The latter, in turn, may be due to some inherent error in the foetus itself, or be due to external stress secondary to an intra-uterine cause.

It must be emphasised, however, that often several different congenital anomalies may be present in the same infant.

A. GENERALISED CONGENITAL ABNORMALITIES

Of these conditions which fall into the hands of the orthopaedic surgeon, three are concerned with errors in epiphyseal bone growth. These are: Achondroplasia, in which the epiphyses fail to grow, Diaphysial Achlasis, in which islands of epiphyseal cartilage are left behind on the surface, where they grow to form exostoses, and Dyschondroplasia, where rests of epiphyseal cartilage remain inside the bone causing enlargement of the bone ends and deficient growth.

(i) Achondroplasia

This is one of the causes of severe dwarfing, sometimes occurring in families. It involves the long bones, so that affected individuals have very short limbs with a trunk and head of normal size. The fingers tend to be rather short and of the same length (*'trident hand'*).

No treatment is possible.

(ii) Diaphysial Achlasis

In this condition, there is failure of the normal process of re-modelling the bone ends which occurs during bone growth. As a result rests of epiphyseal cartilage cells remain on the surface, and as they continue to form bone exostoses appear. These may lead to well-defined rounded lumps, which gradually move down the shaft of a long bone, as epiphyseal growth proceeds. The lumps themselves are covered by bone forming cartilage cells, and tend to point away from the end of the bone from which they originated. At other sites, there is nodular widening of the whole metaphysis. As a result longitudinal growth of the bone is impaired, and deformities follow, particularly as no two epiphyses are affected to a comparable degree. The fully developed condition is rare and often familial, but isolated exostoses are quite common. Growth of the bony knobs ceases when the epiphyseal line fuses. Very occasionally chondro-sarcomatous changes occur, this is manifested by increase in size of the bony lump, which becomes somewhat painful.

Treatment

Exostoses should be excised only if they are causing symptoms from pressure, or look ugly. Most cause no trouble.

(ii) Dyschondroplasia (Ollier's Disease)

In this uncommon condition, rests of epiphyseal cartilage remain behind inside the bone, as the epiphysis grows, causing thickening of the ends and diminution of longitudinal growth. Several bones are often affected, often limited to one limb causing marked shortening. In the 'short' long bones of the hands and feet, the cartilaginous rests produce multiple enchondromata.

Treatment

This is symptomatic, to deal with individual deformities.

(iv) Cranio-cleido Dysostosis

This is a failure of the normal development of membrane bone. Bone arising from cartilage is therefore unaffected.

Clinically, the clavicles are absent so that affected individuals can often bring their shoulder girdles forward until they almost meet in front. There is also delay in closure of skull sutures, leading to a large head. The pubic bones may also be involved, but this is less obvious.

(v) Osteo-genesis Imperfecta (Fragilitas Ossium)

In this disease there is a generalised abnormality of mesenchymal tissues. Clinically, the patients present because of skeletal involvement, though the fact that this affects mesenchymal tissues as a whole is shown by abnormal ligamentous laxity and characteristic blue sclerotics, the latter being due to abnormal translucency so that the reticial pigment shows through the sclera.

Two types occur: Firstly, there may be such gross softening of bone that marked deformities are present at birth, increasing rapidly during early infancy. Secondly, there is a milder type, in which the bones are unduly brittle, so that fractures occur as a result of trivial violence. The latter improves as maturity is reached.

Treatment

In milder cases, no specific treatment is required, individual fractures being dealt with in the normal way, as they occur. In the more severe cases, it is sometimes possible to combine correction of deformities with reinforcement of the bones by threading an intra-medullary pin through the length of the bone.

(vi) Arthrogryposis Multiplex Congenita

This is a condition in which there is abnormal development of striated muscle, with the result that joint deformities are also present. The commonest of these are congenital dislocation of the hip (p. 199) congenital talipes equino-varus (p. 204) and joint contractures.

Treatment is that necessary for the individual lesions, but as, on the whole, they are unusually resistant to conservative measures, operative treatment is often required.

B. LOCAL CONGENITAL ABNORMALITIES

Any part of the locomotor system may develop abnormally, but certain sites are more commonly affected.

(i) Spina Bifida

Originally, in early foetal life, neurological tissue appears as a flat plaque, which later becomes infolded to form a tube, the vertebral column developing in a similar manner.

Arrest of this process can occur at any stage. Thus, in many normal individuals radiological examination of the lumbo-sacral region reveals failure of fusion of the laminae in either the fifth lumbar or first sacral vertebra. This is known as *spina bifida occulta*. Occasionally when it is a little more marked, a bony defect may be palpable clinically, and a minor tuft of hair at that site may be present. In such individuals there may be tethering of the sacral nerve roots to the defect, leading to pes cavus and clawed toes as growth proceeds.

Where the bony defect is more extensive the contents of the spinal canal are exposed on the surface. This may take several forms: firstly a meningeal sac may be present, the nerve roots lying within it. This is known as a *meningocoele*. Secondly, the sac may contain both meninges and nerve root elements. This is known as a *meningomyelocoele*. Lastly, if nerve tissue remains in the primitive state as an open plaque on the back, this is known as a *myelocoele*. In this case, cerebro-spinal fluid leaks on to the surface. Hydrocephalus commonly occurs as a complication in the more severe cases.

Where there is nerve tissue involved, functional impairment will result. This varies up to complete flaccid paraplegia with sensory loss and urinary and faecal incontinence. It is significant that if the exposed nerve tissue is stimulated electrically within the first hours of birth, muscle contractions in the lower limbs can often be obtained, but this disappears as the tissue dries up a few hours later.

As a result of muscle imbalance, various lower limb deformities commonly occur. Where the upper lumbar roots alone survive, unopposed action of the ilio-psoas muscle causes the hips to dislocate. If the lower lumbar roots remain in the hip, flexion contractures follow, in association with paralytic dislocation, in the knee the unopposed quadriceps causes hyper-extension, and in the foot ankle dorsi-flexors lead to a calcaneo-varus deformity. Also, owing to sensory loss, trophic ulceration, and fractures often complicate the picture.

FIG. 116. New born baby with Spina Bifida

Treatment

Spina bifida occulta requires no specific treatment.

In the more severe cases, closure of the defect within twenty-four hours of birth may preserve some of the exposed, functioning nerve fibres. Hydrocephalus is controlled by the insertion of a tube from the sub-arachnoid space into the superior vena vava, having a valve, which permits only the downward passage of cerebro-spinal fluid into the blood-stream. More children, who would formerly have died, survive these days with this treatment and management of their serious disabilities presents a very difficult problem.

Lower limb deformities and paralysis are controlled by suitable apparatus, assisted in suitable cases by surgery. Paralytic dislocation of the hip may be controlled by transplant of the deforming ilio-psoas tendon from the lesser trochanter, through the ilium into the greater trochanter thus transforming it into an abductor.

Management of urinary incontinence and prevention of infection are also very important, though outside the scope of the orthopaedic surgeon.

(ii) Congenital Dislocation of the Hip

In this condition the femoral head becomes displaced upwards out of the acetabulum. The hip is rarely completely dislocated at birth, but the acetabulum is abnormally shallow, so that the femoral head can sublux and displacement increases as the baby becomes more active. Associated with the shallow acetabulum, the femoral neck is rotated forward (*anteverted*) and the labrum acetabulare (*limbus*) is turned into the joint, obstructing reduction.

The aetiology is unknown, abnormal intra-uterine pressure on the limbs and ligamentous laxity have been suggested as possible causal factors. It occurs more frequently in girls than boys, and has a hereditary factor, being common in Austria and northern Italy, and rare among negroid and mongol races.

Clinically, the condition may be suspected at birth if abduction of the hip appears limited, or a click can be felt by a finger placed just above the joint when full abduction is reached, due to the subluxed femoral head slipping down opposite the acetabulum. Later, as upward displacement of the head increases, limited abduction becomes more noticeable and, in unilateral cases, assymetry of the skin creases in the infant's thigh and buttock may be seen. In bilateral cases, the perineum may appear unduly wide. When the child begins to walk an obvious limp is seen in unilateral cases, while when bilateral, the gait is of a typical 'waddling' nature. At this stage *Trendelenburg's Sign* will be positive—when the patient stands on the affected leg, instead of the opposite buttock being raised, it will tend to drop. This is because, having no fulcrum to hold the head in place, stability is lost (Fig. 117).

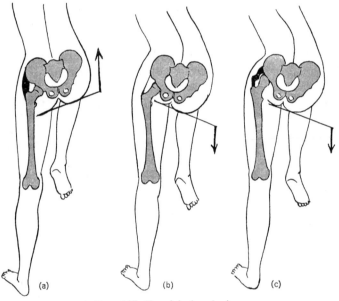

FIG. 117. Trendelenburg's sign

(*a*) Negative in a normal hip
(*b*) Positive due to abductor muscle weakness
(*c*) Positive due to joint instability

Radiologically, in the early neo-natal stage, diagnosis may not be easy, as the epiphysis for the femoral head may not have appeared, but if the legs are held in 45° abduction, some upward displacement may be seen. This is most easily detected if lines are drawn round the upper border of the obdurator foramen of the pelvis, and below the femoral neck. Normally the two are continuous (*Shenton's Line*) but if there is a gap, the head is displaced upwards (Fig. 118).

Later, when the epiphysis for the femoral head has appeared, if displaced it will be seen to lie above a horizontal line drawn through the triradiate

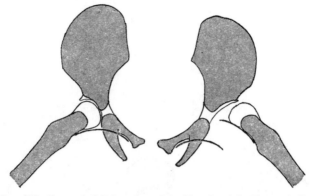

FIG. 118. Congenital dislocation of the hip—break in Shenton's line

cartilage in the acetabulum, and outside a vertical line dropped from its upper border (Fig. 119).

Treatment

This may be conservative or operative. The former is usually successful where treatment commences before the infant begins to walk. Later, surgery is more commonly required.

(a) *Conservative.* This consists in holding the thighs abducted, as in this position the femoral head drops down into the acetabulum, and its constant pressure against the acetabular floor assists in deepening its cavity. In the early neonatal stage, this can simply be achieved by a padded malleable aluminium splint shaped either like an 'X' or an 'H' which is

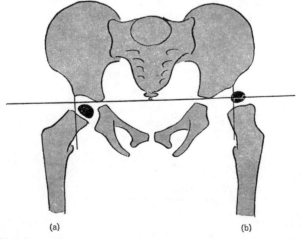

(a)   (b)

FIG. 119. X-ray appearance of a subluxed hip where the femoral capital epiphysis has appeared

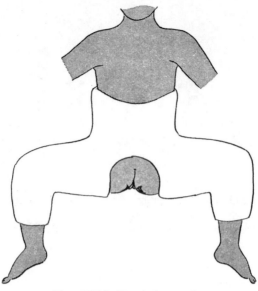

FIG. 120(a). 'Frog' plaster spica

moulded over the shoulders above and under the thighs below, and continued for three to six months. If the infant is a few days old and a little 'clicking' is obtained, it is possible by fixing two large nappies between its legs to keep them abducted without completely immobilising them. More active treatment may not be required at this time. Later reduction is obtained by gradually abducting the child's legs with traction on a metal frame over a period of two to three months, after which a plaster-of-Paris spica is applied holding the limbs in 90° abduction ('*frog*' *plaster*) (Fig. 120(a)). About two

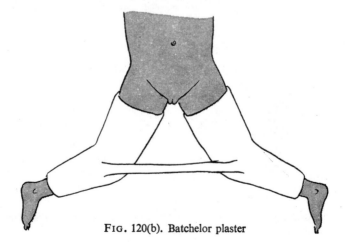

FIG. 120(b). Batchelor plaster

months later this in turn may be modified by holding the legs abducted and internally rotated by plasters joined together by a bar (*Batchelor plaster*) (Fig. 120(b)). Abduction is maintained altogether for about twelve months.

(b) *Operative.* Surgical measures are indicated in infants where conservative treatment fails, and they are therefore directed to overcoming the individual causes of failure.

Firstly, if after fully abducting the hip, the femoral head still fails to reduce, this may be due to blockage by an inturned limbus. This may be well shown up radiologically if some radio-opaque material is injected into the joint (*arthrography*). In such cases the joint should be explored, and the limbus excised.

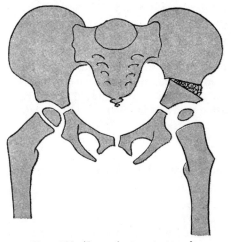

Fig. 121. 'Shelf operation' for later congenital dislocation of the hip

Fig. 122. 'Innominate osteotomy' for later congenital dislocation of the hip

Secondly, excessive anteversion of the femoral neck may mean that reduction is only stable when the leg is held in full internal rotation. If this is so, an osteotomy of the femur just below the trochanters, with external rotation of the limb through about 60° is indicated.

Thirdly, the acetabular roof may be so shallow that persistent subluxation occurs, in which case measures must be taken to make it more efficient. This can be done in two ways: Firstly, a horizontal cut can be made into the ilium immediately above the acetabulum, and the lower portion is lowered downwards to cover the femoral head, being held in place by a wedge of ilium taken from a site higher up ('*shelf operation*') (Fig. 121). Secondly, the ilium may be completely divided just above acetabular level, and the whole lower fragment of innominate bone levered downwards, so that the acetabular cavity is rotated into a more horizontal position ('*innominate osteotomy*') (Fig. 122).

In older persons with unreduced dislocations, osteotomy of the upper end of the femur, with the neck fragment angled into a valgus position, will move the weight-bearing thrust of the leg directly under the pelvis, thereby giving increased stability ('*Schanz*' osteotomy) (Fig. 123).

Complications of Treatment. Interference with the blood supply to the femoral head leading to avascular necrosis, and later collapse of the head similar to that seen in Perthes' disease (p. 239), may result from stretching the joint capsule. For this reason, except in new-born infants where the head is not fully dislocated, and the epiphysis has not yet formed, manipulative reduction should not be attempted and in open operations, care must be taken to minimise stripping the capsule from the femoral neck.

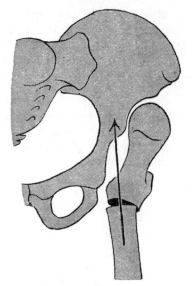

FIG. 123. 'Schanz' osteotomy of the upper femur for untreated congenital dislocation of the hip in adults

(iii) Congenital Talipes Equino-varus (Fig. 124).

This is the third common congenital abnormality of the locomotor system. The name of the condition describes the deformity present. *Talipes* means a deformity involving both ankle and foot. The navicula is displaced medially and downwards so that the head of the talus can be felt on the outer side of the foot. *Equinus* implies that the heel is tucked upwards. *Varus* indicates not only that the whole foot is turned inwards, but also that the forefoot is adducted on the hindfoot. In its mildest

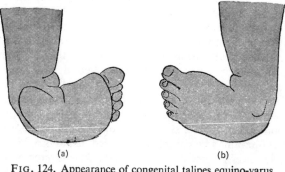

(a)   (b)

FIG. 124. Appearance of congenital talipes equino-varus

(*a*) posterior view   (*b*) anterior view

form, adduction of the forefoot alone may be present—*metatarsus varus*.

The cause is unknown, clinically there appear to be two types. Firstly, there are the milder cases, where full correction is fairly easily obtained and which may be due to the position adopted by the feet in utero. Secondly, there is the more severe group in which complete correction is difficult to obtain, and relapse is very common. The latter may be associated with deformities elsewhere, and is often seen in cases of arthrogryphosis multiplex congenita (p. 197), suggesting that the cause is some abnormality in mesenchymal development.

The condition is commonly bilateral, though both feet are rarely affected to quite the same extent. It occasionally runs in families. Boys are affected more often than girls.

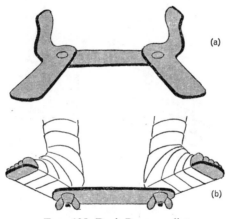

FIG. 125. Denis Browne splint

Treatment

Unlike congenital dislocation of the hip, the condition is obvious at birth, and treatment should commence forthwith. The most important aspect of treatment is to overcome the deformity affecting the hindfoot—the equinus and inversion of the calcaneum, as, if this can be achieved, the main weight-bearing portion of the foot will be plantigrade.

Initially, treatment consists of regular weekly moulding of the foot into a position of dorsiflexion and eversion, maximal pressure being applied to the mid-tarsal region so that the varus deformity is overcome. Following each moulding, the position gained is retained by strapping the foot in eversion, reinforced by a plaster-of-Paris slab. When a reasonable degree of correction has been obtained Denis Browne splints (Fig. 125), to which the foot is strapped, may be substituted. These must also be reapplied at weekly intervals and maintained until the baby is about nine months old, after which he is allowed free by day, but wears leather bootees joined by a bar, in external rotation as night splints. When the child starts to walk, firm boots worn on the opposite feet should be employed for the first year or so. Occasionally if relapse of the metatarsus varus element of the deformity occurs serial below-knee plaster casts may be employed, from each one of which a wedge is cut on the outer side, so that further abduction of the forefoot is possible.

In the more severe group, open operation is often required. Several measures can be employed. Firstly the tight tissues on the inner side of the foot may be released and the tendo Achillis lengthened, thereby allowing the heel to come down. Secondly, either the tibialis anterior or posterior, which by their action as invertors of the foot provide a deforming force, may be transplanted to the outer side of the tarsus, the tibialis posterior tendon being passed through the interosseous membrane in order

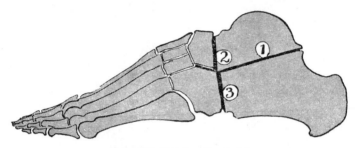

FIG. 126. 'Triple arthrodesis'

to reach the dorsum of the foot. Thirdly, bone surgery may be required. In such cases, in young children, this should be limited either to removal of a wedge from the outer side of the calcaneum—thereby permitting the heel to be everted—or to removal of a wedge from the calcaneo-cuboid joint, which allows the forefoot to be swung outwards.

In cases where deformity persistently recurs, when the growth rate slows down at puberty *triple arthrodesis* (Fig. 126) may be required. This is so named because three joints—the sub-talar, the calcaneo-cuboid, and the talo-navicular—are all fused, by removal of wedges of bone containing the articular surfaces.

Occasionally the reverse deformity to *talipes equino-varus* is seen. In this, known as *Congenital talipes calcaneo-valgus*, the heel points downwards and the forefoot is everted and dorsiflexed. This is a mild postural deformity almost certainly due to intra-uterine pressure on the foetus's dorsiflexed foot. Rapid correction is obtained if the baby's feet are held fully plantar flexed for a few weeks in a plaster-of-Paris dorsal slab.

Congenital vertical talus, which is in fact medial dislocation of the head of the talus, has already been mentioned (p. 186).

(iv) Absence of Parts

Deficient development may affect any region of the body, but is most noticeable in the limbs. Two types are encountered—firstly, congenital amputations, from the distal phalanx of a digit, to complete absence of whole limbs. Sometimes these are associated with intra-uterine constricting bands. Secondly, parts of limbs may be absent, which is most noticeable in the case of bones. In the leg, absence of the tibia may cause grotesque inversion deformities of the foot and knee. Absence of the fibula leads to an extreme valgus deformity of the foot. Gross shortening may be due to absence of the upper part of the femur. In the arm, absence of the radius causes a 'club-hand' appearance, and is often associated with absence of the thumb. Mild congenital shortening of the radius causes dislocation of the inferior radio-ulnar joint known as *Madelung's Deformity*.

Recently, the frequent occurrence of such deformities following the mothers taking thalidomide, has emphasised that the cause is an upset in limb bud development during the first few months of pregnancy.

Treatment will depend upon the nature of the lesion. Prosthetic replacement of absent parts often gives surprisingly satisfactory results.

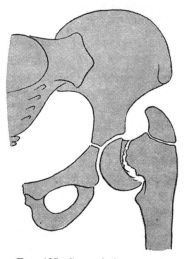

FIG. 127. Congenital coxa vara

(v) Congenital Coxa Vara

In this condition, the lower part of the femoral neck fails to ossify. The head of the femur lies at an abnormally low position relative to the shaft, which increases with growth, leading to an extreme varus angulatory deformity. It probably represents a type of absent development of a part (Fig. 127). Clinically, the appearance, particularly in later childhood, is very suggestive of an untreated congenital dislocation of the hip.

Treatment

This is surgical, and consists of a valgus osteotomy of the upper end of the femur, turning the neck so that it points upwards.

(vi) Abnormalities of the Trunk

Apart from spina bifida, already discussed (p. 198) several other abnormalities may occur in the development of the trunk. Vertebrae may appear wedged (*congenital hemivertebra*), leading to a type of scoliosis, or they may appear to be fused together, which is most frequently seen in the neck, causing a congenital short neck (Klippel–Feil Syndrome).

Several ribs may be fused together, which again is a cause of 'congenital' scoliosis. The scapula may fail to descend from the high position at which the limb bud first appears in early foetal life (*Sprengel's shoulder*).

Of a different type is *congenital torticollis*. This, in fact, does not result from a true developmental abnormality, but is due to a birth injury, which causes fibrosis in one sterno-mastoid muscle and as a result, during growth, the head is pulled down to one side (*torticollis*) and, if left untreated, will cause facial asymmetry in addition.

Clinically, in the early neonatal stage, a lump may be felt in one sternomastoid (*sternomastoid 'tumour'*) due to reaction following the original birth injury.

Treatment

At an early stage, regular stretching of the neck may prevent contraction, but this must be continued by the mother until the infant is $1\frac{1}{2}$–2 years old.

When the contracture is present, division of the sternomastoid near its insertion into the clavicle and sternum gives good results, provided facial asymmetry has not appeared.

(vii) Abnormalities of Digits

Minor developmental abnormalities of the fingers and toes are common. They take these forms:

(*a*) There may be accessory digits, which may take any form from small knobs of flesh on the side to complete extra parts, including fully developed metatarsals or metacarpals as the case may be. The extra digits are usually on the outer side.

Treatment consists of amputation if they cause inconvenience.

(*b*) There may be absence of digits, as has already been mentioned. Absence of a thumb represents a real disability, and a new 'thumb' can often be constructed by deepening the web between the index finger so that it is in opposition to the others—pollicisation of the index finger.

(*c*) Contractures, usually, on the flexor surface may occur, and in the case of fingers, cause sufficient disability to warrant operative correction.

CHAPTER FOUR

INFECTIONS OF BONES AND JOINTS

Summary

A. Bone—Osteomyelitis

   (i) Acute Haematogenous Osteomyelitis
   (ii) Chronic Osteomyelitis
   (iii) Brodie's Abscess
   (iv) Other Bone Infections

B. Joints—Infective Arthritis

   (i) Acute Suppurative Arthritis
   (ii) Acute Septic Arthritis in Infants
   (iii) Gonococcal Arthritis

C. Tuberculosis of Bone and Joint

   (i) General Remarks
   (ii) Local Tuberculous Lesions

      (a) The Spine (Pott's Disease)
      (b) The Hip
      (c) The Knee
      (d) Other Bones and Joints

A. BONE—OSTEOMYELITIS

Like any other living tissue, bone is liable to infection, which may be acute or chronic. Organisms may reach the bone either directly through a skin wound which communicates with it, usually as a complication of a compound fracture, or directly via the blood-stream. The latter tends to be the more acute.

(i) Acute Haematogenous Osteomyelitis

A few organisms often enter in the blood-stream from any focus of infection, but in the majority of cases they do not survive. If, however, they reach an area where tissue vitality is lower than normal they may multiply causing a local infective lesion. In bone, a haematoma resulting from trauma a few days earlier, which is often quite trivial, provides such a site. Acute osteomyelitis occurs most frequently in the medullary cavity of long bones in children, near their growing ends, and, because the knee is most subject to minor injury, it is the lower end of the femur and the upper end of the tibia which are most commonly affected.

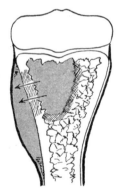

FIG. 128. Acute osteomyelitis showing sub-periosteal abscess

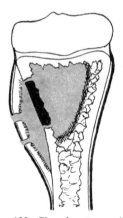

FIG. 129. Chronic osteomyelitis showing the formation of a sequestrum and involucrum

As the medullary cavity cannot expand, considerable tension builds up inside the bone, and pus is forced through the Haversian canals to form a *sub-periosteal abscess* (Fig. 128). When this has occurred, the under-lying bone is deprived of its blood supply, as it has pus on either side. As a result, unless there is early evacuation of the pus, a segment of bone dies and eventually separates to form a *sequestrum*. Meanwhile, the raised periosteum is stimulated to make new bone, so that in severe cases, a large portion of the shaft sequestrates, and is surrounded by a layer of new bone, known as an *involucrum* (Fig. 129). Eventually the abscess bursts through the periosteum and finding its way to the surface forms a chronic sinus. By the time a sequestrum has formed, the disease has reached the chronic stage.

Clinical Features

The patient, usually a child or adolescent, complains of very severe pain in a limb, of rapid onset, with toxaemia and a high temperature. Initially, as the lesion is within the medullary cavity, while tenderness is marked, local heat and swelling are not obvious. These follow rapidly however as the subperiosteal abscess forms. If questioned, a history of some minor injury a few days earlier, and of an apparently insignificant infective lesion, such as a sore throat can often be obtained. There may also be some swelling of the neighbouring joint, suggesting suppurative arthritis (p. 213).

It must be stressed that in the acute phase X-ray appearances are normal. Only when new bone begins to be laid down beneath the raised periosteum does a sub-periosteal shadow appear. With this an area of bony rarefaction appears about the same time. These are the first radiological changes visible. This is two or three weeks after the onset, by which time irreversible bone changes will have taken place.

In infants and young children, several bones may be affected in rapid succession.

Investigations

The white blood cell count will show a marked leucocytosis, and sometimes a positive blood culture of the causative organisms may be obtained.

Treatment

To avoid the loss of blood supply to a segment of bony cortex, and the dangers of sequestrum formation, early drainage of the medullary cavity should probably be undertaken. This is achieved by a skin incision over the most tender area, division of the periosteum, thereby releasing any sub-periosteal collection of pus, and opening the medullary cavity using either a series of drill holes, or gouging out a window in the bone.

A full course of suitable anti-biotics must also be given, and both the patient and the part must be put at rest—the latter by splintage, often consisting of a plaster-of-Paris cast with a window cut to permit dressing of the wound.

If a patient is seen within 24 hours of onset, it may be justifiable to attempt conservative treatment by giving large doses of a wide-spectrum anti-biotic. If, however, there is no marked improvement within a few hours, surgery should be employed.

(ii) Chronic Osteomyelitis

This state occurs after irreversible changes have taken place in the affected bone, and is due to the fact that the causative organisms can lie dormant in avascular necrotic areas, occasionally becoming reactivated, resulting in a flare up. The bone is thickened and sclerotic, often containing an abscess cavity in which a sequestrum may lie.

Clinical Features

During the quiescent phase, which may last for years, the patient has no symptoms, though scars of past sinuses and abscesses are usually to be found. At intervals, however, a flare-up occurs. This may follow some minor trauma to the affected region, but often comes on apparently spontaneously. The patient complains of pain which comes on rapidly, and there is some associated constitutional upset, with pyrexia. Locally, there will be some heat, swelling, and redness. An old sinus scar often breaks down and starts to exude purulent material.

Prolonged discharge of pus, with no other symptoms, may follow, in which case, if the sinus closes, because pus there may build up in pockets, a flare up is liable to occur.

Amyloid disease may complicate cases in which there is prolonged profuse pus formation.

Treatment

It is very difficult to provide a permanent cure for chronic osteomyelitis.

Abscesses, where present, should be drained. If there is an obvious sequestrum, this must be removed, and the surrounding bone gouged away in an attempt to clear out infected material. In severe cases, this should be as radical as possible, when the procedure is known as 'saucerisation'.

In addition, the sensitivity of the causative organism to anti-biotics must be ascertained, and a prolonged course of the appropriate drug given.

(iii) Brodie's Abscess

This is a form of chronic osteomyelitis which appears to come on without a preceding acute attack. There is a persistent boring pain in the bone near one end, with little or no constitutional upset, and an X-ray will reveal a circumscribed cavity in the metaphyseal region of the bone, with dense margins.

Treatment is by radical drainage, the contained pus often proving to be sterile.

(iv) Other Bone Infections

Bone may be affected by many different organisms, either by direct spread through an open wound or via the blood-stream. The typical picture produced is usually that of a sub-acute or chronic, fairly low grade lesion. Causative organisms include the Pneumococcus, B. Proteus, B. Coli, and those in the Typhoid-Paratyphoid group.

Bone infection is a fairly common late complication of *typhoid* fever, bones particularly liable to infection being the vertebral column, or major long bones. In the onset being about the time when the generalised disease appears to be dying out. The radiological appearances often being rather similar to those seen in tuberculosis (p. 216).

Syphilitic infection of bone may occur in the tertiary stage. The tibia is that most frequently affected. It causes a characteristic thickening of the subcutaneous surface—'*sabre tibia*'. A positive Wassermann reaction will confirm the diagnosis.

Treatment

In all cases this consists in the prolonged administration of the appropriate anti-biotic. Surgery being required only to drain an abscess.

B. JOINTS—INFECTIVE ARTHRITIS

Infection may reach a joint by one of three routes. Firstly, by the blood-stream from some distant focus, secondly by direct spread from osteomyelitis in one of the bones, and thirdly, as a result of direct innoculation through a wound in the skin.

(i) Acute Suppurative Arthritis

Like acute osteomyelitis, this is usually due to staphylococcus pyogenes. It is most often seen in children as a complication of acute osteomyelitis. The likelihood of this occurring depends upon the local anatomy of the bone affected. Osteomyelitis normally involves the metaphyseal region, and does not spread across the epiphyseal line. If, therefore, the joint capsule is attached below this, it is possible for pus to find its way into the joint. Thus, suppurative arthritis of the knee is not a very common complication of osteomyelitis of the tibia or femur, in the hip it usually arises as a result of infection in the upper end of the femur.

The pus digests away articular cartilage, so that in untreated cases gross joint destruction ensues, often causing bony ankylosis. Cases due to less virulent organisms, if untreated, cause fibrous ankylosis.

Clinical Features

There is severe pain in the affected joint, together with general malaise and a raised temperature. The joint is hot, tender, and swollen with marked restriction of movement, due to muscle spasm, which may be such that it is held completely rigid. As the synovial cavity becomes distended with purulent fluid, fluctuation may be elicited. Later an abscess may form and rupture through the skin, leaving a chronically discharging sinus.

Investigations

Radiographs at an early stage appear normal. Later some rarefaction will be seen, followed by sub-articular irregularity. There will be a polymorpho-nuclear leucocytosis in the blood, and the erythrocyte sedimentation rate will be markedly raised. Aspiration of the joint yields a fluid filled with polymorphs from which the causative organism may be cultured.

Treatment

The patient is put to bed, and a systematic course of wide-spectrum anti-biotics commenced. As soon as the sensitivities of the causative organism are known, this may be changed to whatever type will be most effective. The joint is put at rest by splintage. This should be in the optimal position of function in case ankylosis supervenes. Effusions are aspirated, and an anti-biotic solution instilled into the joint cavity. Aspirations and anti-biotic instillations are repeated at frequent intervals until the effusion subsides, after which cautious active mobilisation is started. In severe cases, the pus becomes too thick to be aspirated, in which case open drainage of the joint is required. This is to be avoided if possible, because it is liable to increase the residual stiffness after activity has settled down.

(ii) Acute Septic Arthritis in Infants

The hip is the joint most commonly affected, the causative organism being either a staphylococcus or streptococcus. The primary site of infection is some septic focus elsewhere, which in neonatal infants may be the umbilicus. In the young child, the femoral head is largely cartilaginous and is therefore destroyed by the surrounding pus, leading to pathological dislocation of the hip.

Clinical Features

The baby is obviously unwell, but because the hip joint is not near the surface the actual site of infection may be overlooked until an abscess forms in the buttock or thigh. Where pathological dislocation has occurred, marked shortening of the limb occurs with growth.

Treatment

This consists of splintage, in some abduction with traction in older children, together with local and systemic anti-biotics. Later, arthrodesis to give stability and control progressive upward shift of the femur, may be required.

(iii) Gonococcal Arthritis

Acute inflammatory reactions, often in several joints simultaneously, quite frequently occur as a complication of gonococcal urethritis. It usually appears a few weeks after onset of the disease. The affected joints are acutely painful, hot, and swollen, but the constitutional upset is much less marked than with other forms of acute infective arthritis.

(iv) Reiter's Syndrome

This is a combination of mild generalised arthritis, urethritis, and conjunctivitis.

C. TUBERCULOSIS OF BONE AND JOINT

(i) General Remarks

While, with improvements in hygiene and the standards of living through-out the world, tuberculosis is becoming less frequent, it remains an important cause of chronic bone and joint infection.

The organism, which may be either the human or bovine type, but more commonly the former, reaches the site from a focus elsewhere, usually in either the lungs or alimentary tract—in spite of the fact that the primary focus may be so small as to be overlooked, or appear absolutely quiescent. Tuberculous bacilli may primarily infect bone (*tuberculous osteitis*) or synovial membrane (*tuberculous synovitis*), but in the majority of cases eventually both the joint and neighbouring bones are affected together.

The tubercle bacillus at first causes an inflammatory reaction, in which are found the typical *tuberculous giant cells*. Soon, this is followed by tissue necrosis, and the formation of a tuberculous ('*cold*') abscess—a process known as *caseation*. Cold abscesses track along tissue planes, eventually reaching the surface, when a chronic sinus results. Secondary invasion with pyogenic organisms then often supervenes. Eventually fibrous ankylosis of the affected joint occurs. Bony ankylosis only takes place when secondary infection with pyogenic organisms occurs.

Clinical Features

Tuberculosis is a chronic infection, so that some constitutional upset will be present. This is manifest by loss of weight and general lassitude. Often there is an evening rise of temperature causing the characteristic 'night sweats'. Locally, the typical features are pain, particularly on attempted movement of the affected part, which causes muscle spasm. This in turn leads to deformity, which increases with local tissue destruction. Muscle wasting is marked, with swelling at the actual site of the lesion which is associated with thickening of synovial membrane.

Investigations

The erythrocyte sedimentation rate is raised, and when estimated at regular intervals this provides a useful guide to the progress of the disease. The white blood cell count often shows some lymphocytosis. Routine culture and examination of sputum and twenty-four-hour specimens of urine often reveal the presence of tubercle bacilli, even though there is no clinical evidence of active disease in the respiratory or genito-urinary tracts. Where possible any effusion or pus should also be cultured and tested for acid-fast bacilli. This should include guinea pig innoculation in doubtful cases. A *Mantoux test*, which consists of the intra-dermal injection of dead tubercle bacilli, is useful in providing negative information, as, if the patient has never been in contact with tuberculosis, no antigen-antibody reaction will ensue, making it very unlikely that a local lesion is tuberculous. A positive reaction, however, merely indicates that the patient

has never been in contact with tuberculosis, no antigen-antibody reaction will ensue, making it very unlikely that a local lesion is tuberculous. A positive reaction, however, merely indicates that the patient has at some time formed anti-tuberculous antibodies.

Radiographs of the affected area, at first, merely show bony rarefaction and loss of trabecular pattern. Later, actual bony destruction occurs, with erosion of articular surfaces. Soft-tissue swellings, particularly of cold abscesses in the spine, may also be visible.

Treatment

This is subdivided into general treatment of the patient as a whole, and local treatment of the affected part.

General. This consists of measures to build up the patient's strength and resistance to the tubercle bacillus by rest, abundant fresh air, and good food. In addition a course of antituberculous anti-biotics and chemotherapy should commence and be continued for six months. These consist of streptomycin, isonicotinic acid (I.N.A.H.), and para-amino-salicylic acid (P.A.S.).

Local. The basic principle is rest, so that the affected part is splinted in the best position of function should permanent stiffness supervene. Prior to the advent of anti-biotics surgery was only employed as a final measure when the disease was static, and usually consisted of arthrodesis of the affected joint. Now excision of tuberculous granulation tissue and caseous material is practised more often and at an earlier stage.

(ii) Local Tuberculous Lesions

(a) *The Spine (Pott's Disease)*

The spine is the commonest part of the skeletal system to be affected by tuberculosis, the disease usually occurring in the dorsal or lumbar regions. The initial focus is in a vertebral body, near the disc, and it soon spreads across the disc, which it destroys, to involve the neighbouring vertebral body (Fig 130). Caseous material then forms a *para-vertebral abscess* which surrounds the vertebral bodies, giving a fusiform shadow on the radiograph (Fig. 131). In the lower dorsal and lumbar regions, pus commonly spreads into the neighbouring psoas sheath, in which it tracks downwards with the psoas muscle as a *psoas abscess* forming a swelling in the iliac fossa and sometimes extends below the inguinal ligament, where a sinus may occur.

If disease in the thoracic region spreads posteriorly, the spinal canal may be narrowed by granulation tissue or tuberculous debris, causing pressure upon the spinal cord and nerve roots.

Clinical Features

The disease may occur at any age, but is commonest in adolescents and young adults. The complaints are of localised back pain coming on gradually with spasm, and, later, deformity usually consisting of kyphosis secondary to collapse of vertebral bodies. This is most marked in the dorsal spine where it may produce a sharp angular deformity known as a *Gibbus*. On examination, wasting of the erector spinae muscles is noticeable, and swelling may be found. Where there is a psoas abscess, this will produce an abdominal swelling.

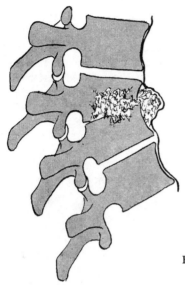

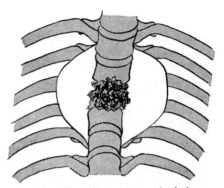

FIG. 131. The spine—paravertebral abscess shadow

FIG. 130. The spine (early)

Complications

Two important groups of complications may occur: firstly, due to pressure on the cord ('*Pott's Paraplegia*'), and secondly, as a result of the immobilisation treatment.

Pott's Paraplegia. Pressure on the spinal cord may occur at any stage in the course of tuberculosis disease in the thoracic spine. The onset is insidious manifesting itself either by motor weakness or sensory impairment in the lower limbs, or loss of bladder or bowel control. For this reason regular neurological examination of patients with thoracic lesions should be carried out. Cases liable to develop neurological complications often show a well marked globular paravertebral abscess shadow, indicating pus under tension.

Complications Due to Immobilisation

These may take three forms. Firstly, *hypostatic pneumonia*, due to accumulation of secretions at the lung bases. Secondly, *urinary* infections and the formation of calculi. Thirdly, *pressure sores*.

Treatment

The basic feature in treatment of a tuberculous spine remains rest. The patient is immobilised either on a frame or plaster bed. To avoid the complications of immobilisation, regular turning, using an anterior plaster stile in the case of a plaster bed, is necessary. The patient's general resistance must be built up by good food and abundant fresh air. For this reason, treatment should be conducted in a country orthopaedic hospital. A full course of antituberculous anti-biotic therapy should commence as soon as the diagnosis has been established.

Surgical measures are practised more often than they were. Where a paravertebral abscess is visible radiologically, particularly if the shadow suggests pus under tension, this should be drained by excision of a transverse process, and the head and neck of the corresponding rib (*costotransversectomy*). When there is much debris in the affected vertebral bodies, this may be removed by a direct lateral approach. Later, when the disease is quiescent, particularly if the residual deformity leaves residual instability, spinal fusion is employed.

Paraplegia, unless spontaneous improvement rapidly occurs, is treated surgically. When there is much fluid pus under tension, drainage by costotransversectomy may suffice, but usually in addition the spinal canal is decompressed anteriorly by excision of the vertebral bodies from the side (*antero-lateral decompression*).

(b) *The Hip*

Tuberculosis of the hip usually commences with an osseous focus either in the femoral neck or acetabulum, from which it spreads to invade the joint cavity. Later, cold abscesses form, which may point anteriorly in the femoral triangle, or posteriorly below the lower margin of gluteus maximus.

Clinical Features

The disease usually affects children, who are often quite young. The complaint is of pain and a limp. The pain often radiates down to the inner side of the knee, in the area of skin supplied by the obturate nerve, because the capsule of the hip joint shares the same nerve supply. The limp is partly due to pain and partly, in the early stages, to muscle spasm. Later, additional causes are stiffness resulting from actual tissue destruction, and deformity. Owing to distension of the joint capsule, the initial deformity may appear to be in ABduction. Later the combined effects of muscle pull and bony destruction will convert this into a flexion-ADduction deformity.

In later cases, a cold abscess if present may rupture, leaving a sinus, down which secondary pyogenic organisms may travel causing bony ankylosis.

Apart from the local sign, some general constitutional upset will be present.

Complications

Premature fusion of epiphyses in the affected limb may occur, not only at the hip, but also at the knee, causing, in young children, gross shortening.

Treatment

In cases which are seen early, before there is radiological evidence of bone destruction involving the joint surfaces, if complete rest, and an intensive course of antituberculous drugs are given, resolution may occur, leaving little permanent damage.

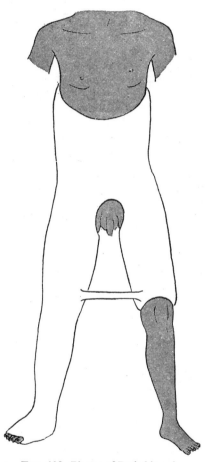

FIG. 132. Plaster-of-Paris hip spica

Rest is obtained by immobilising the hip either on a frame, to which the child's legs are strapped, or in a plaster-of-Paris spica (Fig. 132) for six months. At the conclusion of this period, if X-rays are satisfactory, and the sedimentation rate has returned to normal, cautious mobilisation may be commenced.

Where there is obvious bone destruction, then arthrodesis will give best results. This should, where possible, be performed avoiding opening the joint itself. The ischio-femoral arthrodesis of Brittain (Fig. 133) is ideal in this respect. Arthrodesis, however, should not be performed in young children, as it will impair bone growth.

Excessive shortening, due to premature epiphyseal fusion may, in selected cases, be controlled by delaying growth on the normal side by placing staples across the epiphyseal line of the femur and tibia at knee level (Fig. 162, p. 275).

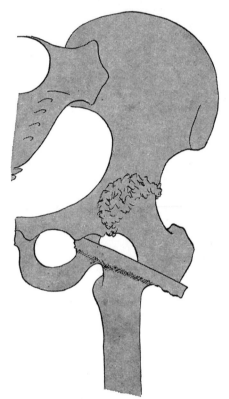

FIG. 133. Brittain's ischio-femoral arthrodesis of the hip

(c) *The Knee*

Tuberculosis of the knee commonly occurs in childhood, and while the actual initial focus may be bony or synovial, often in the early stages involvement of the synovium may be predominant.

Clinical Features

As with other bony tuberculous lesions, the complaints will be of pain and stiffness, but as the knee is a joint that is easily palpable, local heat, swelling, and tenderness can usually be found. Wasting of the thigh muscles will be marked, so that the periarticular swelling becomes more obvious. Stiffness is due to muscle spasm initially but later results from erosion of articular cartilage.

Investigations

Because of the ease of access, direct aspiration of effusions and synovia biopsy for diagnostic purposes are carried out more frequently in the knee than other joints.

Treatment

Immobilisation is ideally carried out on a Thomas's splint, which was originally designed for this purpose, using skin extensions (Figs. 1 and 76). After six months, if all appears quiescent, cautious mobilisation may be commenced. Where there is obvious damage to articular surfaces, arthrodesis is indicated when the disease has settled down though in young children this must be deferred until adolescence—a walking caliper being employed until this stage is reached.

(d) *Tuberculosis of Other Bones and Joints*

Any joint may be infected by tuberculosis, the basic features of which have already been described. Certain specific points, however, require brief mention.

The Shoulder. Adults are more commonly affected than in most sites, and often there is bony destruction, with little or no cold abscess formation. This type of disease is known as *caries sicca.*

Local treatment consists of immobilisation in a plaster-of-Paris shoulder spica (Fig. 31). Arthrodesis is commonly required later.

The Elbow. Tuberculosis is comparatively uncommon in the elbow. Treatment is along standard lines, except that arthrodesis is less frequently employed as a fibrous ankylosis in the case of the elbow usually gives reasonably a satisfactory result.

The Wrist, Carpus, Ankle, and Tarsus are also occasionally affected by tuberculosis. In all, treatment, local and general, is along routine lines, though arthrodesis eventually is usually necessary.

The Metacarpals and Metatarsals are affected occasionally, being examples of pure tuberculous osteitis. This condition is known as *Tuberculous dactylitis.* Local excision of the affected bone is sometimes employed under suitable antituberculous drug cover.

ARTHRITIS

Summary

GENERAL REMARKS

Arthritis is a term used to describe any lesion of a joint. This may be due to some purely local abnormality in one joint, or to some more widespread condition affecting several joints and possibly other structures in addition. Broadly, there are four groups:

(i) Infective Arthritis

This is due to some specific organism and has already been discussed (p. 213).

(ii) Osteo-arthritis

This results from age changes and the effects of repeated mechanical stresses and strains. Weight-bearing joints are therefore those usually affected.

(iii) Poly-arthritis

In these cases, whose aetiology is unknown, there is widespread joint involvement, with inflammatory changes and proliferation in the periarticular tissues. The commonest type to fall into this category is *rheumatoid arthritis*, though ankylosing spondylitis is also one of this group.

(iv) Miscellaneous

A group in which joint manifestations occur as a complication of some specific pathological process. Examples are joint changes associated with gout or haemophilia.

A. OSTEO-ARTHRITIS

General Remarks

Degenerative changes in joints are a normal result of the repeated stresses thrown upon aging tissues, and therefore in elderly persons some degree of osteo-arthritis is present in all joints. If, however, this process is exaggerated, symptoms may arise. In practice osteo-arthritis may be classified as:

(a) *Primary*—where it appears in a joint which has been otherwise normal, in which case several joints may be affected simultaneously.

(b) *Secondary*—where owing to some previous abnormality in the joint, the two articulating surfaces do not fit together congruously, abnormal wear inevitably will follow. Examples are osteo-arthritis following fractures involving the joint surfaces, or resulting in their mal-alignment, congenital abnormalities, such as incompletely reduced congenital dislocation of the hip, or loose bodies in the joint.

Pathology. The moving parts of the joint are primarily affected, so that the first change is in the articular cartilage, which becomes roughened and then eroded, leaving bare bone. By the time this occurs, owing to frictional forces on the exposed bone it becomes sclerosed, with grooves on the surface in the line of movement. This is known as *eburnation.* At the same time, cystic spaces often appear beneath the sclerosed bone surfaces.

As the process continues, new bone is thrown out at the joint margins, producing lipping. Often definite nodules (*osteophytes*) are formed. Sometimes these break away, and if they have no soft tissue attachment they may become loose bodies in the joint. At a later stage some fibrosis in the capsule occurs. At certain sites, notably the hip joint, pathological changes are precipitated by some softening of the bone probably as a result of impaired blood supply.

Investigations

As osteo-arthritis is not a constitutional disease, unless there is some underlying generalised condition which has changed the stresses thrown upon the joint surfaces, all blood tests will be normal. Radiographs are characteristic. The first change is narrowing of the joint space, because erosion of articular cartilage allows the bone surfaces to come closer together. With this cyst changes and increased density, due to sclerosis, is seen in the sub-chondral bone. Lipping and marginal osteophyth formation can also be seen.

Clinical Features

The main complaints are of pain and stiffness. The onset is insidious, coming on for no known cause, in a middle-aged or elderly individual, unless there has been a previous history of injury or trouble with the affected joint several years before, in which case the patient may be slightly younger. As the condition progresses, limitation of movement increases often more in one direction than another, so that a fixed deformity may result. The usual cause of the deformity being that, because of the pain, some muscle spasm follows, and the more powerful groups therefore restrict movement to a greater degree than their less powerful opponents. Thus in the hip the flexors, adductors, and external rotators are stronger than their opponents, and in the knee, the hamstrings are stronger than the quadriceps.

On examination, some stiffness will be obvious, and often some crepitus due to the irregularities in the opposing articular surfaces can be felt, on movement. In the more superficial joints bony thickening is often palpable and a small effusion due to irritation of the joint lining may be present, but no actual soft tissue thickening or local heat will be found. Minor degrees of muscle wasting also often occur.

Treatment

This will depend to a large extent upon the individual joint affected. It is not possible to reverse the changes in the articular surfaces which have already occurred.

Conservative treatment is usually mainly employed. These aim at firstly controlling the symptoms caused by the changes already present, and secondly limiting as far as possible the progress of the degenerative process. They can be subdivided into local and general measures.

Local treatment consists of, firstly, the use of exercises to improve the tone of muscles acting upon the affected joint, thereby retaining the range of movement and protecting the joint from some of the minor strains to which it is subject in the course of everyday life. Secondly, heat in some form, which may relax muscle spasm and relieve some of the local pain. Thirdly, where marked changes or a fixed deformity are already present, the use of some light splint or appliance may help to control pain and help the patient to compensate for the disability.

General treatment consists firstly in the use of analgesics to limit pain. Usually these should be of the soluble aspirin type, taken as required when pain is troublesome. Occasionally limited courses of anti-rheumatic drugs such as Phenylbutazone ('Butazolidin') may be prescribed, but as they may have unpleasant side-effects, they should only be used for restricted periods in carefully selected patients. Secondly, where obesity is present, weight reduction to reduce the strains on affected joints is necessary. Thirdly, in younger patients, a course of rehabilitation, including resettlement in more suitable employment, may help them to overcome their disabilities.

Operative treatment depends very much upon the individual joint. *Arthrodesis* by fusing the affected joint, completely relieves all pain. Neighbouring joints must however be in good condition to compensate for that which is stiffened, so that its use must be restricted to younger patients. *Arthroplasty* aims at restoring a useful range of painless movement in the affected joint. Where deformity is present, in weight-bearing joints, it may be possible to redistribute the strains by corrective *osteotomy*. Operations upon soft tissues have little part to play in the treatment of osteo-arthritis.

Individual Joints

(i) **The Spine.** Because man has adopted an upright posture, considerable strains are thrown upon the spine, particularly at the junctions of the mobile portions with the rigid—at the base of the neck and lower lumbar regions. Degenerative changes therefore invariably occur at these sites, but most individuals pass through life unaware of them. Symptoms arise if changes at one level are different from those elsewhere, as if a longstanding disc lesion or minor structural anomaly has been present. They consist of aching pain at the affected level, worse with movement and relieved by rest, often with radiation along the course of a related nerve root.

Examination will show local tenderness and restriction of movement. Often some slight asymmetry between the two sides may be seen when the erect patient is viewed from the side. Evidence of nerve-root irritation may be present, but will be less marked than in a patient with an acute prolapse of an inter-vertebral disc (p. 176).

Treatment

Heat, exercises, and weight reduction often suffice to bring symptoms under control in younger patients. In the middle aged or elderly a support-

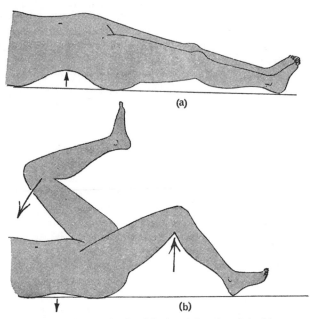

(a)

(b)

FIG. 134. Test for fixed flexion deformity of the hip

ing corset often provides the best solution. Occasionally in younger patients with a marked local lesion, spinal fusion may provide the best solution. This may be achieved either from behind by fusing the laminae of the affected vertebrae, or from in front by fusing their bodies.

(ii) The Hip. Osteo-arthritis of the hip is very common, partly because of the strains thrown upon the joint, and partly because minor changes, either due to congenital anomalies such as a shallow acetabulum, or epiphysitis (Perthe's disease, p. 239) frequently occur.

Clinically, a limp and deformity are common features. Examination will confirm the limitation of movement, though it is important to remember that movement of the pelvis on the spine may mask this unless a hand is placed upon the opposite anterior superior iliac spine. Flexion deformities of the hip may be demonstrated when by fully flexing the opposite hip. Normally the limb does not move, but if it also rises then some fixed flexion is present (Fig. 134). Some true shortening of the limb, as measured from the tip of the medial malleolus to the anterior superior spine may be present, but where there is an adduction deformity, this may cause '*apparent shortening*', which can be measured by the difference in length from the umbilicus to the respective medial malleolus (Fig. 135).

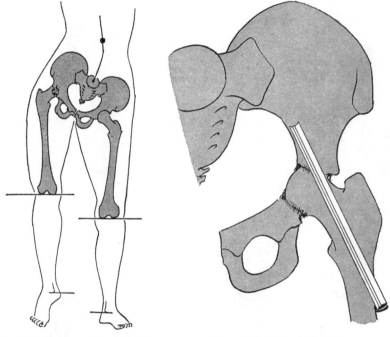

FIG. 135. 'Apparent shortening' due to adduction deformity of hip

FIG. 136. Arthrodesis of hip

Treatment

Conservative measures as described may help, often, where shortening whether true or apparent is present, this may include a small raise to the heel of the shoe. A stick, held in the opposite hand helps to distribute the weight away from the affected side in walking.

Surgical measures are often employed. In younger patients, with advanced unilateral disease, and normal joints elsewhere, *arthrodesis* provides a very satisfactory solution. In these cases, the joint is exposed, all remaining articular cartilage removed and the head of the femur and acetabular cavity reshaped so that the one fits snugly into the other. Internal fixation using a stout screw or trifin nail is then employed (Fig. 136). Where deformity is present, and in early cases, where obvious bony changes are present radiographically, and pain is marked, are helped by *subtrochanteric osteotomy* (McMurray), followed by internal fixation using a nail and plate (Fig. 137). This is a very useful procedure, though why it is effective is not fully understood.

Arthroplasty is a useful measure when there is disease in both hips and it is, therefore, important to restore a good range of movement. Various methods have been employed, firstly, the head and neck of the femur and the acetabular cavity may be totally replaced by metallic prostheses,

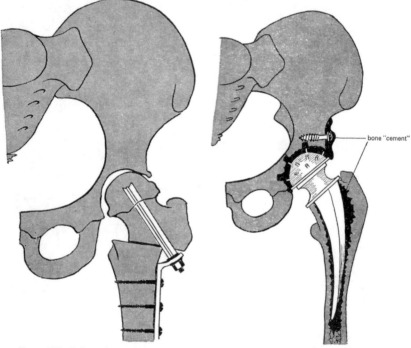

FIG. 137. Subtrochanteric osteotomy of hip (McMurray)

FIG. 138. Total hip replacement (McKee-Farrar): the cup and femoral head prosthesis are anchored by 'cement'

anchored by bone cement, the acetabular prosthesis being either anchored by cement (McKee-Farrar total hip replacement—Fig. 138) or, the acetabular prosthesis may be made with a long screw which is driven into the ilium, right up to the sacro-iliac joint (Ring prosthesis).

Another hip replacement (Charnley's total hip replacement) is the insertion of a smaller metal head into the upper femoral shaft combined with a polyethylene socket in the acetabulum.

The Austin–Moore Vitallium prosthesis (p. 112, Fig. 72) is also sometimes used, in which case the acetabular cavity has to be reamed out to provide a smooth well-fitting surface, or a metallic cup may be inserted between the femoral head and the acetabulum (Smith–Petersen Cup). When artificial prostheses are inserted, however, owing to the mechanical strains imposed upon them, wear may cause trouble some years later, though this is getting less likely with the more modern prostheses.

Finally, where there is widespread disease in younger people, or when other measures have been attempted, and have failed, the head and neck of the femur may be excised. This leaves a fairly mobile, though unstable joint (Fig. 139 (*a*)) (*pseudarthrosis*). Stability may be somewhat improved if an osteotomy of the upper end of the femur is performed at the same time (Fig. 139 (*b*)). As the space normally occupied by the femoral head and neck fills with fibrous tissue, the improvement gained is permanent.

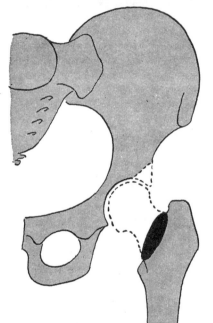 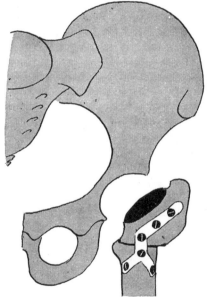

FIG. 139(*a*). Pseudarthrosis of hip
(Girdlestone)

FIG. 139(*b*). Pseudarthrosis of hip
combined with osteotomy (Batchelor)

(iii) The Knee. As has been mentioned in the section on injuries (p. 122), the knee is man's largest joint, and is subject to great strains. For this reason internal derangements which upset the mechanics of the joint are very common, and ordinary wear and tear is considerable, so that both 'primary' and 'secondary' osteo-arthritis frequently occur. Common predisposing factors are deformities such as a genu varum and valgum (p. 184), chondromalacia patellae (a condition in which the growing articular cartilage becomes soft, and therefore wears away), osteo-chondritis dissecans, (p. 244), and recurrent dislocation of the patella (p. 125). In addition, as a result of trauma residual ligamentous laxity in either antero-posterior or the lateral plane, mechanical upsets due to long standing meniscus injuries frequently occur. Osteo-arthritic changes, at first, are often restricted to one part of the joint.

Clinically, as the joint is large and superficial, bony thickening and crepitus are easily felt. Often the patella is relatively immobile, and effusions can be easily detected. Because the quadriceps passes over the knee, via the patella, it works at a slight mechanical disadvantage, so that a slight flexion deformity often occurs. Some quadriceps wasting is also often to be found.

Treatment

In early cases the maintenance of powerful quadriceps tone by regular exercises, coupled with weight reduction, may keep the disease under con-

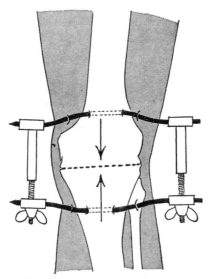

FIG. 140. Charnley compression arthrodesis of the knee

trol for long periods. Later, a supporting bandage may provide some protection.

Surgery has limited application. Where the disease is unilateral, *arthrodesis* in severe cases affords a very satisfactory solution. This is best achieved by using Charnley's compression method (Fig. 140). Occasionally, where the changes are limited to the knee cap, simple patellectomy may give good lasting results. Where changes are more marked in one compartment of the joint, especially where there is an associated genu valgum or varum deformity, osteotomy of the upper end of the tibia to throw the weight on to the opposite side of the joint gives good results.

Occasionally where there are gross degenerative changes present in both knees and several other joints, a total joint replacement, using a metal hinge—the rod of which is inserted upwards into the femoral shaft and the other part of which is inserted downwards into the tibia—is indicated. This is known as a 'Sheir's' prosthesis; after which active mobilisation of the knee is indicated. This should only be used in cases of gross general disability after careful assessment as the prosthesis inevitably has a limited 'life'.

(iv) **Other Joints.** (*a*) In the *upper limb*, osteo-arthritic changes are not so severe, and usually follow trauma. Minor changes rarely requiring very active treatment are quite frequently seen in the acromio-clavicular and elbow joints. True osteo-arthritis of the shoulder joint is rare. Symptoms from osteo-arthritic changes most commonly occur when the wrist or carpus are affected. Osteo-arthritis of the wrist most commonly follows fractures of the scaphoid, where non-union and avascular necrosis have taken place (p. 88). In the carpus, apart from trauma, the commonest site for osteo-arthritis is in the joint between the base of the first meta-carpal and trapezium. This is most frequently seen in women, and is probably due to underlaxity in this joint. If conservative measures fail, in younger patients, arthrodesis gives good results. In the more elderly, where prolonged plaster fixation is undesirable, the trapezium may be excised. The other common cause of carpal osteo-arthritis is avascular necrosis of the lunate (*Keinboch's disease*, p. 243). Where there is a generalised tendency to osteo-arthritis, changes are frequently seen in the terminal inter-phalangeal joints, with osteo-phyte formation (*Heberden's nodes*). Symptoms are rarely severe, the changes often being noticed by chance in patients who report complaining of osteo-arthritic changes elsewhere.

(*b*) In the *lower limb*, osteo-arthritis of the ankle usually follows severe fractures involving weight-bearing articular surfaces. If symptoms prove severe enough, arthrodesis gives good results. Osteo-arthritis of the tarsus may be due to deformities, such as incompletely corrected congenital talipes equino varus or trauma. Often, carefully made arch supports to distribute the weight evenly is sufficient to control symptoms. If this fails, 'triple arthrodesis' (p. 206) will be effective. Osteo-arthritis of the meta-tarso-phalangeal joint of the big toe (Hallus Rigidus) has been discussed elsewhere.

B. POLY-ARTHRITIS

In the conditions which make up this group, the joint manifestations, while usually the dominant feature, are in fact merely part of a generalised disease. This is shown by the fact that the erythrocyte sedimentation rate is invariably raised and involvement of other tissues can usually be found. Rheumatoid arthritis and ankylosing spondylitis are the two commonest conditions.

(i) Rheumatoid Arthritis

This is a generalised disease, commoner in women, which may appear at any age, but usually in early middle life.

Pathology

Initially there are oedema and chronic inflammatory changes in the synovial membrane. As a result some effusion in the joints also occurs, though this is not marked. Later, this oedematous proliferative tissue spreads over the articular cartilage, or, in the case of tendon sheaths, on to the tendons themselves. The articular cartilage is slowly eroded, so that ultimately the joints are completely disorganised. Attrition rupture of tendons may also occur.

Clinical Features

The onset is insidious consisting of vague joint pains, often associated with some general malaise. This is followed by soft tissue swellings of joints—the smaller peripheral joints of the hands and feet being those

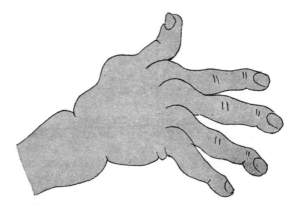

FIG. 141. Typical appearance of rheumatoid arthritis in the hand

affected first. Later it spreads centrally to the elbows, knees, shoulders, and hips, until ultimately in severe cases all joints throughout the body are involved. In addition, there is swelling of the synovial sheaths of tendons, and subcutaneous 'rheumatic' nodules appear beneath the skin. Progress tends to be variable, but eventually often when considerable damage has been done, the active disease becomes 'burnt out'. Nevertheless, in view of the mechanical damage inflicted upon individual joints, osteo-arthritic type of changes often supervene.

The appearance of the hands and feet are often typical. In the hands (Fig. 141) there will be marked swelling of the proximal inter-phalangeal and metacarpo-phalangeal joints. In advanced cases the latter become markedly ulnar deviated. The thumb tends to be flexed at the metacarpo-phalangeal and hyper-extended at its inter-phalangeal joints. The fingers tend to be hyper-extended at the proximal and flexed at the distal inter-phalangeal joint, the latter is thought to be due to fibrosis in the intrinsic muscles which causes shortening of their attachments. There is often associated swellings of the extensor and flexor tendon sheaths at the wrist, and owing to attrition rupture of the extensor tendons at this level, there may be inability to extend the metacarpo-phalangeal joints, particularly of the little and ring fingers.

In the feet, a gross hallux valgus deformity is common, with clawing of the lesser toes, owing to their being dorsally dislocated at the metatarso-phalangeal joints. As a result of this severe pain under the metatarsal heads may be troublesome.

As the disease progresses it may assume one of two forms—the 'wet' form, where gross oedema and effusions round joints are a feature, or a 'dry' form where joint swelling, while present, is not so marked as the bony destruction which accompanies it.

Investigations

The erythrocyte sedimentation rate is invariably raised. To some extent, the level provides an indication of the degree of activity in the disease. Specific investigations such as the latex fixation test will be positive in fully developed cases. Often some anaemia will be present.

Radiographs at first show osteoporosis, which will be patchy near involved joints. Later actual bone destruction may be seen.

Complications

Occasionally iritis and uveitis may occur in severe cases of rheumatoid arthritis leading to marked visual disturbances.

Psoriasis of the skin occasionally occurs along with a type of arthritis that resembles rheumatoid arthritis in some respects.

Treatment

Rheumatoid arthritis is a constitutional disease, the patient must therefore be kept generally as fit as possible by avoidance of fatigue and a good well-balanced diet.

Various medicaments may be employed. Salycilates of the soluble aspirin type are useful in controlling pain, and being safe can be used over long periods. Anti-rheumatic drugs such as phenylbutazone ('Butazolidin'), indomethacin ('Indocid') or mefanamic acid ('Ponstan') may help to control the disease during its more active phases, but as they may produce adverse side-effects, their use should be restricted to definite courses separated by intervals of several months. Steroids, in selected cases, produce a rapid remission of symptoms. But, as they have important side effects, their indiscriminate use is unwise.

Locally, in the acute phase, affected joints should be put at rest. Light plastic splints, worn especially at night, relieve pain and discourage the development of deformities. Later, when more quiescent, quite active exercises and heat may assist in preserving joint function. The occasional local injection of hydro-cortisone into individual joints may be useful in reducing pain and muscle spasm.

Surgery is indicated in carefully selected cases. This may be of three types—excision of proliferating synovial tissue (*synovectomy*) from either joints or tendon sheaths, arthrodesis of severely disorganised and painful joints, and repair of ruptured tendons.

In the *hand*, synovectomy of swollen metacarpo-phalangeal joints may limit progress of the disease, and help to control the ulnar deviation of the fingers. Excision of enlarged bursae and synovial tendon sheaths at the wrist are sometimes required. Excision of a deformed lower end of the ulna may be indicated, if extensor tendon rupture has occurred at this level.

In the *foot*, often most satisfactory results are obtained by surgical shoes made from a plaster-of-Paris cast of the deformed part and incorporating built-in arch supports. Marked hallux valgus may be treated by Keller's operation (p. 192), and clawing of the toes by excision of the metatarsal heads.

In the *knee*, if there is marked synovial swelling, but not much radiological evidence of bony damage, synovectomy may yield good lasting results. Failing this, arthrodesis is useful.

In the *hip*, in rheumatoid arthritis where joint damage elsewhere is almost always present, it is important to preserve movement, so that excision of the head and neck of the femur gives best results. In carefully selected cases, complete hip replacement (McKee-Farrar or Charnley) produce excellent results.

(ii) Ankylosing Spondylitis

This is a form of polyarthritis which differs markedly from rheumatoid arthritis, inasmuch as the disease commences centrally, in the spine, and from there spreads peripherally, and is almost confined to young adult males. The local pathological process is similar to rheumatoid arthritis except that, as the name implies, affected joints normally go on to bony fusion. Eventually the disease burns itself out.

Clinical Features

The onset is insidious, consisting of persistent low back pain with stiffness, worse on rising in the morning. It rapidly spreads upwards to affect the thoracic and cervical regions, and in severe cases may then spread outwards to involve the shoulder, hips, knees, and occasionally the tempero-mandibular joints. Because the costo-vertebral joints are closely linked with the spine, an early physical sign will be marked restriction in chest expansion. Later, in untreated cases, as the effect of gravity and muscle spasm, a severe rigid flexion deformity in the spine and neck may occur. Because, at this stage, breathing is entirely abdominal, the added restriction of a fixed flexion deformity adds to the risk of respiratory infection.

Investigations

The sedimentation rate will be raised, and provides a useful guide to the degree of activity present. Radiographically, the first changes will be seen in the sacroiliac joints, partly because these are the largest joints in the spine and therefore most easily visualised. The earliest signs are loss of the sharp bony outline. Later the joints become completely fused. New bone joining the vertebral bodies anteriorly may be seen radiologically later (Fig. 142(a)).

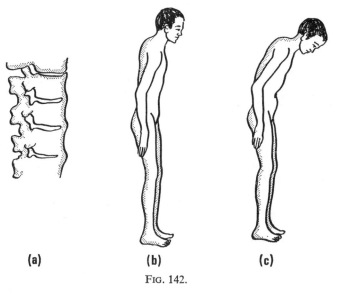

(a)   (b)   (c)

FIG. 142.

Treatment

In the early stages, exercises to preserve mobility and minimise the risk of deformity, coupled with courses of anti-rheumatic drugs such as phenyl-butazone may be sufficient. In severe progressive cases, a course of wide-field radiotherapy is sometimes useful in controlling pain and delaying the progress of the disease, but it carries a slight risk of leukaemia developing a few years later. A Plaster-of-Paris shell for recumbancy in bed at night, and also, if painful for use during the day, is advisable.

Flexion deformities may be prevented by supplying the patient with a spinal brace, and using a plaster-of-Paris shell for recumbency. When markedly present, and the disease is in a quiescent phase, a corrective osteotomy of the spine may be carried out (Fig. 142(b) and (c)).

Stiffness in the hips is best treated by excision of the head and neck of the femur.

(iii) Still's Disease

This is a rare type of poly-arthritis occurring in childhood, which may be identical to rheumatoid arthritis in adults. It tends to be virulent, often with low-grade pyrexia and anaemia, and affected joints tend to become ankylosed, so that gross crippling may result.

Treatment is along the lines already described.

C. OTHER JOINT CONDITIONS

Joints may be secondarily affected in several types of disease.

(i) Neuropathic (Charcot's) Joints

In generalised neurological diseases, where the normal protective pain sensation is lost, gross disorganisation of one or more major joints may complicate the picture.

The usual causal neurological lesions are either neuro-syphilis (tabes dorsalis) or syringomyelia. The actual changes as far as the joints are concerned is an exaggerated form of degenerative arthritis, due to the fact that owing to absent pain sensations, following minor trauma, all the normal protective responses do not take place. The usual complaints are of instability and swelling of the affected joint. Those most frequently involved are the knee, hip, ankle, shoulder, and elbow. Neuropathic joints in the upper limb are usually associated with syringomyelia.

Treatment is by supports where possible. Occasionally, particularly in the knee, arthrodesis is carried out.

(ii) Gout

This is an abnormality of purine metabolism, whereby the blood uric acid level is raised, and sodium biurate crystals are deposited in soft tissues, particularly near the smaller joints.

Clinical Features

The patient, usually middle-aged, complains of sudden pain in a joint, most commonly the metatarso-phalangeal joint of the big toe, and starting at night. On examination there is heat, redness, and swelling of the affected joint, which is acutely tender.

After a few days symptoms subside, to recur again, possibly in a different joint later. Owing to the deposition of urate crystals, rapid disorganisation of affected joints follows. Deposits also occur in soft tissues elsewhere—particularly the external ears, where they are known as *tophi*.

Treatment is medical, the affected joints being rested in the acute phase. Surgery is contra-indicated as it often provokes fresh attacks.

(iii) Haemophilia

This is a blood dyscrasia, in which owing to a deficiency in the clotting factor, a marked tendency to bleed from very minor trauma, or even spontaneously occurs. It is entirely restricted to males being transmitted by females. As a result haemarthroses often occur in major joints. If repeated several times, fibrosis of the joint lining and severe damage to the articular cartilage occurs, leading to marked stiffness and deformity.

Treatment

This is entirely conservative and consists of rest and protective splintage.

Owing to the risk of precipitating further bleeding, aspiration without special precautions should be avoided. Transfusions of fresh blood are often required to replace the deficient clotting factor.

(iv) Osteo-chondromatosis

This is an uncommon condition which may affect any joint, in which as a result of synovial proliferation leading to the formation of multiple cartilaginous loose bodies.

Treatment must consist not only in the removal of loose bodies, but also, to prevent their recurrence, a synovectomy must be carried out.

CHAPTER SIX

AFFECTIONS OF EPIPHYSES

Summary

A. Osteo-chondritis Juvenilis

   (i) Femoral Head (Perthes' Disease)
   (ii) Metatarsal Head (Freiberg's Disease)
   (iii) Vertebral Body Epiphyses (Scheuermann's Disease)
   (iv) Apophysitis of Tibial Tubercle (Osgood-Schlatter Disease)
   (v) Apophysitis of Calcaneum (Sever's Disease)
   (vi) Osteo-chondritis of Tarsal Navicular (Köhler's Disease)
   (vii) Osteo-chondritis of a Vertebral Body (Calvé's Disease)
   (viii) Avascular Necrosis of the Lunate (Kienböck's Disease)

B. Osteo-chondritis Dissecans

C. Slipped Upper Femoral Epiphysis

EPIPHYSES are the growing ends of long bones. At first the ends are covered by cartilage, but at specific intervals during the child's growth, depending upon the individual bone concerned, osseous epiphyseal centres appear within the cartilage. These grow until they entirely replace the cartilaginous ends, leaving only a line between them and the parent bone. This is the epiphyseal line, which remains until the age when bone growth is complete, at which time the cartilage disappears, and the epiphysis fuses with the parent bone.

At certain sites, several separate centres appear at the growing ends of bones. Those which do not directly articulate with the neighbouring bones are known as apophyses.

Congenital anomalies in epiphyseal structure which alter bone growth have already been discussed (p. 196).

A. OSTEO-CHONDRITIS JUVENILIS

Occasionally lesions occur in certain individual bone centres, in which a cycle of changes takes place. The actual cause appears to be interference in the normal blood supply to the affected part, but the reason why this should happen is unknown.

Pathology

The first change, as a result of interference with the blood supply, is that the avascular bone becomes relatively more dense than its neighbours, because there is no blood flow to wash out the calcium. Then the dead bone begins to crumble and collapse. Later new blood vessels grow into the area, so that its density disappears, and slowly the affected part returns to normal texture, but owing to the softening the shape is distorted.

In theory any portion of any growing bone may be affected, but in practice the condition is largely restricted to certain sites. These are:

Epiphyses:
    (i) The femoral head—Perthes' Disease.
    (ii) The head of the second or third metatarsal—Freiberg's Disease.
    (iii) The ring epiphysis of vertebral bodies—Scheuermann's Disease.

Apophyses:
    (i) For the tibial tubercle—Osgood-Schlatter Disease.
    (ii) For the calcaneum—Sever's Disease.

Main bony centres:
    (i) For the tarsal navicular—Köhler's Disease.
    (ii) For vertebral bodies—Calvé's Disease.
    (iii) (though not occurring in a growing bone). The carpal lunate—Kienböck's Disease.

(i) Osteo-chondritis of the Femoral Head—Perthes' Disease

This occurs in growing children between the ages of four and ten. Boys are affected more commonly than girls. It usually is limited to one side, but occasionally is bilateral, when the onset on one side often does not coincide with that of the other.

Clinical Features

There is an insidious onset of a limp with some pain, more marked when the child is tired, and increasing as the disease progresses. The pain is often referred down a nerve to the inner side of the knee, so that a child complaining of pain in the knee with a limp should always have its hips carefully examined.

On examination some limitation of movement, notably of abduction and internal rotation at the hip may be found, and in later cases, where collapse of the femoral head has already taken place, some true shortening will be present.

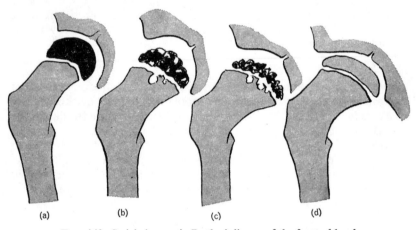

(a)   (b)   (c)   (d)

FIG. 143. Serial changes in Perthes' disease of the femoral head

Investigations will all be normal, except for the X-rays. These show a sequence of changes (Fig. 143). Firstly, there is uniform increase in density of the epiphysis, with some widening of the joint space. Secondly, the dense femoral head fragments, followed by apparent cavitation in the metaphyseal region. Thirdly, there is rarefaction of the fragmented epiphysis. Finally the epiphyseal bone texture returns to normal, though unless all stresses have been kept off the joint throughout, the shape will be flattened and the femoral neck widened.

The whole cycle often takes up to three years to complete.

Treatment

This consists of removing all upward weight-bearing thrusts through the hip until the cycle of changes is complete.

In practice the child is put to bed, with skin traction on the affected limb for a few weeks until the pain and spasm have subsided. After which provided that the child never puts the unprotected leg to the ground, ambulation is permitted using a pattern-ended caliper (Fig. 144).

Various operative procedures are being tried to encourage revascularisation of the femoral head including drilling and sub-trochanteric osteotomy, but results are still too early to assess.

Later, if osteo-arthritic changes develop in young adult life, arthrodesis of the hip gives good results.

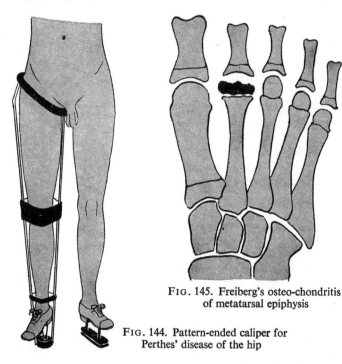

FIG. 145. Freiberg's osteo-chondritis of metatarsal epiphysis

FIG. 144. Pattern-ended caliper for Perthes' disease of the hip

(ii) Osteo-chondritis of a Metatarsal Head (Freiberg's Disease)

Either the second or third metatarsal head is affected, changes occurring in adolescence. Symptoms consist of pain at the base of the affected toe, and in the sole under the metatarsal head. Often symptoms are mild, and the condition is missed until osteo-arthritic changes lead to symptoms in adult life.

Radiological changes consist of flattening and fragmentation of the metatarsal head (Fig. 145).

Treatment

As this is not strictly a fully weight-bearing area, strict rest, as practised in Perthes' disease is not called for. The metatarsal head should be protected by the supply of a metatarsal arch support (Fig. 104, p. 154) worn in a firm shoe, and athletic activities should be curtailed.

If symptoms recur later in life, resection of the affected metatarsal head gives good results.

(iii) Osteo-chondritis of Vertebral Body Epiphyses (Scheuermann's Disease) (Adolescent Kyphosis)

In this type of osteo-chondritis, several vertebrae are affected, usually in the thoracic region. Onset is about the time of puberty, when the ring epiphyses which surround the margins of the vertebral bodies appear.

Complaints are of minor back-ache, and a 'round-shouldered' posture, so that attention is often drawn to the condition by the child's parents or schoolteacher.

Radiologically, fragmentation of the epiphyses can be seen (Fig. 146) with apparent narrowing of the disc spaces anteriorly. Later in life some wedging of the affected vertebrae may be seen.

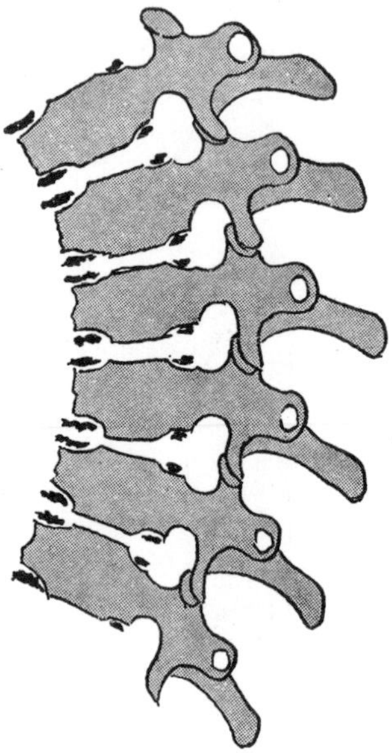

FIG. 146. Osteo-chondritis of vertebral body epiphyses (Scheuermann's disease)

Treatment

In most cases a course of exercises to encourage an upright posture suffice. Where the deformity is more marked, or symptoms troublesome, a supporting spinal brace may be prescribed. Very occasionally a period of recumbency on a plaster bed is necessary.

Many patients only get symptoms when osteo-arthritis changes have occurred in later life. In them, if exercises fail, a supporting corset usually succeeds in bringing symptoms under control.

(iv) Apophysitis of the Tibial Tubercle (Osgood–Schlatter Disease)

This is the commonest site for osteo-chondritis, and as the apophysis for the tibial tubercle takes no part in weight bearing, it is not at all serious. It usually occurs in boys between the ages of eleven and fourteen; both knees may be affected. Symptoms consist of pain over the tibial tubercle, with some enlargement and local tenderness.

Radiographs show fragmentation of the apophysis.

Treatment

This is purely symptomatic. In most cases avoidance of trauma while the tenderness is present is all that is required. When the pain is more severe, a short spell in a plaster-of-Paris cylinder allows the acute phase to subside.

(v) Apophysitis of the Calcaneum (Sever's Disease)

Painful heels in childhood are fairly common, the site of tenderness being just below the insertion of the tendo Achillis. The age of onset is between eight and twelve years. Radiographs at this time show the apophysis of the calcaneum to be dense and fragmented. There is some doubt, however, if this can be true apophysitis, because X-rays of normal calcanea at the same age also often show fragmentation.

Treatment

This is symptomatic. Usually mere avoidance of trauma, and wearing of comfortable shoes alone is required. If pain is more severe, a short spell in a below-knee walker plaster case will allow it to subside.

(vi) Osteo-chondritis of the Tarsal Navicular (Köhler's Disease)

This is an example of osteo-chondritis affecting the main bony nucleus. Onset is therefore earlier than when an epiphyseal centre is involved. It

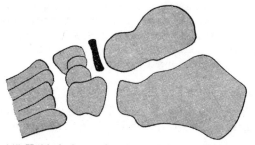

FIG. 147 Köhler's Osteo-chondritis of the Tarsal Navicular

usually occurs in children between the ages of three and five years. Clinically, the child complains of pain in the foot, and develops a limp, and on examination some tenderness along the inner side may be elicited.

Radiographs will show density and flattening of the navicular, so that it appears like a disc (Fig. 147). Later, even without treatment, the bone returns completely to its normal shape.

Treatment

While the pain is present, a below-knee walking plaster-of-Paris cast is worn, usually for two or three months.

(vii) Osteo-chondritis of a Vertebral Body (Calvé's Disease)

This, being osteo-chondritis in the main bony nucleus of a vertebra rather than an epiphysis, also occurs at an early age usually before seven years old. There is marked flattening of the affected vertebral body (Fig. 148), commonly in the lower thoracic region, and as a result a slight angular kyphosis, with prominence of one spinous process may be found. This, coupled with the complaint of back-ache in a young child, is suggestive of tuberculosis, though the radiograph, which shows a dense, very flat, vertebral body with normal disc spaces above and below is characteristic, and excludes any infective lesion.

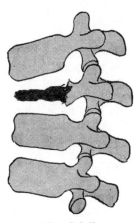

Treatment

This consists merely of keeping the child recumbent until the symptoms have subsided. In the course of time, when the cycle is completed, the vertebral body returns almost entirely to its normal shape.

FIG. 148. Calvé's osteo-chondritis of vertebral body

(viii) Avascular Necrosis of the Carpal Lunate (Kienböck's Disease)

While not a true example of osteo-chondritis, in as much as this condition occurs in adult bones, it is conveniently considered at this point, because the cycle the bone undergoes is the same as that occurring in osteo-chondritis. The probable cause of the avascular necrosis is some minor trauma which interrupted the blood flow to the lunate.

Clinical Features

Young adults are usually affected. The complaint being of increasing pain and stiffness in the wrist, with local tenderness in the region of the lunate.
Radiographs are characteristic. Initially they show density in the lunate, which later becomes distorted and fragmented.

Treatment

At an early stage, the hand should be immobilised in a scaphoid type of plaster cast, which is maintained for three to six months. Later, if symtoms persist, the lunate may be excised. Sometimes an acrylic prosthesis is used to replace the excised bone. If there are severe osteo-arthritic changes in the wrist, arthrodesis gives best results.

B. OSTEO-CHONDRITIS DISSECANS

This is a condition in which a segment of the articular surface area of a bone becomes separated as a result of local avascular necrosis, and after the overlying articular cartilage has given way, forms a loose body within the joint cavity (Fig. 149). It usually occurs towards the end of the growing period, the lower ends of the femur and humerus being most frequently affected. Less commonly it occurs in the body of the talus and the head of the femur.

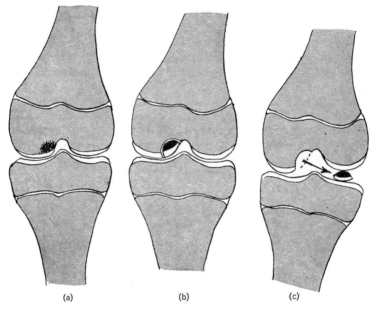

(a) (b) (c)

FIG. 149. The formation of loose body in osteo-chondritic dissecans

Clinical Features

The patient, usually a boy aged from twelve to eighteen, at first complains of discomfort and catching inside the joint, which cannot be accurately located. This continues for some time, slowly increasing, until the loose body separates. When this occurs there will be sudden locking, usually followed after a short time by equally sudden unlocking of the joint, which usually occurs spontaneously. This locking will recur, but in different positions, depending upon the position in which the loose body becomes jammed between the articular surfaces.

In the knee, in this respect, it differs from the locking due to a meniscus injury (p. 130), which always occurs in the same position with pain at the same site. Sometimes, in the knee, the loose body may be palpated beneath the surface if it comes to lie in the supra-patellar pouch.

In the elbow, because the weight of the forearm distracts the bone ends slightly, locking is less painful and more transient.

In the hip and ankle, loose bodies are less likely to cause locking as they only occasionally become jammed between the articular surfaces. Pain will be the predominant feature.

Radiographs are characteristic. At an early stage the separating portion will be seen as a dense fragment of the bone surrounded by a clear line. In the knee this is usually in the medial femoral condyle near the intercondylar notch, slightly behind the mid-line. In the elbow it usually arises from the capitulum of the humerus. If the separating fragment is large, particularly in the knee, it may break into two or more smaller pieces.

Treatment

If detected at an early stage, immobilisation of the joint in a plaster cast may allow the separating fragment to become revascularised and reattached.

Later, when the fragment has separated and formed loose bodies, exploration is indicated. Usually the loose bodies are removed, and the sharp edges of the cavity from which they came are pared down. Sometimes, in the knee, if seen when separation is just beginning to occur, or where the fragment is large and consists of one single loose body, it may be freshened and held in place by a metallic spike.

C. SLIPPED UPPER FEMORAL EPIPHYSIS (ADOLESCENT COXA VARA)

In this condition, the epiphysis for the femoral head becomes displaced. At first it moves backwards, throwing the limb into external rotation, subsequently it is shifted downwards, causing shortening of the limb.

Pathology

The cause is not known, but as it occurs most commonly just before growth ceases in individuals, usually overweight, due to endocrine imbalance, of the hypo-pituitary Frohlich's type. As epiphyses fuse a little earlier in girls than boys, females tend to be affected at a slightly earlier age. The displacement may be gradual or sudden, following an external rotational twist to the limb. The latter occurs rather more commonly in apparently normal individuals. Displacement of the epiphysis appears to stimulate the normal process of fusion to the shaft.

Occasionally, slipping of the upper femoral epiphysis complicates other general conditions of epiphyseal abnormality such as renal osteo-dystrophy (renal rickets, p. 290).

Why, in cases of generalised growth abnormality, the upper femoral epiphysis alone becomes displaced is not clear. It is possible that this is because it is the only major weight-bearing epiphysis which is constantly exposed to oblique mechanical stresses.

Clinical Features

The patient is usually aged between twelve and sixteen—twelve to fourteen in girls, and fourteen to sixteen in boys. Sometimes the slip is sudden, following a twisting injury, when the patient is in acute pain, unable to move the affected leg, which is held in a position of adduction and external rotation. More commonly, displacement is gradual, where the complaints are of a limp and pain—the latter may be referred to the knee. Examination of the affected joint shows at first an increase of external rotation, with a corresponding decrease in external rotation. Later abduction is also limited.

Often the condition is bilateral, though both hips may not be affected simultaneously. Slipping of the second hip may occur insidiously while the first is under treatment, so that both sides should be checked regularly.

Radiographs

Because the initial displacement is backwards, little abnormality may be visible in routine antero-posterior views. Early displacement is much more evident in good quality lateral films (Fig. 150(a) and (b)).

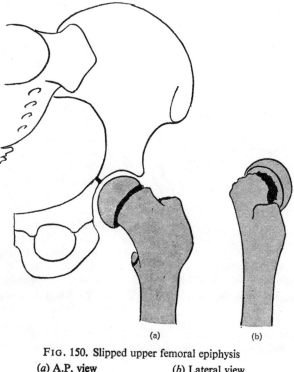

(a)   (b)

FIG. 150. Slipped upper femoral epiphysis
(*a*) A.P. view   (*b*) Lateral view

Complications

Avascular necrosis of the epiphysis may occur, usually following in judicious attempts at reduction, either by manipulation or open operation. This leads to collapse of the femoral head and very marked stiffness in the joint. Osteo-arthritis is an inevitable sequel to cases in which marked displacement persists.

Treatment

This can be considered under three headings:

(*a*) If gradual slipping is taking place, and has been detected early. In these cases, internal fixation by means of threaded pins (Crawford-Adams) will prevent further displacement and stimulate epiphyseal fusion in a still acceptable position (Fig. 150(c)).

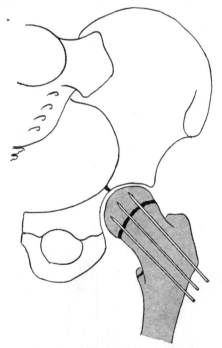

(*b*) If displacement is too great to accept. Here, there are two lines. Firstly, the patient may be kept on traction until the epiphysis has fused in the displaced position—usually four to six months, and then a corrective osteotomy at sub-trochanteric level is performed, thereby avoiding the risk of causing avascular necrosis of the femoral head. Secondly, open reduction may be carried out, followed by threaded pin fixation. This carries the risk of avascular necrosis. If, however, a wedge is removed from the femoral neck so that the soft tissue attachments of the displaced epiphysis (which carry its blood supply) are not stretched, this is decreased.

(*c*) If there has been sudden complete displacement, and the head is obviously mobile, very gentle manipulative reduction may be employed, followed by fixation using threaded pins.

FIG. 150(c). Threaded pin fixation for slipped upper femoral epiphysis

In later cases, corrective sub-trochanteric osteotomy gives best results, and often helps even when osteo-arthritic changes are beginning to appear.

CHAPTER SEVEN

AFFECTIONS OF SOFT TISSUES

Summary

A. Tendon Sheaths

  (i) Tenovaginitis

    (*a*) Trigger Finger
    (*b*) De Quervain's Disease
    (*c*) Carpal Tunnel Syndrome

  (ii) Traumatic Tenosynovitis
  (iii) Infective Tenosynovitis

    (*a*) Acute Suppurative Tenosynovitis
    (*b*) Chronic Infective Tenosynovitis

B. Musculo-tendinous Lesions

  (i) Tennis Elbow
  (ii) Golfer's Elbow
  (iii) Plantar Fasciitis

C. Painful Shoulders

  (i) Supra-spinatus Tendinitis
  (ii) Frozen Shoulder
  (iii) Bicipital Tendinitis
  (iv) Calcification in the Supra-spinatus

D. Bursitis

  (i) Pre-patellar Bursitis
  (ii) Tibial Tubercle Bursitis
  (iii) Olecranon Bursitis
  (iv) Ischial Bursitis
  (v) Gluteal Bursitis

E. Ganglion

F. Dupuytren's Contracture

G. Hand Infections

  (i) Nail-bed (Paronychia)
  (ii) Pulp-space
  (iii) Deep Fascial Space

A. TENDON SHEATHS

(i) Tenovaginitis

Tendon sheaths are liable to mild chronic inflammatory thickening known as tenovaginitis. The entrance is usually the site where thickening is most marked. The cause is usually unknown, occasionally repeated mild traumatic irritation may be a factor, as sometimes the patient can recall doing some repetitive movement involving some strain a short time prior to the onset of symptoms. Rarely, particularly if more than one site is affected simultaneously, tenovaginitis may be the first sign of rheumatoid arthritis.

The tendon sheaths in the hand is one of the commonest sites, either where the finger or thumb flexors enter their synovial sheaths at the level of the metacarpal head (*trigger finger*), or where the abductor pollicis longus and extensor pollicis brevis cross the lower end of the radius at the wrist (*de Quervain's disease*).

(a) *Trigger Finger*
Clinical Features

The patient becomes gradually aware of a clicking sensation at the base of the affected digit, with some local tenderness. It is usually worse in the morning. Gradually this increases, until eventually on flexion the finger snaps suddenly shut, and then only with difficulty can it be extended, which it also does with a snap. When this occurs very definite thickening can be felt opposite the entrance to the sheath.

The thumb is also frequently affected (*trigger thumb*).

Occasionally a similar condition is met with in infants, usually affecting a thumb. It is most often discovered by accident, when the mother notices an inability to extend the inter-phalangeal joint.

Treatment

In Adults. At the early stages before true 'triggering' has begun, an injection of hydrocortisone suspension into the tendon sheath may abort the process and afford lasting relief. When, however, it has reached the stage of really catching, surgical division of the constricting sheath is a simple operation and gives very satisfactory results.

In Infants, division of the tight sheath using a small tenotomy knife is usually possible, thus avoiding an incision.

(b) *Tenovaginitis of the Radial Styloid* (*de Quervain's Disease*)

The patient complains of pain at the base of the thumb, localised to the radial styloid, worse when the thumb is extended. The range of movement is not sufficient to result in clicking, but a definite localised tendon lump can be felt corresponding to the tendon sheath.

Treatment

In early stages, a hydrocortisone injection may relieve symptoms, but usually division of the tendon sheath gives good results. The terminal branch of the radial nerve lies nearby, and therefore should be looked for and avoided.

(c) *Carpal Tunnel Syndrome*

In this condition, the median nerve is compressed by the transverse carpal ligament as it passes from the forearm into the hand. The cause may be obvious, such as osteo-arthritis of the wrist, a mal-united fracture of the lower radius, or external pressure from a ganglion in the region. Usually, however, no direct cause is found, in which case the nerve is irritated by a thickened transverse carpal ligament, presumably subject to the same changes as occur in tenovaginitis.

Clinical Features

Middle-aged women are usually affected. The complaint is of pain, numbness, and parasthaesia in the palmar aspect of the thumb, index, middle, and radial side of the ring fingers corresponding to the area supplied by the median nerve. Symptoms tend to be worse at night. In several cases, the thenar muscles are somewhat wasted.

The condition must be differentiated from the nerve root irritation secondary to cervical spondylosis (p. 180).

Treatment

If symptoms arise at the wrist, a plaster-of-Paris palmar slab worn at night will give considerable relief, and this affords not only useful palliative treatment, but also a simple diagnostic test. Cure can only be obtained by open division of the transverse carpal ligament, which is a quite minor operative procedure.

(ii) Traumatic Tenosynovitis

This consists of an inflammatory reaction around a tendon as a result of repetitive movements which impose a strain upon it, particularly if performed by an individual who does not normally use that muscle group very much. This usually affects the deep extensors of the wrist on the radial side, though it may occur over the front of the ankle, or in the tendo Achillis.

Clinical Features

The patient is usually a fit young adult who has been doing something involving excessive use of the affected part. Pain on movement is the complaint, and on examination, in addition to slight local tenderness, some different swelling and characteristic crepitus can be found.

Treatment

The part is put at rest in a plaster-of-Paris cast for about three weeks, after which cautious mobilisation is commenced.

(iii) Infective Tenosynovitis

This may be acute or chronic, depending upon the causative organism. Tendon sheaths in the hand and wrist are those most commonly affected, and, because any residual disability in the hand is serious, they are the most important.

(a) *Acute Suppurative Tenosynovitis*

Organisms enter the tendon sheath either as a result of a direct puncture wound, or, more commonly due to deeper extension of a sub-cutaneous digital infection. Once infection is in the tendon sheath it rapidly spreads through its length. In the index, middle, and ring fingers this extends from the distal inter-phalangeal joint to the metacarpal head, but in the fifth finger, the sheath is continuous with the common flexor sheath at the wrist. In the thumb, the tendon sheath also extends to wrist level (Fig. 61, p. 101).

Clinical Features

There is severe pain in the affected finger which will be hot and swollen on the palmar aspect throughout its length. It will be held semi-flexed, and any attempt, active, or passive is acutely painful. Some general constitutional upset is also present.

Treatment

Early drainage is required. An incision is made into the distended tendon sheath proximally and distally and the pus evacuated. It is then frequently irrigated with the appropriate anti-biotic solution for two or three days. Systematic anti-biotics are given in addition. As soon as the acute phase has subsided, cautious gentle mobilisation is commenced to minimise adhesion formation between the tendon and its sheath. In the case of the fifth finger and thumb, an incision proximally near the wrist is often also required.

(b) *Chronic Infective Tenosynovitis* (*Compound Palmar Ganglion*)

This is usually, but not invariably, due to the tubercle bacillus. In the latter case infection is blood borne, as with other tuberculous lesions. The flexor tendon sheaths at the wrist are those usually affected.

Pathology

The tendon sheaths are oedematous and thickened, containing a considerable quantity of fluid, in which are characteristic fibrinous 'melon seed' bodies. If the cause is tuberculous, characteristic giant cells will be present in the thickened sheaths, and acid-fast bacilli can often be cultured.

Clinical Features

There is a gradual onset of swelling and discomfort usually in the palm of the hand, which spreads beneath the transverse carpal ligament to reach the flexor aspect of the lower forearm. As this increases, fluctuation between the palmar and forearm swellings may be obtained. The fingers become progressively stiffer.

Treatment

When the tuberculous nature of the lesion has been proved a full course of streptomycin, isomazid, and P.A.S. (para-amino salycilic acid) is commenced and continued for six months. In the early stages, the wrist may be rested in a plaster cast, but where swelling is marked, surgical excision of the entire affected tendon sheaths, followed by cautious gentle mobilisation, gives best results.

B. MUSCULO-TENDINOUS LESIONS

At certain sites, areas of marked local tenderness occur, the cause of which is often speculative. They are usually located at points near where a muscle is attached to bone, and there may be a history suggesting some mild repetitive trauma as the original cause, possibly due to rupture of some muscle fibres. As with tenovaginitis, occasionally these painful areas are a prelude to the appearance of typical rheumatoid arthritis.

The commonest regions affected are the elbow either near the lateral or medial epicondyles, or in the sole of the foot near the heel.

(i) 'Tennis Elbow'

This is used to describe a point of tenderness near the lateral epicondyle of the elbow. It often appears spontaneously but may be caused by some twisting movement of the forearm as the joint is extended, such as when serving at tennis—hence the name.

Clinical Features

The onset may be sudden or gradual, usually middle-aged adults are affected. On examination there is a point of marked local tenderness usually just in front of the lateral epicondyle. Extending the elbow with the wrist pronated (which increases the tension on the common extensor origin which is at the lateral epicondyle) acutely exacerbates the pain—this is known as Mills' manoeuvre. Raising the arm with the wrist pronated, as when holding a cup of tea, is also often very painful.

The condition must be differentiated from pain referred down the outer side of the arm, as in cases of cervical spondylosis.

If no treatment is given, eventually, after about two years, spontaneous remission occurs.

Radiographs are usually normal. Very occasionally a small shadow of new bone can be seen in the region of the tender spot.

Treatment

In most cases an injection of hydrocortisone suspension exactly into the tender spot affords rapid relief. If this fails, a period of rest with the elbow flexed to a right angle in a plaster-of-Paris case for four to six weeks should be tried. Sharp extension of the elbow with the wrist flexed and pronated under general anaesthetic, presumably by completing a partial tear of the muscle fibres, is often very helpful. Should all else fail, very occasionally, open stripping of the common extensor attachment to the lateral epicondyle is required.

(ii) 'Golfer's Elbow'

This uncommon lesion is the exact opposite to 'Tennis Elbow' consisting of acute pain over the medial epicondyle, aggravated by extension of the elbow with the forearm supinated. Golf, in fact, is rarely associated with the condition.

Treatment consists of local hydrocortisone injections into the tender spot. Surgery is rarely required.

(iii) Plantar Fasciitis

This is a condition usually occurring in middle-aged men consisting of pain under the heel. Onset is insidious, and the cause is unknown. Sometimes it may be bilateral. The tender spot is most commonly just anterior to where the weight is taken, and corresponds to the site of attachment of the plantar fascia to the calcaneum. The pain is aggravated by weight-bearing, and, provided no pressure reaches the tender spot, is often almost absent at rest.

Radiographs are usually normal. Occasionally a spur is seen pointing forwards at the site of attachment of the plantar fascia, but these also occur in symptomless heels, so their significance is doubtful.

Treatment

Spontaneous remission usually occurs after one to two years, so that often if a soft padded longitudinal arch support is fitted which extends across the full width of the shoe, and thereby distributes weight away from the tender area, marked relief is obtained. A local injection of hydrocortisone into the tender spot sometimes gives dramatic relief.

C. PAINFUL SHOULDERS

Because man uses his forelimbs mainly for lifting, the weight of his arm exerts a distracting force on the shoulder. This anatomically is a ball-and-socket joint, but, to permit a wide range of movement, the socket is very shallow. Stability is largely dependent upon the muscles and tendons which surround it, particularly upon the muscles which are inserted into the tuberosities of the humerus, which together ensheath the humeral head, forming the '*rotator cuff*'. The supra-spinatus segment of the cuff is that subjected to the greatest mechanical strains.

(i) Supra-spinatus Tendinitis

The subacromial bursa lies beneath the acromion and deltoid, and thereby allows the supra-spinatus tendon beneath it to glide freely. If either as a result of minor injury, or inflammatory change the bursa is not functioning

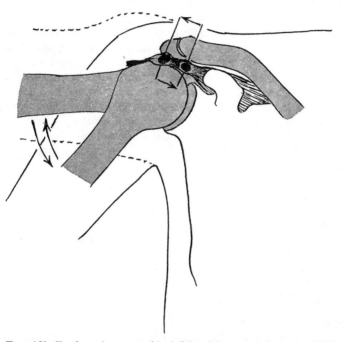

FIG. 151. To show the cause of 'painful arc' in supra-spinatus tendinitis

normally, when the arm is abducted the great tuberosity will make contact with the acromion and be painful. When the arm is elevated beyond this point so that the bones are no longer touching, pain will be relieved. This is known as a '*painful arc*' (Fig. 151). It may also occur with incomplete rupture of the supra-spinatus tendon.

Clinical Features

There will be pain in the shoulder, with some limitation of movement in all directions, but the 'painful arc' will be the most striking feature. On palpation, a tender spot will be found just below the tip of the acromion, but no other abnormality will be found. Radiograph and blood investigations will be within normal limits.

Treatment

If there is one local tender spot, an injection of hydrocortisone suspension often gives great relief. In addition, local heat and gentle exercises should be prescribed.

(ii) 'Frozen Shoulder' (Periarthritis)

This is a condition in which all shoulder movements are restricted and painful.

Clinical Features

The patient is usually a middle-aged adult. Males and females are equally affected. The onset may be associated with some minor direct injury to the shoulder, but usually is gradual. Often, if there has been some injury to the lower arm, such as a Colles' fracture of the wrist (p. 83), the shoulder becomes stiff and painful unless active movements are practised regularly. On examination very little actual gleno-humeral movement is possible, most movement of the upper limb being due to the scapula altering its position on the chest wall. Diffuse tenderness will be present, more marked anteriorly. There is no local heat or wasting of muscles. Investigations are normal.

Diagnosis

Pain from true frozen shoulder must be differentiated from that referred from the cervical spine. In fact, often referred pain from the fifth and sixth cervical roots cause spasm of the rotator cuff musculature, which in turn leads to a degree of periarthritis, so that both conditions may be present together. If cervical spondylosis is a factor in causing symptoms, neck movements, especially extension, will be restricted and painful. X-rays of the cervical spine will show changes.

Treatment

Preventative. When an arm injury is present, or pain due to cervical spondylosis is referred to the shoulder region, swinging exercises for the shoulder must be regularly carried out.

Curative. When true shoulder stiffness is present, in the acute phase, the arm should be rested in a sling for a few days. As soon as the pain starts to diminish exercises should commence, preceded by heat to reduce the muscle spasm. At first these should consist of gentle swinging within the limits of pain, the tempo being stepped up gradually as pain diminishes.

(iii) Bicipital Tendinitis

The tendon of the long head of the biceps crosses through the shoulder joint, to pass via the bicipital groove into the upper arm. As age increases degenerative changes take place in the tendon which becomes frayed, and may rupture.

Clinical Features

There will be tenderness over the humeral head, which will be aggravated if supination of the forearm is attempted against resistance with the elbow flexed.

Rupture of the long head of the biceps may occur after an interval, or, in an elderly man, may take place quite spontaneously, often with very little pain, so that sometimes it is discovered by chance. The appearance is characteristic as, when the elbow is flexed, a marked bridge will appear over the lower part of the biceps muscle (Fig. 152).

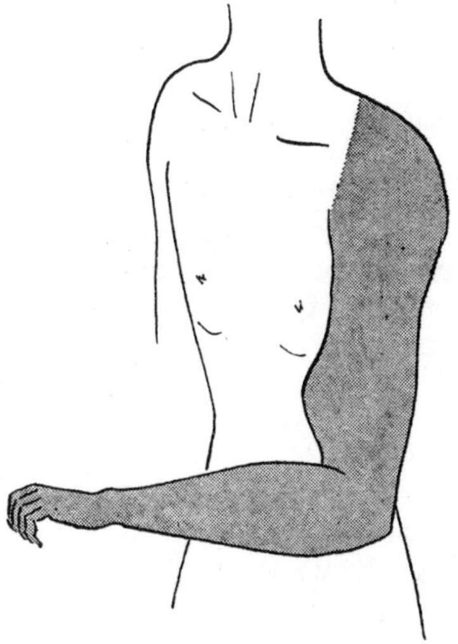

Treatment

When in the painful phase, the arm should be rested. Heat may reduce some of the pain. If rupture of the long head has occurred, this should be accepted as surgical repair would be extremely difficult and there is no real disability.

FIG. 152. Clinical appearance of ruptured long head of biceps muscle

(iv) Calcification in the Supra-spinatus

Occasionally calcareous deposits form within the supra-spinatus tendon near its insertion into the great tuberosity. The cause is unknown, it may sometimes result from a partial rupture of the tendon.

Clinical Features

Middle-aged adults are affected. Often the calcification is discovered as an indefinite shadow on routine X-ray for what appears to be a mild frozen shoulder, but usually the condition presents as very acute pain in the shoulder of rapid onset, and examination will show some heat and swelling in addition to very marked tenderness and pain on any movement.

The acute pain usually settles after a few days, and it is thought that it occurs when a pre-existing calcareous deposit ruptures through its lining, thereby causing an acute foreign body reaction with hyperaemia.

Radiographs in the acutely painful phase show a vague shadow over the humeral head. When this subsides, the size is much reduced, and the outline more definite.

Treatment

In the acutely painful stage, local exploration and curettage of the calcareous deposit, which looks like rather coarse toothpaste, gives rapid relief. When in a quiescent phase heat and exercises only are required.

D. BURSITIS

Bursae occur wherever the skin across a prominent bone is subject to pressure. Such points include the patella (pre-patellar bursa), the tibial tubercle, the olecranon, the ischial tuberosity, and the great trochanter. In addition a bursa is liable to form over any bone which is abnormally prominent—that occurring in hallux valgus (p. 192) being the commonest example.

(i) Pre-Patellar Bursitis ('Housemaid's Knee')

This results from pressure on the knee when kneeling on a hard surface, leaning forwards. Clinically there will be a tender fluctuant swelling over the knee-cap, which may be warm and hot. Occasionally it results from a simple sharp blow on the knee-cap, in which case the swelling will be due to blood within the bursa.

Treatment

The swelling should be aspirated, after which a pressure bandage is applied. Occasionally open drainage may be necessary, in which case, if possible, the incision should not correspond exactly to where pressure is normally taken, as the scar is liable to be adherent. If recurrence rapidly follows, excision of the bursa may be necessary.

(ii) Tibial Tubercle Bursitis ('Parson's Knee')

This follows pressure from kneeling upright on a hard surface. It is more liable to occur if the tibial tubercle is unduly prominent, as may follow apophysitis (Osgood–Schlatter's disease, p. 241).

Treatment is as for pre-patellar bursitis.

(iii) Olecranon Bursitis ('Student's Elbow')

This, occurs following prolonged pressure of the point of the elbow on a hard surface, such as a desk or table. Treatment is as described.

(iv) Ischial Bursitis ('Weaver's Bottom')

Pain over the ischial tuberosity may follow prolonged sitting on a hard surface. It is not as common as bursae elsewhere, and as it is situated at a deeper level, aspiration is not so easy.

Treatment

This, therefore, normally consists of avoiding the position which caused the pressure.

(v) Gluteal Bursitis

Bursae at this site—where the gluteus maximus crosses the tip of the great trochanter are sometimes of traumatic origin, but really correspond in the hip to the subacromial bursa in the shoulder. Occasionally they may contain a calcareous deposit.

Infection, including tuberculosis, sometimes occurs at this site.

Treatment

Where a swelling is present excision is required, including often some bone from the great trochanter.

E. GANGLION

This is a tense cystic swelling arising from synovial tissue. The wall is composed of synovial cells, and it contains a clear jelly-like material, which is secreted by the surrounding cells. It probably arises as a result of local hesination of synovial tissue through its fibrous lining, whereupon enlargement takes place.

Common sites for ganglion are in the hand and foot. In the hand they are most frequently seen over the dorsum of the wrist, at the bases of digits on their palmar aspects, and near the lower ends of the radius and ulnar anteriorly. In the foot they usually occur over the dorsum of the tarsus but may be found in the toes. Cystic degeneration in the semilunar cartilages of the knee have the same histological appearances (p. 131).

Treatment

If ganglion are causing no symptoms, no treatment is required, and occasionally spontaneous disappearance occurs. Sometimes they can be dispersed by a direct blow, which ruptures the cyst and always disperses its contents, but recurrence is common. Sometimes they may be dispersed by puncture with a hypodermic needle, followed by the injection of 'Hyalase'. The only certain way to prevent recurrence, however, is by careful excision of the whole swelling, including the pedicle to which it is attached to the deeper tissues.

F. DUPUYTREN'S CONTRACTURE

This is a condition affecting the palmar aponeurosis, in which thickening, fibrosis, and contracture occurs. The cause is not known. It is commoner in men than women, and heredity appears to play a part. Trauma may also be a factor, however, because while frequently bilateral, the dominant hand is usually the worst affected, and occasionally it occurs in some minor pre-existing scar.

Clinical Features

Dupuytren's contracture usually starts in middle age, in the ulnar side of the palm. The first sign is a small hard subcutaneous nodule near the base of the ring finger, in the distal palmar skin crease. As it extends, the skin gets increasingly puckered and adherent, and thick subcutaneous strands can be felt roughly corresponding to the bands of the palmar aponeurosis as it splits on either side of the base of the finger. Eventually the metacarpo-phalangeal and proximal inter-phalangeal joints become flexed down (Fig. 153). The distal joint remaining unaffected. Both the ring and little fingers may be affected equally, but usually one is more involved than the other. In time, in severe cases, the condition spreads to affect the middle finger, and later the index. Occasionally nodules occur early at the base of the thumb and index fingers.

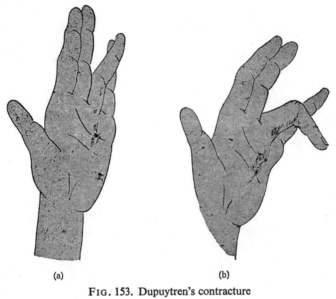

(a)   (b)

FIG. 153. Dupuytren's contracture
(a) Early   (b) Later

Often in persons prone to Dupuytren's contracture, there is subcutaneous thickening over the dorsum of the proximal inter-phalangeal joints, known as 'knuckle-pads'.

Rarely, the plantar fascia of the foot is also affected.

Treatment

Surgery affords the only cure. This must involve excision of all the affected palmar fascia. Skin flaps can usually be raised by careful dissection but incisions must nowhere cross the skin creases (Fig. 154). The digital nerves, as they pass through the tight bands, must be carefully dissected free.

Where there is a gross flexion deformity of one digit, permanent contracture of the joint capsules may have also occurred, in which case a stiff finger will remain, and amputation gives the best result.

Post-operatively, when sound skin healing has been achieved, a prolonged course of mobilising exercises and careful stretching is required to restore full movement.

G. HAND INFECTIONS

The hand, being the part that is most subjected to injury in humans, is peculiarly liable to infection as a result of some minor trauma such as a prick. In addition, because of its specialised nature, hand infections differ from the boils and abscesses met elsewhere in the body. Tendon sheath infections have already been discussed (p. 250). Other sites requiring consideration include infection of the nail beds, the finger pulp, and the potential deep spaces in the palm, situated between the metacarpals and interostei on one side and the flexor tendons on the other. The causative organism is usually the staphylococcus pyogenes.

(i) Nail-bed Infections (Paronychia)

This usually begins as an infection of one side of the base of the nail fold, from whence it spreads across beneath the nail fold, and sometimes also under the base of the nail itself.

Treatment

In early cases, local incision, rest, and the administration of wide spectrum anti-biotics may abort the attack. If the infection has spread, however, the nail fold must be raised by incisions on either side, and often the base of the nail itself must also be removed (Fig. 155).

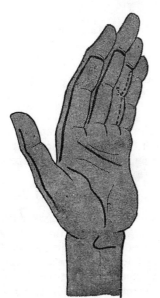

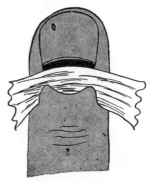

FIG. 155. Incision of base of nail in treatment of paronychia

FIG. 154. Lines of incisions for use in hand surgery

(ii) Pulp Space (Fig. 156(*a*))

These infections follow direct innoculation of organisms, as by a prick. Because the finger pulp has many strands connecting the skin to the bone, spread of pus does not at first occur and considerable tension is built up. This, coupled with the normal large number of sensory nerve endings in a finger-tip, makes a pulp space infection extremely painful. In addition, unless the tension is rapidly relieved, osteomyelitis of the terminal phalanx may follow.

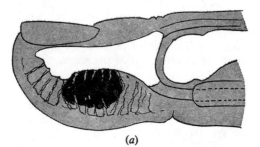

(*a*)

(*b*)

FIG. 156. Pulp space finger infection

(*a*) Site of the pus formation
(*b*) Incision for drainage

Treatment

In early stages it may be possible to abort the attack by anti-biotics. If the abscess is obviously pointing beneath the surface a direct incision is required, but otherwise, to avoid scarring on the sensitive finger-tip, a lateral incision should be made (Fig. 156(*b*)).

(iii) Deep Fascial Space Infections

Because the potential space deep to the flexor tendons is divided into two parts by a vertical septum running along the length of the third metacarpal, there are two 'spaces'—that on the radial side being known as the *thenar space*, and that on the ulnar side being known as the *mid-palmar space* (Fig. 157). The spaces extend superficially to the webs between the fingers. Infection may reach these spaces by direct innoculation as a result of

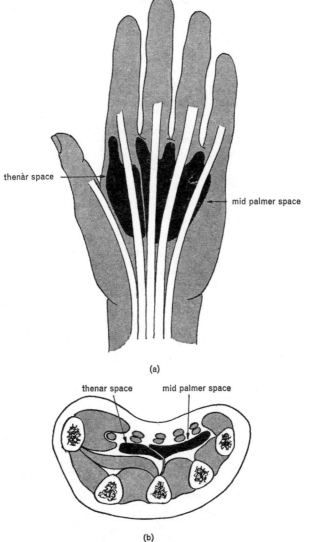

(a)

(b)

FIG. 157. Anatomy of the palmar fascial spaces
(a) AP view   (b) In section

wounds at the bases of the digits, or as a result of spread proximally from more superficial lesions.

Clinical Features

Because the infection is deep, pointing of the pus is unlikely to occur until late. There will be marked pain and swelling in the palm of the hand, with stiffness of the fingers, and oedema of the dorsum of the hand. In thenar space infections there will be swelling in the web of the thumb.

Treatment

Drainage is by incisions into the web spaces of either between the thumb and index finger in the case of thenar space infections, or between the middle and ring or ring and little fingers (depending upon where the swelling is most marked) in the case of the mid-palmar space.

CHAPTER EIGHT

NEOPLASMS

Summary

I. BONE NEOPLASMS

A. Benign Growths

(i) Osteoma
(ii) Osteochondroma
(iii) Chondroma
(iv) Other Bony Growths

Osteoid Osteoma
Simple Bone Cyst
Aneurysmal Bone Cyst

B. Intermediate Growths

Osteoclastoma (Giant-cell Tumour of Bone)

C. Malignant Growths

Primary Malignant Bone Growths

(i) *Osteogenic Sarcoma*
(ii) *Par-osteal Sarcoma*
(iii) *Chondro Sarcoma*
(iv) *Malignant Endothelioma* (*Ewing's Tumour*)
(v) *Multiple Myeloma*

Solitary Plasmocytoma

Secondary (Carcinomata)

II. SOFT-TISSUE NEOPLASMS

A. Fatty Tissue

Lipoma
Liposarcoma

B. Musculo-Tendinous Tissue

Rhabdomyosarcoma

C. Synovial Tissue

Giant-cell Tumours
Maligant Synovioma

D. Nervous Tissue

Neurofibroma
Neurofibromatosis (Von Recklinghausen's Disease)

E. Blood-vessels (Haemangioma)

Capillary
Cavernous

NEW growths of the locomotor system may be conveniently subdivided into those affecting bone, and those affecting soft tissues. In each case they may be benign or malignant.

I. NEOPLASMS OF BONE

Neoplasms originating in bone may arise from osseous tissue, or from cartilaginous cells associated with the epiphyses, or from the blood forming elements contained in red bone marrow.

A. BENIGN BONE GROWTHS

(i) Osteoma

This is a benign growth arising from true osseous tissue. It is comparatively uncommon and usually occurs in the membranous bones of the skull, where it produces a smooth swelling, which is dense and hard (*'ivory osteoma'*). Sometimes it causes symptoms from pressure, in which case simple excision is indicated.

(ii) Osteochondroma (Exostosis)

This growth, which is not a true neoplasm, arises from rests of epiphyseal cells which are left upon the bone surface, and as a result they continue to grow until the parent epiphysis fuses. With growth of the bone,

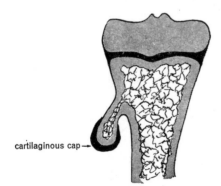

the epiphyseal line moves away from the growth, and the exostosis itself forms a pedicle and points away from the end of the bone from which it originated. If examined before bone growth has ceased, a cartilaginous cap will be found covering the surface farthest away from the pedicle (Fig. 158).

Osteochondromata may be solitary or multiple. In the latter case the condition is known as *diaphysial aclasis* already described (p. 196).

cartilaginous cap →

FIG. 158. Exostosis

Complications

Apart from pressure affects upon neighbouring structures such as peripheral nerves, malignant change occasionally occurs, so that the onset of pain or enlargement of the lump after skeletal growth has ceased should be viewed with suspicion.

Treatment

Simple excision of the exostosis through its pedicle gives good results where the bony mass is causing symptoms, or is increasing in size, but often no treatment beyond observation at intervals is necessary.

(iii) Chondroma

This is a true benign tumour composed of cartilaga cells arising in a bone, though it originates from the epiphyseal cartilage. It is commonest in the 'short' long bones of the hands where it tends to occupy the medullary cavity and is known as an *enchondroma*. Occasionally they occur in flat bones, such as the ilium, where they bulge outwards forming an *ecchondroma*.

Clinically enchondromata in the bones of the hand often pass unnoticed until, after the cortex has been eroded, spontaneous fracture occurs. A chondroma in a major long bone may present as a chondrosarcoma, having undergone malignant change.

Multiple cartilaginous cell rests may occur in the major long bones, leading to widening of the bone ends and marked shortening. This condition, known as *dyschondroplasia* or Ollier's Disease has been already described (p. 197).

Treatment

Where an enchondroma is causing cortical erosion of a major bone, it should be curetted out, and the cavity filled with cancellous bone chips, but usually no treatment is required. Spontaneous fracture appears to stimulate new bone formation, so that often not only does union occur, but regression of the tumour follows.

(iv) Other Bony Growths

Osteoid Osteoma

This consists of a small nidus of osteoid tissue which forms, usually in the cortex of a bone, and is surrounded by an area of sclerosis. It can occur anywhere in the skeleton, but is commonest in the major long bones. It usually occurs in young adults, and the main clinical feature is a deep boring pain, worse at night. Radiologically there is a fusiform area of sclerosis with a small central area of rarefaction. Treatment consists of excision of the rarefied area.

Simple Bone Cyst

This is a condition usually found in children or adolescents, in which a cyst forms in the substance of a bone, often the humerus, and sometimes the lunate or scaphoid. It is often discovered by chance, but in major long bones may lead to a pathological fracture.

Treatment is only required if the cyst is large and may lead to fracture, in which case it should be curetted and the cavity filled with bone chips.

Aneurysmal Bone Cyst

This is an uncommon condition in which a cystic state develops within a bone due to blood vessels contained within. Its actual nature remains obscure.

Treatment consists of curettage.

B. INTERMEDIATE GROWTHS

Osteoclastoma (Giant-cell Tumour of Bone)

This is a tumour situated near the ends of major long bones. It is commonest in the tibia or femur near the knee, but is also frequently seen in the

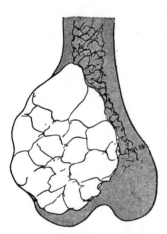

lower end of the radius. The age of onset is usually early adult life, after the epiphysis has fused.

Histologically there is a spindle-cell stroma, in which characteristic multi-nucleate giant cells similar to osteoclasts are to be found.

Clinically, there is a firm smooth swelling arising from the end of a major long bone. Some aching pain may be present and has drawn attention to it. Owing to the thin bony lining, firm palpation may elicit typical 'egg-shell crackling' as the bone is crushed, though this should never deliberately be sought. Local recurrence after removal is common, and sometimes blood-borne metastatic spread to the lungs occurs.

FIG. 159. Osteoclastoma of bone

Radiologically, a thin walled translucent mass will be seen arising in the bone near its end, and traversing the site of the epiphyseal line. Fine bony trabeculae may often be seen crossing the translucent area (Fig. 159).

Differential Diagnosis

Osteoclastoma may be confused with a Brodies' abscess (p. 212), localised fibrous displasia of bone (p. 295) and a metastatic deposit from a neoplasm elsewhere.

Treatment

Where possible, local excision of the affected bone should be carried out. Often, however, this is not practicable, in which case the lesion should be completely curetted out, after which a course of super-voltage radiotherapy is given.

C. MALIGANT TUMOURS OF BONE

These may be primary, arising in the bone itself, or be secondary metastatic deposits from a malignant growth elsewhere.

Primary Malignant Bone Growths

(i) *Osteogenic Sarcoma*

This is the commonest primary malignant new growth of bone. It is called osteogenic because it has its origin from bone cells, not because the tumour forms bone, though, in fact, this is often also the case. It is commonest near the growing ends of major long bones, especially the lower femur and upper tibia. It most frequently occurs in older children when bone growth is most active, and young adults. There may be an association with previous trauma, which could explain its common site near the knee. In adult life osteogenic sarcoma is rare, it may appear in bones affected by Paget's disease (p. 294) probably because normal osseous metabolism is already disturbed in these cases.

Histologically, the tumour consists of masses of poorly differentiated round or spindle cells and often with elements of connective tissue such as cartilaginous, myxomatous, or fibrous tissue, interspersed with sinusoidal blood spaces. While eventually the growth bursts through the periosteal lining and spreads into the surrounding soft tissues, the epiphyseal line appears to provide a barrier to its spread within the bone.

Clinical Features

The presenting symptom is *pain* of a constant aching nature, and this in turn will draw attention to bony *swelling*. Later, as the growth progresses, and destruction of normal bone increases, pathological fracture may occur. Metastatic spread is by the blood-stream, and often takes place at quite an early stage. The lungs are mainly affected, but spread to other bones sometimes follows.

The prognosis is poor, only about one quarter of the cases survive, but where evidence of spread has not appeared within about three years of the onset of symptoms, the likelihood of later recurrence diminishes.

Investigations

Radiography. There will be signs of bony destruction within the diaphysis, with erosion of the bony cortex, at first restricted to one side. Evidence that the periosteum has been raised is visible at the margins of the lesion, where new bone forms beneath it (*Codman's Triangle*). The quantity of new bone visible outside the bone cortex in the main bulk of the tumour will vary according to whether the growth is predominantly osteolytic (bone destructive) or osteoblastic (bone forming). Sometimes characteristic strands of bone radiating vertically from the cortex ('*sun-ray spicules*') may be seen (Fig. 160).

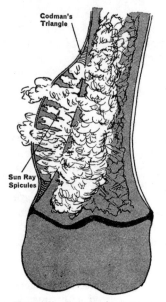

Codman's
Triangle

Sun Ray
Spicules

FIG. 160. Osteogenic sarcoma

Radiographs of the chest should be taken at the same time, for evidence of pulmonary metastases.

Blood investigations will be required to exclude an infective lesion of bone.

A *biopsy* will be needed to confirm the nature of the condition, before radical treatment is carried out.

Differential Diagnosis

Infective lesions of bone, particularly those due to syphilis or the colityphoid group of organisms, may produce a clinical and radiological picture similar to osteogenic sarcoma. Other bony neoplasms such as chondrosarcoma, osteoclastoma, or a carcinomatous metastatic deposit in bone from a primary growth elsewhere may require to be excluded.

Treatment

Radical amputation through a site well clear of the tumour, and including the whole of the bone affected is the accepted method of treatment. This implies disarticulation through the hip for growths of the lower femur, or above-knee amputation for upper tibial tumours.

With the advent of super voltage radiotherapy, the tumour cells, if subjected to heavy dosage, may be killed, and survivors so isolated by fibrous tissue that their activity is curtailed. Many surgeons therefore advocate a preliminary course of radiotherapy, with amputation four to six months later. The advantages of this method are, firstly, that by then small pulmonary metastases present, but not detectable, when the tumour was first diagnosed, will then be manifest and a dying patient saved from a serious and mutilating operation. Secondly, the danger of releasing neoplastic cells into the blood-stream at the time of operation is markedly reduced.

(ii) Parosteal Sarcoma

This is a more benign, but less common form of bony new growth arising from sub-periosteal bone. The clinical features are identical with true osteogenic sarcoma, and treatment is also the same, but the prognosis is very much better.

(iii) Chondrosarcoma

These are on the whole rather less malignant than osteogenic sarcomata. They occur in middle adult life, arising either from the ends of the major long bones, or from flat bones such as the pelvis or scapula. Chondrosarcoma may arise in a preceding enchondroma such as in dyschondroplasia (Ollier's disease) or appear in previously normal bone.

Clinically there will be pain and swelling over the affected bone, and the latter may grow to a large size. Radiologically the bone end will be enlarged and can be seen to be filled by a blotchy destructive tumour.

Treatment

In most instances radical amputation is indicated. Occasionally, if the tumour is slow growing and affects the end of a major long bone, notably the humerus, the whole bone end may be excised, including attached muscle insertions, and replaced by a metallic prosthesis.

(iv) Malignant Endothelioma (Ewing's Tumour)

This is a highly malignant neoplasm which appears to originate from endothelial tissue within the marrow of long bones, most commonly the femur or humerus. As it penetrates the cortex, it produces a fusiform swelling in the midshaft of the affected bone in which, as a result of attempts by the periosteum to lay down new bone as it is raised by the tumour, layers of osseous tissue are formed. This gives a characteristic 'onion peel' appearance on X-ray (Fig. 161).

Clinically the tumour usually occurs in childhood causing pain and a bony swelling together with some local heat, which may be suggestive of low grade osteomyelitis. Spread is through the bloodstream and pulmonary metastases therefore rapidly follow.

Treatment

Preliminary biopsy is necessary to confirm the diagnosis.

Amputation was the treatment of choice, but with the advent of super-voltage radiotherapy, and because pulmonary spread may have already occurred when the patient is first seen, even though the deposits cannot then be detected, high dosage radiation is being employed with increasing frequency.

(v) Multiple Myeloma

This is a malignant neoplastic condition affecting plasma cells, and therefore rapidly attacks red bone marrow generally. The outcome is uniformly fatal,

FIG. 161. Malignant endothelioma (Ewing's tumour)

though the rate of progress varies considerably, and with suitable treatment advancement can be delayed, sometimes for several years.

Pathologically, there are multiple foci of bone destruction, often appearing as small punched-out areas, involving chiefly ribs, sternum, vertebrae, skull and pelvis, together with the upper ends of the femora and humeri. Histologically, sheets of cells resembling rather immature plasma cells will be seen.

Clinical Features

The patient is usually a middle-aged adult, and pain is the common presenting symptom. This may be a widespread ache due to the multiple bony deposits, or of sudden onset at a single site, due to pathological fracture, particularly in the back as a result of a vertebral body collapse. Later, bone marrow destruction leads to severe anaemia.

Investigations

Apart from the punched out areas visible on X-rays of bones containing red bone marrow, routine *urine* testing usually reveals a protein-like substance which appears as a cloud when the urine is heated, but re-dissolves when boiling point is reached, this is due to the presence of a proteose known as *Bence–Jones Protein.*

Blood tests will show a great increase in the erythrocyte sedimentation rate, and raising of the serum globulin level. *Sternal puncture*, to obtain a specimen of red bone marrow, will reveal a great increase in plasma-cells.

Treatment

Local lesions respond well to radiotherapy, which, in the case of pathological fractures of long bones, may be combined with internal fixation. General measures to prolong life consist of the use of cytotoxic drugs of the nitrogen mustard group, and the administration of steroids in large doses. Anaemia may be controlled by repeated blood transfusions.

Solitary Plasmocytoma

This is an atypical variety of myelomatosis, in which a single tumour arises in a bone from the plasma cells in its marrow. After an interval it usually spreads, and the picture changes to typical multiple myelomatosis. Occasionally, if seen early, arrest of the disease may be achieved by an intensive local course of radiotherapy.

Secondary (Metastatic) Malignant Bone Growths

Metastatic bony deposits arising from primary carcinomata at certain sites are common. Usually they occur late in the disease, but occasionally, notably in carcinoma of the bronchus, a pathological fracture through a secondary deposit may be the first sign of the disease. Bony metastases are always blood borne, and therefore occur most frequently where there is red bone marrow—in the vertebrae, pelvis, and the upper ends of femur or humerus. The common primary sites are the *breast, bronchus, prostate, kidney*, and *thyroid*.

Treatment

In the large majority of cases, this is palliative, and consists of local radiotherapy and internal fixation of pathological fractures where possible. Sometimes, when X-ray suggests that a fracture is imminent, prophylactic intra-medullary nailing of the femur or humerus may be employed. The general spread of the disease may be slowed down by the use of cytotaxic drugs or steroids. Where the primary is in the *breast*, adrenalectomy and even removal of the pituitary (hypophysectomy) may delay progress markedly. A solitary deposit from a hypernephroma may occur, and occasionally removal of both the kidney and the metastasis may arrest the disease process.

II. SOFT TISSUE NEOPLASMS

On the whole, in the locomotor system, serious neoplastic disease is less common in soft tissues than in bone.

A. FATTY TISSUE

Lipoma

These are common tumours occurring anywhere in the body where fatty tissue is present. Subcutaneously they form a soft, painless, lobulated nodule. Deeper, they are not so easy to recognise. Very occasionally mild pressure effects results in neighbouring structures. Treatment is only indicated where symptoms warrant surgical interference.

Liposarcoma

Very rarely maligant change occurs, in which case an indurated lump is found. Diagnosis depends upon biopsy results, and very wide excision is indicated.

B. MUSCULO-TENDINOUS TISSUE

True tumours of muscles and tendons are rare. Very occasionally malignant new growths of striated muscle—*rhabdomyosarcoma*—occurs. It is highly malignant and metastasises rapidly.

C. SYNOVIAL TISSUE

New growths arising from synovial tissue may affect either joints or tendon sheaths.

(i) Giant-cell Tumours (Benign Synovioma)

These are benign tumours arising from the synovial tissue in tendon sheaths, usually in the hand, especially the flexor sheaths of the fingers. They cause local lobulated swellings often confused with ganglion.

Treatment consists of complete excision. Occasionally they may recur.

(ii) Malignant Synovioma

This is a highly maligant growth arising from synovium, usually a major joint, such as the knee. It produces a firm fleshy mass which spreads widely in the surrounding soft tissues, but rarely invades the bone. It is composed of ill-developed fusiform cells, among which are spaces suggesting attempts to form synovial cavities.

Clinically indurated swelling of the affected joint lining is the main feature. Movements often being largely unaffected. Pulmonary metastases occur early. The prognosis is bad.

Treatment

Where possible amputation offers the best hope of a cure, but if this is difficult wide excision coupled with large doses of radiotherapy is indicated.

D. NERVOUS TISSUE

Neurofibroma

This is a tumour arising from the fibrous tissue lining of the peripheral nerve. It forms a firm swelling, but usually the conduction of the nerve from which it arises is not affected unless it is situated in an area where space is restricted.

Neurofibromatosis (Von Recklinghausen's Disease) (not to be confused with Von Recklinghausen's parathyroid hypertrophy, p. 293).

This is a condition in which there are multiple neurophomata on nerves, associated with patches of skin pigmentation. It appears to be familial, and the skin pigmentation is often first seen in early childhood. It appears to be associated with severe scoliosis (p. 182) and a neurofibroma causes pressure on the spinal cord or canda equina where it may cause cord or nerve root irritation.

Treatment

Excision of individual neurofibromata which are causing symptoms should be undertaken. No treatment for the overlying general disease is possible.

E. BLOOD VESSELS (HAEMANGIOMA)

These are probably not true tumours, but a local congenital anomaly of small blood vessels, which become overgrown. There are two types, depending upon the size of the blood spaces.

Capillary

In which there are a mass of fine vessels, which if near the skin, causes a red blotchy area.

Cavernous

In which large blood cavities are present, causing a swelling. In these cases, firm pressure over the mass causes it to disappear and it then fills up again when the pressure is released.

Because diffuse haemangiomas cause an increase in local blood flow, if they are situated in a growing limb, epiphyseal overgrowth may occur.

Treatment

This may be difficult. Capillary haemangiomata may require excision, if on the skin surface, from the cosmetic angle. Cavernous haemangiomata may sometimes also be excised, but this may be difficult, when injection of some sclerosing fluid or local radiotherapy may arrest their progress.

Overgrowth in a limb may sometimes require epiphyseal arrest by stapling (Fig. 162).

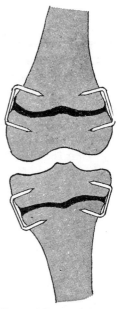

FIG. 162. Epiphyseal stapling to retard bone growth

CHAPTER NINE

NEUROLOGICAL DISORDERS

Summary

A. Spastic Paralysis

  General Remarks

   (i) Infantile Cerebral Palsy
   (ii) Spinal Cord Lesions

B. Flaccid Paralysis

   (i) Anterior Poliomyelitis
   (ii) Obstetric Paralysis

      (*a*) The Upper-arm Type (Erb–Duchenne)
      (*b*) The Lower-arm Type (Klumpke)
      (*c*) Whole-arm Type

NEUROLOGICAL cases requiring orthopaedic assistance are those primarily affecting the locomotor system. In the majority, permanent changes have already occurred and the main problems are preservation of function, and the correction of deformities.

Paralysis is of two types—Spastic, where the causative lesion is in the central nervous system, either the brain or spinal cord, or Flaccid, where the lesion is either in the peripheral nerves, nerve roots as the fibres leave the cord, or the anterior horn cells in the cord, where the peripheral nerve cells have their origin.

A. SPASTIC PARALYSIS

This may present in four ways:

(i) Paraplegia—in which as a result of some lesion in the spinal cord, both lower limbs are affected, the extent of involvement depending upon the level.

(ii) Quadriplegia—in which all four limbs are involved, due to some lesion either high in the cervical part of the cord, or at the base of the brain (also called Tetraplegia).

(iii) Hemiplegia—where two limbs on one side are affected. This is usually due to some condition in the central cortex, when there may be facial weakness on the opposite side.

(iv) Monoplegia—where a single limb is involved. This also is usually due to a lesion in the brain itself, but can result from a condition affecting only half the spinal cord, though this is uncommon.

Where the lesion affects the spinal cord, there will be both sensory and motor loss, whereas in brain lesions, as the sensory and motor areas are unrelated, there is motor paralysis alone.

Where there is spastic paralysis, all muscle groups in the involved area are in a state of spasm, with the result that deformities are liable to occur, because in opposing muscle groups, one side is more powerful. Thus, in the foot, the calf muscles are stronger than the anterior tibial, so that an equinus deformity occurs. In the knee, the hamstrings have a greater mechanical advantage over the quadriceps, with the result that flexion deformities are common. In the hip, the adductors and flexors are more powerful than the abductor–extensor group. Similarly in the wrist and hand, flexion deformities occur, the elbow loses full extension, and the shoulder is held to the side.

(i) Infantile Cerebral Palsy

This condition is due to brain damage occurring either in late pregnancy, due to some maternal upset, or as a result of a prolonged and difficult labour, and may follow a forceps delivery. Cerebral anoxia is a feature, and it is commoner in premature infants whose skulls are soft. Post-natally, severe jaundice is a frequent case, and in later childhood it may follow encephalitis.

The clinial appearances will depend upon the site of damage. If the cerebral hemispheres are affected, spastic paralysis will occur, which may be monoplegia, hemiplegia, or quadriplegia, depending upon the extent of damage. If the brain stem is the site of injury, generalised involuntary movements (*athetosis*) will be the main feature. Some degree of mental retardation is also often present, but, particularly in the severely athetoid child, this may be less than would appear, because incoordination may make speech difficult.

Clinical Features

Attempts at sitting, standing, and walking will be delayed, and at the time when a normal baby would be taking these steps, incoordination of movement, with rigidity in the affected limbs becomes obvious. In the hemiplegic case, the limbs on the affected side assume a characteristic appearance. In the arm, the elbow is flexed, and the wrist flexed and pronated. In the leg, the foot is in rigid equinus, with the knee flexed, and the hip both flexed and adducted. The face is often rather expressionless. Where both legs are involved, walking may be almost impossible because hip adductor spasm causes the legs to cross each other ('scissors gait').

In the athetoid case, constant involuntary movements affecting the face, and all four limbs increase when any purposeful action is undertaken, so that in severe cases the patient is almost unable to do anything for himself.

Treatment

As the brain damage is permanent, a cure is impossible, and treatment must be directed towards assisting the patient to overcome his disabilities by re-education and careful training. In the severely affected spastic child of fairly normal intelligence, institutional management may give the best results.

Orthopaedic treatment is concerned with individual lesions, and it is important to bear in mind that as the basic cause is central, in the brain, therefore, too enthusiastic correction of individual deformities may upset the overall pattern, and thereby impair rather than improve function. Corrective splints and supporting appliances to control deformities are useful in selected cases.

Surgery is sometimes of value. Procedures include fusion of joints, operations on tendons and division of nerves.

Arthrodesis is of most value in the wrist, where, by correcting an extreme flexion deformity, the patient may be able to use his fingers to better advantage. To test the functional advantage to be gained, before operating a trial should be made with the wrist in a plaster case applied in the desired position when the patient is anaesthetised.

Tendon operations are of value where there is deformity, particularly in the foot, where elongation of the tendo-Achillis is useful in controlling severe equinus deformity, though overlengthening must be avoided as a fixed 'calcaneus' represents a severe disability.

In the hip, subcutaneous tenotomy of the adductor magnus is a minor procedure which may help to diminish adductor spasm. Division of the hamstrings near their insertion into the tibia assists in overcoming a flexion deformity in the knee. Flexion deformity at the hip may be improved by release of the muscles originating from the iliac spines.

Neurectomy is occasionally of value in releasing adductor spasm in the hip. The obturator nerve is divided intra-pelvically, as it enters the obturator foramen.

Severe athetoid movement may be diminished by destruction of the globus pallidus, usually by alcohol injection under direct vision.

(ii) Spinal Cord Lesions

Apart from traumatic paraplegia (p. 34), and external pressure on the cord such as may follow tuberculous disease of the spine (p. 216). Various conditions affecting the spinal cord itself occur, in which spastic paralysis in some form may be a feature. These include *syringomyelia*, in which there is cystic degeneration in the cord, *disseminated sclerosis*, in which there is demyelination of plaques of nervous tissue in both cord and brain, *tumours of the cord*, such as neurinomas and meningiomas, and *Friedreich's atakia*, where there is sclerosis of the posterior columns. The latter may present with either scoliosis or pes cavus, before any other neurological signs are apparent.

B. FLACCID PARALYSIS

Apart from direct injury, peripheral nerves are subject to trauma and pressure at certain sites. When the nerves themselves are affected, there will be sensory disturbances as well as motor weakness, whereas if the anterior horn cells in the cord are site of the lesion, motor paralysis alone will occur.

(i) Anterior Poliomyelitis (Infantile Paralysis)

This is an infection of the anterior horn cells caused by a filter passing virus. Since the advent of active immunisation, it is less common than it was, but it is still a common cause of permanent motor paralysis, and epidemic outbreaks may occur. They are rather more common in later summer or autumn than in winter months.

The virus enters through the naso-pharynx and spreads via the bloodstream to the anterior horn cells in the central nervous system. Initially there is round-cell infiltration of the affected areas, with local oedema, thereby impairing the function of the horn cells. Later this may resolve, with recovery of function, or the anterior horn cells may be destroyed leading to permanent paralysis.

In certain cases, the central nervous system is unaffected, the patient having merely a 'summer cold'. During the stage of active infection, the virus is excreted in the sputum and faeces, so that the non-paralytic case is liable to be a carrier of the disease.

As the name 'Infantile Paralysis' implies, the age of onset is often early childhood, though in recent years it has become more common in later childhood and early adult life.

Clinical Features

The course of the disease may be subdivided into three phases:

(i) The stage of activity, corresponding to when the virus is producing active infective changes.

(ii) The stage of recovery, when the anterior horn cells affected by the virus, but which survived its attack, resume function.

(iii) The stage of residual paralysis, which is permanent, and is linked with the number of anterior horn cells that have been actually destroyed by the disease.

Stage of Activity

At the commencement, there is fever, lassitude, and general malaise. Rapidly, when the virus reaches the central nervous system, these are followed by signs of meningeal irritation, consisting of headaches, neck rigidity, and vomiting. Paralysis, if it is going to occur, appears a day or two later. At this stage it is often widespread, and is associated with pain in the muscles which may be severe. The extent of the initial paralysis is almost always considerably more extensive than that which will be present finally. It may be virtually complete affecting both respiratory and pharyngeal musculature, which will require urgent treatment.

During this phase, which lasts about six weeks, when the virus itself is actively present in the body, the patient may transmit the infection, and should be isolated.

Stage of Recovery

This stage may last up to two years. During this time, firstly, nervous activity returns to the anterior horn cells which were involved in the disease process, but survived it. This is followed by recovery of function in the nerve fibres, and then return of muscle tone. Some improvement also results from hypertrophy of any muscle fibres which retained their nerve supply.

If, however, after about three months, no return of function in a completely paralysed muscle group can be found, the likelihood of any useful recovery is remote.

Stage of Residual Paralysis

This is the final state, resulting from the actual destruction of the anterior horn cells in the cord. Accurate assessment cannot be made under two years, but a fairly clear idea of what will be the final pattern of residual paralysis may be obtained a few months after the onset of the disease.

Investigations

During the stage of activity, *lumbar puncture* will reveal an increased cell content in the cerebro-spinal fluid.

The extent of initial paralysis, and its subsequent progress should be assessed regularly by a *muscle chart*. The power in each muscle is tested, and placed in one of six categories:

0 = No contraction whatever.
1 = Flicker of contracture insufficient to produce any movement.
2 = Active movement possible, if the effects of gravity are eliminated.
3 = Active movement possible against gravity.
4 = Active movement weaker than normal, though possible against resistance.
5 = Normal muscle power.

Complications

Apart from chest problems occurring when there is respiratory paralysis, three main complications are found in poliomyelitis.

(i) *Vascular*. Widespread muscle paralysis leads to vascular stagnation, which causes coldness, cyanosis, and chilblains, which may be very troublesome.

(ii) *Shortening*. Because of the diminished blood flow in the affected limbs, epiphyseal growth is liable to be retarded in young children.

(iii) *Deformity*. Where there is partial paralysis, the less affected muscles will tend to pull the part in the line of their fibres. At first this can be passively overcome, but eventually joint fibrosis follows, and a fixed deformity occurs.

Treatment

This will depend upon the stage of the disease.

The Stage of Activity. The patient should be isolated and put to rest in bed. Paralysed limbs should be supported in the position of function. In the arm, the shoulder should be held slightly abducted, by resting the limb on a pillow, the elbow should be maintained semiflexed, and the wrist slightly dorsiflexed on a light cock-up splint, made either of plastic or plaster-of-Paris. In the leg, a light splint is employed to hold the knee in about 160° of extension, and the ankle and foot at a right angle to the tibia in both planes. To prevent rotation of the hip, a cross bar is incorporated which keeps the foot pointing upwards.

Once every twenty-four hours all affected joints are gently passively put through a full range of movement. If muscle pain is troublesome, local heat is often helpful.

Respiratory paralysis calls for the use of an artificial respirator, together with measures to reduce and clear bronchial secretions.

The Stage of Recovery. When this stage is reached, treatment is concerned with aiding recovery in partially paralysed muscles, and preventing the onset of deformity due to muscle imbalance. Exercises, gradually increasing in tempo for the muscles where some residual power remains forms the most important aspect in management. Together with this,

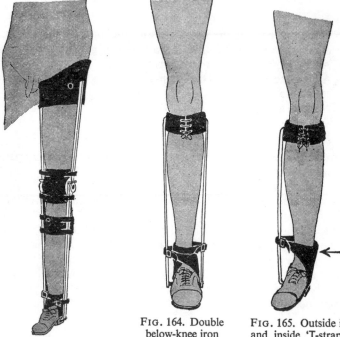

FIG. 163. Full length caliper with knee lock

FIG. 164. Double below-knee iron

FIG. 165. Outside iron, and inside 'T-strap' to control valgus deformity of ankle

splintage is employed to protect the weaker muscle groups, thereby per venting the development of a fixed deformity.

If possible, the patient should become ambulant, if necessary by the use of walking aids. To observe progress accurately muscle power should be charted at regular intervals.

Stage of Residual Paralysis. Where no further recovery in muscle power can be expected, treatment is directed towards minimising the permanent disability. Where there is marked residual paralysis, general measures include rehabilitation to enable the patient to become as independent as possible, and training for a suitable form of employment.

Local treatment may be conservative or operative.

Conservative. This may take two forms—the use of appliances to replace paralysed muscles externally, and the gradual correction of fixed deformities—of which the former has the widest application.

Paralysis of trunk musculature may necessitate the use of a corset or spinal brace.

In the *upper limb*, if the elbow flexors are paralysed, a moulded leather or plastic splint to hold the joint at a right angle will improve function, as will a splint to support the wrist, if this is weak. Where opposition of the thumb is lost, a light splint holding the metacarpal forward is also useful.

In the *lower limb* splints and appliances are used extensively as stability of the leg is essential for walking. Where there is extensive paralysis a full length caliper is employed (Fig. 163) this should be fitted with knee locks, so that the joint can be passively flexed when sitting. If the hip muscles are also paralysed the caliper may be attached to a firm pelvic hand by a hinge which also incorporates a locking device. Where there is extensive below-knee paralysis, a double below-knee iron is used (Fig. 164) in which a spring is fitted to allow a certain degree of elasticity between the foot and the leg. Where the invertors are weak, causing marked valgus deviation of the foot on weight bearing, a single outside iron with a 'T-strap' to hold the foot against it may be employed (Fig. 165). Similarly, peroneal weakness leading to an inversion deformity of the foot may be controlled by an inside iron and outside 'T-strap'. If dorsiflexion of the foot alone is weak, then a toe raising spring may be used (Fig. 166).

FIG. 166. Toe raising
spring

Correction deformities at certain sites may be carried out gradually. The two commonest being fixed flexion at the knee, which is achieved by the use of a plaster-of-Paris cylinder from which serial wedges are cut opposite the joint, and at the hip, where a flexion deformity may be overcome by flexing the patient in a plaster cast holding the trunk and normal hip in full flexion. The deformed leg is then held in a Thomas's splint which is slowly lowered, thereby extending the hip.

Operative. Surgical measures may be directed towards muscles and tendons or bones and joints. Operations upon *muscles* may take two forms: *tendon transplantation*, in which the tendinous insertion of a functioning muscle, which may therefore be causing a deformity, is transferred and made to act in the direction of its paralysed opponent. Where there is a fixed deformity, the muscle attachments may be divided so that the deformity can be overcome. This is most frequently employed to correct flexion contractures of the hip and knee.

In the upper limb, tendon transplantation is useful at several sites. Thus a paralysed biceps muscle may be replaced by detaching the origin of part of pectoralis major from the chest wall, and reinserting it into the upper arm. Wrist and finger extensors may be replaced by attaching the tendon of flexor carpi ulnaris into the extensor digitorum and pollicis longus tendons, and flexor carpi radialis into extensor carpi radialis and abductor pollicis longus tendons. Opposition of the thumb may be restored by transplanting the flexor digitorum sublimis of the ring finger to the head of the first metacarpal.

In the lower limb, hip abduction and extension may be improved by transplantation of the ilio-psoas tendon into the great trochanter of the femur (an operation most commonly employed in children with spina bifida, p. 198). Quadriceps power may be improved if the biceps femoris or semitendinosus tendons are re-inserted into the patella. Eversion or inversion deformities at the ankle may be corrected by transplanting either a peroneal tendon to the inner side or tibialis anterior or posterior to the outer side of the tarsus respectively. Claw toes may be corrected by transplanting the long flexor tendons to the extensor expansion on the dorsum, and a dropped first metatarsal, by moving the extensor hallucis tendon to the metatarsal neck.

Operations upon *bones* usually take the form of *arthrodesis*, where, by stiffening one flail or deformed joint, the remaining muscle power may be

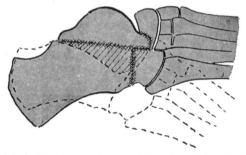

FIG. 167. Triple fusion of tarsus to correct foot drop deformity (Lambrinudi's operation)—cf. Fig. 126

employed to utilise some other part of the limb. Thus, in the *upper limb*, fusion of a flail shoulder enables the scapulo-thoracic group of muscles to move the arm as a whole. In the hand, fusion of the first metacarpal to the second in a position of opposition, employing a bone graft to bridge the gap, is useful where sublimis tendon transplant is not possible. In the *lower limb*, arthrodesis of the hip and knee should be approached with caution as it may merely add to the strains imposed upon weakened muscles elsewhere. Fixation of a paralysed ankle in slight equinus may be very useful where there is widespread muscle weakness in the leg, because where weight is put upon the limb, the knee is locked in an extended position. Instability of the foot may be corrected by triple arthrodesis of the tarsus (p. 206). If there is weakness of dorsiflexion causing a drop foot deformity, this may be corrected at the same time by cutting a wedge from the lower surface of the talus, having its base anteriorly, so that where the foot is horizontal, the ankle articular surface is in a plantar-flexed position (Fig. 167). Sometimes arthrodesis of both the ankle and sub-astragaloid joints (pantalar arthrodesis) may be useful in providing stability where the foot is completely flail. Claw toes may be corrected by inter-phalangeal arthrodesis instead of the flexor to extensor tendon transplant already described.

Arthrodesis of joints should not be employed until growth is reaching maturity, or premature fusion of epiphyses will be caused.

Treatment of Complications

Apart from deformities resulting from muscle imbalance, whose management has already been discussed, the two main complications occurring in poliomyelitis are those due to vascular stagnation, which affect mainly the lower limbs, and shortening due to impaired epiphyseal growth when the disease occurs in young children.

If chilblains and other affects of vascular stagnation are troublesome, occasionally lumbar sympathectomy is carried out where the lower limbs are affected. Also, in the legs, discrepancy in length may, in selected cases, be corrected by arresting epiphyseal growth on the normal side by placing metal staples across the epiphyseal cartilages of the lower femur and upper tibia (Fig. 162).

(ii) Obstetric Paralysis

This is an injury to the brachial plexus occurring in infants during a difficult delivery. It is due to traction forces applied to the baby's head when it is laterally flexed to one side, with the shoulder on the opposite side pulled downwards. It is slightly commoner in breach presentations.

There are three types, depending on the portion of plexus affected.

(a) The Upper-arm Type (Erb–Duchenne)

In this, the commonest form, the injury affects the upper trunk of the plexus, composed of the fifth and sixth cervical nerve roots. This causes the shoulder to be adducted, and the arm internally rotated, with the elbow extended, and the wrist pronated and flexed. It is usually fairly obvious as soon as the baby is born.

(b) The Lower-arm Type (Klumpke)

This form is less common, and is due to an abduction strain, pulling the lower trunk of the plexus—composed of the eighth cervical and first thoracic nerve roots. This causes a claw-hand deformity due to paralysis of the intrinsic muscles. The sympathetic trunk is also often affected causing narrowing of the pupil and recession of the eyeball on the affected side

(Horner's syndrome). This is less likely to be noted at birth, and may only be observed when the baby fails to grasp objects normally.

(c) *Whole-arm Type*

In this, the whole brachial plexus is injured, leaving a completely flaccid anaesthetic arm.

Treatment

Some spontaneous recovery usually occurs.

Initially, therefore, the baby's arm should be held, by bandaging the limb to a light metal splint in the opposite position to that in which it tends to lie. In the upper arm type this means maintaining the shoulder abducted, with the arm externally rotated, and the elbow flexed. The wrist is extended and spinated. When the baby is washed, and the splint removed, the mother should put the limb through a full range of passive movement.

Later, reconstructive operations such as arthrodesis of the shoulder or tendon transplant of the pectoralis major to replace the biceps, and of wrist flexors to replace the extensors, may be useful.

GENERALISED DISORDERS OF BONE

Summary

APART from developmental abnormalities in bone structure, such as achondroplasia (p. 196), and widespread skeletal neoplastic deposits, whether primary, as in multiple myelomatosis, or secondary, generalised disorders of bone fall into three categories:

(i) Metabolic, including those due to deficiency diseases.
(ii) Hormonal.
(iii) Conditions of unknown aetiology.

I. METABOLIC DISORDERS OF BONE

A. DEFICIENCY DISEASES

Deficient intake of vitamins C and D can upset the normal formation of bone.

(i) Vitamin C—Scurvy

Deficient intake of Vitamin C (Ascorbic Acid) causes bleeding. This affects all parts, notably the oral mucous membrane and skin, but in young children massive haematomas are common, and occasionally epiphyseal separation occurs. Following both these, extensive ossification occurs due to periosteal stripping. Ascorbic Acid is a water soluble vitamin contained in fresh fruit, vegetables, and lean meat. It is rapidly destroyed by heat. Infantile scurvy (*Barlow's disease*) may occur in babies who are artificially fed on cow's milk that has been sterilised by boiling unless fruit juice is also given. In breast-fed babies it may occur at the time of weaning.

Clinical Features

There is a liability to bleeding from the gums, which may upset the normal dentition. In the limbs, there will be pain and swelling of rapid onset, as a result of which the infant holds the limb immobile, a state known as 'pseudo-paralysis'. The clinical picture may closely resemble acute osteomyelitis.

In modern life, the disease is rare in older children and adults, and the skeletal system is not often affected.

Treatment consists of the liberal administration of Vitamin C.

(ii) Vitamin D

Vitamin D (Calciferol) is a fat soluble substance concerned in phosphorus metabolism, so that its deficiency impairs the formation of calcium phosphate in bone. The bones, therefore, are abnormally soft, and may bend. In children, whose bones are growing, the condition is commoner, and is known as Rickets. In adults it is known as Osteomalacia.

In both, not only is the cause actual vitamin D deficiency, but an identical clinical picture results from other causes of impaired phosphorus metabolism, such as certain types of chronic renal disease, or inability to absorb fat from the digestive tract.

(a) *Rickets*

Vitamin D is present in animal fats, vegetable oils, and milk. The body also synthesises it when the ergostorol contained in skin is exposed to the ultra-violet rays in sunlight. True vitamin D deficiency is, therefore, now uncommon in civilised countries.

Not only are the long bones liable to bend under weight bearing stresses, but also, because normal calcification is impaired, osteoid tissue in the epiphyses tends to hypertrophy, leading to enlargement detectable clinically, and widening and irregularity of the epiphyseal lines visible radiologically.

Clinical Features

If the mother is healthy, infants are usually born with sufficient Vitamin D to last the first six to twelve months of life. After which the child's growth is retarded, the head becomes enlarged, and there is generalised enlargement of epiphyses. The ribs become flared and the costo-chondral junctions appear enlarged ('rickety rosary'). In addition, the abdomen is prominent.

Treatment

This consists of the administration of Vitamin D in liberal doses. Severe deformity may require correction by surgical intervention, either by open division of bone (Osteotomy) or closed manipulative fracture of the bone (Osteoclasis).

(b) *Vitamin Resistant Rickets*

Occasionally, in spite of apparently normal Vitamin D intake, the skeletal changes typical of rickets may appear in a young child. The actual cause of the failure to utilise Vitamin D in the ordinary way is unknown, but symptoms can be controlled if massive doses of the vitamin are administered.

(c) *Osteomalacia*

This is the adult equivalent of rickets, in which there is deficient calcification of bone, with excess osteoid formation within the trabeculae, in contra-distinction to osteoporosis where the trabeculae themselves are thinned, and osteoid is absent.

As a result, the bones are softened and may bend. In women, distortion of the pelvis may lead to obstruction in childbirth.

(d) *Coeliac Disease*

This is a condition occurring in young children, in which there is inability to utilise fat. As a result, because Vitamin D is fat soluble, rickety changes appear in the bones. In addition, owing to the infant's inability to absorb the fat in its diet, marked general wasting and underdevelopment occurs. The cause appears to be an abnormal reaction of the intestinal villi to gluten, which is contained in flour. Treatment, therefore, consists of abundant Vitamin D intake, and a diet free from gluten.

(e) *Idiopathic Steatorrhoea*

This is inability in the adult to utilise the fat in the diet, and like coeliac disease in infants is due to an intestinal reaction to gluten. If left untreated, the prolonged inability to utilise Vitamin D in the diet, leads to the bone changes seen in osteomalacia.

(iii) **Renal Osteo-dystrophy (Renal Rickets)**

Chronic kidney disease will impair the calcium–phosphorus metabolism and lead to bone changes similar to those seen in rickets if occurring in childhood, or osteomalacia in adults. Two types occur depending upon the site of the renal damage.

(a) *Renal Glomerular Rickets*

Where there is impairment of glomerular function, whether due to local pathological changes, as in chronic nephritis, or as a result of back pressure from ureteric obstruction leading to hydro-nephrosis, there will be phosphorus retention in the blood-stream and the surplus will be excreted into the bowel, where it combines with the calcium contained in the intestine to form calcium phosphate, which being insoluble, cannot be absorbed and is excreted. The serum calcium level therefore falls, and this stimulates the parathyroid glands to mobilise calcium from the skeleton.

(b) *Renal Tubular Rickets (Fanconi's Syndrome)*

In this condition there is failure of the normal reabsorption of substances from the renal tubules that have been excreted through the glomeruli. As a result, phosphates, glucose, and amino-acids are passed into the urine, and the serum phosphorus level is lowered. This reduces the phosphates available for bone formation, leading to rachitic changes in the skeleton. Acidosis also follows.

Clinical Features

The child will be dwarfed, with epiphyseal enlargement and bony deformities, such as coxa vara, genu valgum, and flat feet. In addition to which there will be the signs of chronic renal failure consisting of excessive thirst, polyuria, and general debility.

Treatment

Where possible the renal disorder is treated. In addition, large doses of Vitamin D and calcium are given, with alkalis if necessary to control the acidosis.

B. LIPOID GRANULOMATOSIS

This is a group of uncommon conditions affecting the reticulo-endo-thelial system, in which there are deposits of granulomatous tissue, often containing lipoid material. There is proliferation of the histiocytes, and where intra-cellular lipoid deposition is present characteristic 'foam cells' are found. The aetiology is unknown. Three forms occur.

(i) Eosinophil Granuloma

This is a local condition, found in young adults, in which a granulo-matous deposit is present in a bone, filled with eosinophils. Occasionally several deposits are present. Affected bones are usually the skull, verte-brae, ribs, pelvis, femora, or humeri. Attention is often drawn to the condition by the occurrence of a pathological fracture.

Treatment is often unnecessary, but radiotherapy will hasten resolution.

(ii) Hand–Schüller–Christian Disease

This is a more generalised type of granulomatosis affecting chiefly the skeleton. Cholesterol is found in the deposits, giving them a yellowish colour. Histologically the intra-cellular cholesterol produces large numbers of 'foam-cells'.

The skull is often chiefly involved, and often deposits near the orbits or pituitary fossa cause exophthalmos or diabetes insipidus.

Treatment

While no treatment is possible for the disease as a whole, individual deposits causing pressure symptoms will regress if subjected to radio-therapy.

(iii) Gaucher's Disease

In this type of granulomatosis which affects young children, the main features are enlargement of the liver and spleen due to deposits of the lipoid kerasin in reticulum cells. Similar changes are found in bone mar-row, leading to deposits particularly in the skull and vertebrae.

Treatment

This is largely symptomatic. A grossly enlarged spleen may be removed, and local radiotherapy causes regression of bony deposits causing pressure symptoms.

C. HYPERTROPHIC PULMONARY OSTEO-ARTHROPATHY

Characteristic clubbing of the fingers is characteristic of chronic cardiac and pulmonary lesions. Sub-periosteal thickening of the more distal long bones is also usually found. The actual cause is not known, but it must be associated with the chronic peripheral circulatory congestion present.

II. HORMONAL DISORDERS AFFECTING THE SKELETON

Bone growth and structure, together with the rest of the body as a whole, is largely controlled by the hormones secreted by endocrine glands. Those particularly concerned with the skeleton are the pituitary, the thyroid, and parathyroid glands.

A. THE PITUITARY

Both the eosinophil and basophil cells produce internal secretion which affect the skeletion.

(i) Eosinophil Cell Overactivity

This usually results from a small adenoma in the anterior lobe of the pituitary, and causes skeletal overgrowth. The effects depend upon whether or not growth has ceased.

(a) In children, *gigantism* results, in which there is generalised increase in growth of all the bones.

(b) In adults, *acromegaly* occurs. Growth in length after epiphyseal closure is impossible in long bones, but an increase in bony thickness takes place. This is particularly marked in the hands, feet, and mandible. The skin is also thickened, leading to a coarsening of the facial appearance.

(ii) Basophil Cell Overactivity

Increase in basophil activity, which may result from an adenoma of the cells in the pituitary itself, or from secondary simulation as a result of excessive activity in the adrenal cortex, causes a condition known as *Cushing's syndrome*. In this there is adiposity, hyper-tension, amenorrhoea in women, and generalised osteoporosis. As a result of the latter, vertebral collapse causing back-ache often occurs. A similar clinical picture may follow the prolonged therapeutic administration of cortisone or its derivatives.

B. THE THYROID

Thyroid deficiency in children causes *cretinism*, which is usually congenital. There is a general retardation in growth, leading to mental deficiency and dwarfism, with delay in the appearance of epiphyseal centres. Marked improvement follows the administration of thyroid hormone.

In thyrotoxicosis, calcium excretion is abnormally high, so that osteoporosis may result.

C. THE PARATHYROIDS

Parathormone, excreted by the parathyroid glands, controls metabolism. Where the hormone excretion is excessive, usually due to the adenoma in one of the glands, calcium is mobilised from the bones, causing generalised osteoporosis, and local cystic changes. Where these occur, the histological picture may be almost identical with giant-cell tumours of bone (Osteoclastoma, p. 268) or fibrous dysplasia (p. 295). This condition is known as *osteitis fibrosa cystica*, or *Von Recklinghausen's disease of bone*. As a result of the raised urinary calcium content, renal calculi are common.

Treatment

This consists of removal of the causative parathyroid adenoma.

III. SKELETAL DISORDERS OF UNKNOWN AETIOLOGY

A. SENILE OSTEOPOROSIS

In the elderly the bones tend to become osteoporotic. The cause is probably partly due to reduction in endocrine activity, as it is commoner in women after the menopause, and partly to a general reduction in metabolic activity. The whole skeleton is equally affected, but bone subject to stresses are those which draw attention to the condition. The bony cortex becomes thinner, and the size and number of the trabeculae are reduced. Osteoid is absent, which is the reverse of that seen in osteomalacia where the bone attempts to correct the loss of calcification by forming excessive osteoid tissue.

Clinical Features

Collapse of vertebral bodies is the most common presenting feature, leading to back-ache and kyphosis. The collapse may occur suddenly, causing acute back pain often associated with more distant pain in the trunk or lower limbs due to irritation of nerve roots. Often it is more insidious, when it leads to chronic back pain, with increasing deformity causing general shortening of the trunk and a stoop.

Fractures of long bones result from reduced violence when there is senile osteoporosis. This is particularly common at the wrist, where fractures of the lower end of the radius (Colles' fractures, p. 83) often follow minor falls in old people, and in the upper end of the femur due to comparatively trivial rotational strains (p. 109).

Treatment

General measures consist of supplementing the calcium intake in the diet, and in severe cases the administration of anabolic hormones, notably Dianabol ('Durabolin') and methyl testosterone. Back-ache, if severe, may be controlled by a light spinal support and mild analgesics. Fractures— except for sub-capital fractures of the femoral neck (p. 110) where the blood supply to the head fragment may be impaired—unite readily.

B. PAGET'S DISEASE (OSTEITIS DEFORMANS)

This is a condition occurring during the second half of life, in which changes affecting certain bones occur. There is a slight male predomin-ance, and the cause is unknown. The distribution varies widely from a solitary bone to a large portion of the skeleton. Affected bones have initially increased vascularity so that they become decalcified and softened. They also become generally thickened with marked coarsening of the trabe-cular pattern. Later, recalcification occurs often causing the bone to be more brittle than normal.

Any bone may be involved, but the condition tends to be commonest in the skull, vertebrae, pelvis, femora, and tibiae.

Clinical Features

The condition may cause mild boring pain in bones during the early vascular stage, particularly in the back or pelvic regions. Often attention is drawn to it by the slow development of deformity—such as bow legs or increasing kyphosis—or skeletal thickening which is most noticeable in the tibiae or skull, where the need for larger headwear may be noted by the patient. Frequently Pagetoid changes in bone are discovered by chance on routine radiographical check for some other condition.

Complications

Pathological fractures, particularly of the upper femoral shaft are com-mon, and often may be the first sign of the condition. Osteogenic sarcoma is a rare but very serious complication of the disease, occurring during the early active hyperaemic stage. Rarely, when a large portion of the skeleton is affected, in the early active stage, right-sided heart failure may occur, owing to the marked increase of blood flow through the bones.

Treatment

No specific measures are possible. Local treatment consists of supports —such as light spinal corsets and analgesics where pain is troublesome. Fractures unite readily.

C. POLYOSTOTIC FIBROUS DYSPLASIA

This is a condition of unknown aetiology, in which there is fibrous replacement affecting portions of several bones. The appearance radiologically and histologically is similar to that often seen in hyper-parathyroidism, though the serum calcium levels are within normal limits and there is no other evidence of parathyroid overactivity. The onset is probably in childhood, though symptoms rarely appear until adult life is reached. In some cases there is associated skin pigmentation, and in females, occasionally, there is precocious puberty (Albright's Syndrome).

If a single bone alone is affected, this is known as *monostotic fibrous dysplasia*.

Clinically, as a result of the bony softening, shortening and deformity occur in the affected limbs. Occasionally pathological fracture may occur.

Treatment is symptomatic only, consisting of supports for the deformed parts.

INDEX

INDEX